A Woman's Place

A Woman's Place

MY LIFE AND POLITICS

Audrey McLaughlin

with
Rick Archbold

MACFARLANE WALTER & ROSS
TORONTO

Macfarlane Walter & Ross
37A Hazelton Avenue
Toronto, Canada M5R 2E3

Canadian Cataloguing in Publication Data

McLaughlin, Audrey, 1936-
  A woman's place : my life and politics

ISBN 0-921912-39-0

1. McLaughlin, Audrey, 1936-   .   2. Women legislators — Canada — Biography.   3. New Democratic Party.   4. Canada — Politics and government — 1984-   .*
I. Archbold, Rick, 1950-   .   II. Title.

FC631.M25A3 1992   971.064'7'092   C92-095290-9
F1034.3.M25A3 1992

The publisher gratefully acknowledges the support of the Ontario Arts Council

Printed and bound in Canada

To the memory of Pauline Jewett,
a passionate Canadian and a true leader
who helped break the trail for the rest of us

C O N T E N T S

Preface   xi

ONE / **Stepping Forward**   1

TWO / **The Men's Club**   25

THREE / **Leadership**   50

FOUR / **Another Beginning**   76

FIVE / **Stalemate and Stand-off**   100

SIX / **War or Peace?**   132

SEVEN / **Remaking the Country**   160

EIGHT / **A Future That Works**   173

NINE / **A Woman's Place**   195

PREFACE

WHEN WORD GOT OUT that I was working on this book, a reporter challenged me. What had I accomplished that I should be writing about myself so soon? Shouldn't I wait until I retired? It struck me that these questions were variants on a question many women hear over and over again: what makes you think you should be listened to? The simple answer is: because we have something important to say.

Because I'm a new leader on the national scene, many Canadians wonder who I am and what I believe. My primary aim in the pages that follow is to acquaint readers with someone named Audrey McLaughlin, a woman who feels she's qualified to become the next prime minister of Canada. The road that has brought me to this point has been in some ways typical for a woman of my generation: an early marriage, two children by the time I was twenty, divorce and single parenthood. But some of the forks I've chosen have taken me in unusual directions — including to West Africa and to my current home in the Yukon.

As the poet Robert Frost wrote in the "The Road Not Taken," I have sometimes followed "the one less travelled by, and that has made all the difference."

This book is not a conventional political autobiography, but a statement that is part personal and part political — an attempt to describe some of the events and episodes in my life that have led me here and to explain the foundations of my political philosophy. While it contains some discussion of policy, it is not intended to serve as a comprehensive political platform. Rather it indicates some of the important policy directions I believe Canada must take in the near future. And while I have tried to be honest about myself in these pages, I have also tried not to invade the privacy of those closest to me. I feel strongly that, while I may have chosen to enter politics, my friends and family have not.

The book's title plays, of course, on the old saying "a woman's place is in the home." During my life I have ventured into many areas where women were once prohibited — and are still admitted with reluctance. The world of electoral politics is certainly one of these. But I am proud to have earned the privilege and responsibility to show that a woman's place is not only in the House of Commons, or at the head of the cabinet table, but wherever she chooses to be.

• • •

Many people helped make the writing of this book possible, and to all I offer my heartfelt thanks. First I want to acknowledge those who generously agreed to be interviewed: Gayle Annett; Dawn Black; Margaret Brown; Jane Kerrigan-Brownridge; Pam Bryden; Julie Cruickshank; Sarah Davis; Ginny Devine; Marion Dewar; Max Fraser; Dave Godfrey; Tessa Hebb; Margaret Joe; Tracy Kane; Joy Langan; Michael Lewis; Howard McCurdy; Laurie McFeeters; Jennifer Mauro; Cathy Opler; Carol Phillips; Valerie Preston; Bernice Rambert; Doug Rody; Sarah Steele; Sharon Vance; Janice Tripp; Dave Wright.

A number of people read all or part of the manuscript and made useful suggestions: Pam Barrett; Dal Broadhead; Ted Jackson; Steve Lee; Carmen Neufeld; Jill Rutherford.

Members of my staff, both in Ottawa and Whitehorse, were helpful in countless ways: Francesca Binda; Les Campbell; Paul Degenstein; Brenda Gehringer; Louise LeBlanc; Susan Murray; Diane Olsen; Glen Sanford; Toby Sanger; Bob Vandenberg; Sue Wilms.

Ben Cashore orchestrated research and fact checking with cheerful enthusiasm. The Library of Parliament speedily answered every request for information. And many individuals provided or confirmed information, among them Jim Butler; Chris Dray; Sharon Clarke; Bob Dewar; Max Fraser; Stephen Lewis; David Mackenzie; Peter Kuitenbrouwer.

I would also like to express my appreciation to Sharon Gignac, who transcribed many hours of taped interviews, and to Susan Crean, who allowed me access to her extensive research on women in Canadian politics.

Thanks also to my co-writer, Rick Archbold, whose skill, never-flagging energy, and unfailing sense of humour made him a joy to work with; to my publisher, Jan Walter, and editor, Judi Stevenson, who made perceptive comments and constructive suggestions that immeasurably improved the final result; to our copy editor, Wendy Thomas; and to literary agent Denise Bukowski, who brought publisher and author together.

CHAPTER ONE

STEPPING   FORWARD

A S I WALKED IN THE REAR DOORS of the old gym at the Yukon Indian Centre in Whitehorse on the evening of July 20, 1987, two hundred people erupted in a deafening combination of cheers, whistles, and applause. Inside the room, with its worn, wood-panelled walls and wire-meshed windows, a wet blanket of sweltering air enveloped us all, but in that mood of ecstatic exhilaration, no one seemed to notice. I worked my way slowly towards the stage, stopped by dozens of hugs and handshakes en route. I had just won the Yukon federal by-election, and there was a wonderful feeling in the room, a sense that in politics, as in life, anything is possible.

With my mother beaming proudly beside me, I stood at the microphone in the glare of lights from the television cameras, trying to quiet the crowd. I was smiling from ear to ear: it felt great to have worked hard and achieved a goal. I take particular pleasure in exceeding other people's expectations, and since no one had expected me to capture the New Democratic Party nomination, let alone win the by-election to become the Yukon's next member of parliament (the first NDPer to do so), I was experiencing a great sense of satisfaction. But it's not in my nature to savour the moment of victory for long. When I found out I'd won, my first thought was, "Now I'm actually going to have to do this."

I thanked those who'd helped on the campaign and promised to be a full-time representative of the Yukon — a poke at my predecessor, Erik Nielsen, who had seldom been seen in the riding in the latter part of his twenty-nine-year tenure. So many people had worked to make my victory possible, and I felt an enormous sense of responsibility; I didn't want to let these people down.

What lay ahead would be tougher than what had just been accomplished. The Tories were due to call a general election sometime in the next two years. Winning the Yukon in a by-election was one thing; holding it in a general election was another. Certainly mine wasn't the face Yukoners had come to expect in the job. Nielsen, the crusty Tory who'd earned the nickname "Velcro Lips" for his legendary ability to keep a secret, was a politician of the old school — something I most definitely was not. And I'd managed to squeak in by barely three hundred votes. Clearly I had my work cut out for me.

When I finished speaking, there were more cheers, more hugs, more congratulations. The victory party went on into the wee hours as people celebrated not only my win but the NDP sweep of all three federal by-elections that day. But I'd been campaigning non-stop since early April, and more than anything else I needed a good night's sleep.

That evening one chapter of my life came to an end. The next morning marked the start of another: "Audrey McLaughlin, member of parliament." Now there's an unlikely story.

It's unlikely because a woman like me — in fact, any woman — seldom gets far in politics. The fact that Audrey McLaughlin was the one standing in front of the cheering crowd that night, going to Ottawa in a few weeks, surprised nobody more than me. I had had no special advantages, no exemption from the lessons about "being a girl" that shaped and limited so many of the women of my generation. In fact, when I was growing up, girls were taught to let the boys take the stage, and I'd always found it uncomfortable to put myself forward. And even though I'd come a long way by 1987, I still found it hard to play a leading role.

Before my campaign for the NDP nomination, I'd never given a political speech, never really given a formal speech of any kind. Now I would be making speeches in the House of Commons. It was as if I were stepping from obscurity onto centre stage of the country's major concert hall.

As I write these words, I've been an elected politician for barely five years. I won't pretend that it has always been easy, or fun. I've been dismissed and discounted; time and again I've been given the unmistakable message that I had overstepped some sacred yet invisible boundary. Those things are frustrating, and sometimes hurtful. But if I've learned one thing, it is never to devalue myself or my experience just because I don't fit the conventional politician's mould or because my resumé is filled with unexpected entries.

It wasn't always thus. I haven't always felt so confident in myself. If self-esteem means recognizing your own worth in spite of society's negative messages, I believe it is won, piece by piece, through personal and collective actions that show you that you have some power to affect your world, that you have choices.

• • •

When I look back over my life, I see that there are specific turning points, certain defining moments and experiences that have made me the person I've become. One that came to mind in the aftermath of my by-election victory dates back to the late spring of 1964. I was a twenty-seven-year-old mother with two young children, helping my husband run a mink farm near the village of Wroxeter in southwestern Ontario. I hadn't managed to finish high school, but there I was, at the graduation ceremony of the University of Western Ontario, about to receive my B.A. in English and Psychology.

It may not sound extraordinary, but it was. All through high school, I'd heard mixed messages. On the one hand, I was told that I "wasn't living up to my potential"; on the other, I was told in subtle ways that I wasn't going far, because women just didn't. At that time, most girls learned that we didn't quite measure up, that we were second best, that we should keep our places and let the boys do the important things.

It wasn't just one thing — it was an accumulation of experiences and images, piled up over months and years: a teacher who discouraged risk taking in girls but praised it in boys; a classroom where the girls kept quiet and the boys did all the talking; movies where women almost always deferred to men; a world where almost every position of power and responsibility was held by a man. The signals were everywhere — in the media, in the books we read in school, in the unconscious assumptions of our parents and our teachers. How could we not believe them?

Not surprisingly, my husband believed them, too. When I'd first started to take university correspondence courses, he didn't object; he just wasn't particularly supportive. I'm sure he couldn't see what possible use university would be to a housewife; for that matter, I wasn't sure myself. I simply had a restless curiosity that needed an outlet. I wanted more than being a wife, a mother, and a mink farmer — not that these three weren't full-time jobs.

Mine was an unhappy marriage. I married too young and for the wrong reasons. When I was seventeen and living away from home for the first time, I started dating a slightly older man, Don McLaughlin. At eighteen I became pregnant — typical of the times, I'd never heard anything about contraception. The shame and fear are as real in memory as they were then. Of course there were options to marriage, including raising a child on my own, but they seemed impossible. I worried about my parents' reaction and what my friends would think. There seemed to be no one I could discuss it all with; it was one of the loneliest periods of my life. A schoolmate in a similar predicament had simply walked in front of a train. The only acceptable solution for me was marriage.

My son, David, was born in 1956; my daughter, Tracy, followed two years later. At the tender age of twenty, I found myself in a run-down farmhouse with two infants to look after and a couple of hundred mink to help tend. Money was scarce; the business was always on the verge of failing. The correspondence courses were something to keep my mind alive, not a way of escape. I never expected to earn a degree, not at the beginning. But I kept on taking more courses and doing well in them, and one thing led to another. I loved new ideas, the sense that there was so much to discover. Once I entered these new worlds — philosophy, literature, psychology, history, economics — I couldn't turn back.

My whole family was at Western that graduation day: my mom and dad, my husband and my children, and my mother-in-law (sadly, my father-in-law had recently died). It was a significant event for my parents, since I was the first person on either side of the family to graduate from university. And my mother-in-law, who had always treated me like the daughter she never had, was as proud of me as my own mother. (Lorna McLaughlin was one of the important role models in my early life, a pillar of compassion and strength. Even after my husband and I were divorced, Lorna and I remained close.)

Looking back now, I realize that something changed when I was handed that scroll of paper. From that moment on, I began to question the idea that I would never amount to anything. The transformation didn't take place overnight. For a long time, I continued to doubt myself even as I took on new challenges, steadily expanding the circles of my experience. I often heard a little voice saying, "You can't do that; you don't belong in that world." It would be many more years before I learned to ignore that voice, but at least I had begun to talk back.

•   •   •

As I began to change, I had to overcome not only the barriers within myself but also the obstacles that society puts in the way

of anyone who steps beyond his or her designated place. Those
barriers were still around in the spring of 1987 when I decided
to run for the NDP nomination in the upcoming Yukon by-election. This was an election the party thought it could win — with
the right candidate. But few within the party at that time were
thinking the right candidate might be a woman.

Their belief had less to do with sexism in the Yukon NDP
than with a general perception that Yukoners would never vote
for a woman, that a woman wouldn't fit with their self-definition
as pioneers living on the rough, tough frontier. This myth ignored
the fact that the Yukon was in reality a very complex and sophisticated society, that its "macho" image was more image than
substance. There had already been a woman commissioner of the
Yukon, Ione Christensen, and there were women cabinet ministers
then in the territorial government. If anything, the openness of
Yukon society had permitted an unusual number of women to take
on non-traditional jobs — driving trucks or working in mines or
running government departments. Yet somehow the perception
remained that a woman couldn't win a federal election.

In January 1987, when Erik Nielsen announced he was
resigning as MP, I was nearing the end of a six-month sabbatical
in foreign parts — three months volunteering with an economic
development organization in Barbados and three months travelling alone through South and Central America. In March, when
I returned to Whitehorse, a number of my women friends urged
me to run for the nomination. My reaction was astonishment. I
had been active in the party since the early 1970s, but my only
experience as a candidate was in 1982 when I ran for Whitehorse
city council — and lost. However, as more and more people
suggested it, I began to consider the idea. If they all believed I
could do it, how could I be the doubter? Then, too, I was at a
point in my life where I wanted to take on something new,
something that would really stretch me. My children were grown,
a long relationship had recently ended, and my consulting business had been put on hold while I was away. As I argued with
the voice in my head that said, "You can't do it," I began to
realize that my qualifications were actually rather good.

By then, I'd been involved for many years in community advocacy, helping people confront government or corporate systems that were not serving their needs. In the Yukon, I'd worked on projects ranging from improving child welfare legislation to research on land claims and aboriginal self-government. I'd travelled to almost every corner of the territory. I'd also earned my credits as a member of the territorial NDP, stuffing envelopes and canvassing door to door, serving on the party executive and running several successful election campaigns. (In 1985, when the Yukon NDP surprised everybody and took power in the territorial legislature, I ran my friend Margaret Joe's campaign. She eventually became Canada's first aboriginal justice minister.) I had also spent much time and energy trying to bring more women into the party and, once there, into positions of responsibility.

Before making such an important decision, I wanted to talk to people. I went around to my close friends and asked what they thought. Together we weighed the pros and cons. One of my major initial concerns was money — a perennial barrier for most women who seek political office. Because donations to nomination campaigns aren't eligible for tax credits, it can be very difficult to raise the funds to run a serious race. But my friends assured me they would personally raise the money I needed, so I wouldn't have to go into debt.

My other big concern was the sheer hard work — often gruelling work — of an election campaign. I remember standing in Jennifer Mauro's kitchen (at the time she was a local businesswoman; later she became Premier Tony Penikett's principal secretary) as she pointed out the other logical possibility: that I might actually win the nomination and then the election. That seemed such a long shot, I hadn't given it much thought. But she was right: I had to be prepared for the chance that I might win, which would mean spending much of my time away from cherished friends, the Yukon, and the life I'd built there.

Of course, there was more to consider than just myself. What sort of representative did the territory need? The answer, it seemed to me, was someone who could solve problems by building bridges between people, something I had long experience at doing. In my eight years as a Yukoner, I'd built quite a few bridges of my own, becoming acquainted with our various solitudes — rural and urban; rich and poor; aboriginal and white; newcomer and oldtimer. For much of my life, I seem to have been working at bringing people together to resolve conflict or increase understanding. What better opportunity to do this than as a federal member of parliament?

Finally, after talking the whole thing over with a lot of friends and people I respected, it came down to whether I had the courage to take the risk. I remember having an image of myself thirty years later, sitting in a rocking chair and asking, "Why didn't I go for it? What held me back? What did I miss?" That image decided it.

I suspect a lot of people in the party were quite relieved when I decided to go after the nomination. By 1987, the NDP had come far enough that it would have been embarrassing not to have a woman in the race. While I was still deliberating, Premier Tony Penikett approached me and suggested I become a candidate. I later learned that he'd been getting some heat from the federal party about the absence of a woman on the slate. Veteran MP Pauline Jewett had telephoned him and made it crystal clear that she expected there to be a woman in the contest. My candidacy solved that problem.

It soon emerged that the choice of the NDP party establishment was Maurice Byblow, a businessman from the mining town of Faro who had previously served as a member of the territorial legislature. I knew Maurice well and respected him. He would be a very tough opponent to beat. However, once I decided to run, I decided to run flat out. That meant I would campaign full time and that my core group of supporters would need to contribute many, many hours of their time. Fortunately, my small team was made up of people who had done much of the organizing and volunteer work that had helped put the NDP in power in the Yukon. If anyone knew how to operate an effective nomination campaign on a shoestring, they did.

When I think of this group, mostly women, who had already become both my friends and political soulmates, I'm struck by the sheer range of their life experiences and accomplishments. There was a psychologist, an anthropologist, a lawyer, an aboriginal film maker, a nurse, and the first female diamond driller in the Yukon. (For those not familiar with mining jargon, a diamond driller is a hard-rock miner who operates a diamond drill.) Many had travelled widely; several had worked extensively in developing countries. They were wily and creative campaigners, too, a real joy to work with.

Because the party had a solid chance of winning the seat in the by-election to come, the nomination was more fiercely contested than usual. As well as me and Maurice Byblow, the front runner, two other candidates declared: Robb Ellwood, an engineer, and Tom Burke, a plumber. There was a great deal of interest in the outcome, and many new party members were signed up during the membership drive that ended in early April, thirty days before the nomination meeting.

Our team knew that the only chance for a long-shot candidate like myself to win was to out-organize the opposition. To start with, we signed up more new members than anyone else. As the campaign got under way, we distributed literature, organized coffee parties, and worked the phones. But we realized that wouldn't be enough. So at the beginning of April, I hit the road in my pick-up truck to take my quest to the communities outside Whitehorse. Part of the reason for the trip was that it was the only way to reach some of our potential supporters: many people in the Yukon don't have phones. But beyond this, in a nomination campaign, personal contact is paramount.

My supporters had raised $5,000 to cover campaign expenses, but I had to travel cheaply. Sometimes I stayed with friends and sometimes I slept in my sleeping bag in the back of the truck. By the end of April, I was able to say that I'd talked to almost every member of the territorial NDP. Meanwhile, our team had been working incredibly hard, both in Whitehorse and in the rural areas. They were feeling good about my chances, but the proof would be in the ballot box. I had no idea what to expect.

On May 3, the other three candidates and I addressed the closing session of the Yukon NDP annual convention in

Whitehorse. Then we packed into a borrowed Suburban van and headed off for what was essentially a travelling nominating convention. Since the riding encompasses the entire Yukon, it is simply too vast for all party members to come to Whitehorse for a nominating convention. For example, it's a six-hour drive from Dawson City to Whitehorse. In the past, this meant that those people who couldn't afford to come — namely most members in rural communities — were effectively disenfranchised. This time the party had decided to try an experiment that would include everyone in the nominating process: we took the meetings to the membership. The only important community we missed was Old Crow, a native settlement above the Arctic Circle that is accessible only by air and that had only one signed-up NDP member at the time. (For this and other remote places we weren't able to reach, we used mail-in ballots.)

In each town or village we held a full nomination meeting — usually in a local community centre or union hall. The turnouts varied from as few as a handful in small places like Burwash and Ross River, to as many as forty in Faro, Maurice's home base. Each of us gave a short speech and answered questions. Then we waited while voters ranked us from one to four by secret ballot. Finally the ballot box was sealed and loaded into the back of the van for us to take back to the final nomination meeting at the end of the week in Whitehorse. We repeated this process fifteen times in seven days.

Although it was something of a crash course in public speaking for me, the week turned out to be a lot of fun. I was running against friends, people with whom I basically agreed, so the atmosphere was cordial. We joked and told stories as we drove along — and enjoyed the scenery. May is the month of the spring break-up on Yukon rivers, a beautiful time of year, although the roads are usually in pretty rough shape as they thaw out after the long winter. Between the tiny settlements on our itinerary, the territory is still very much a wilderness. It's not uncommon to round a bend and spot a moose, a caribou, or a lynx. The landscape is a spectacular succession of snow-capped mountains reflected in glassy, green lakes.

By the time we returned to Whitehorse on May 9, several members of my campaign committee believed I had a chance to win; they were confident that at the very least the final tally would be much closer than most people were expecting.

Our small but tenacious team had run the nomination fight like an election campaign, which meant identifying our supporters and making sure every one of them cast a ballot. If it was going to be close, every vote mattered. Some who had pledged to vote for me were involved in local theatre. When we phoned them one last time to make sure they would be at the nomination meeting, they said, "Sorry, there's a play on in town and we're going to the theatre." This is where organization and determination count. We said, "Fine, go to the play, but at intermission we're coming to get you for the vote." They were good-natured about this soft-arm tactic — and they did show up for the balloting.

The meeting was held in the Takhini Arena in Whitehorse. To make the place less cavernous, the organizers cut it in half with a curtain, placing a stage in front and arranging several hundred chairs on the concrete rink floor. The vote tabulation would take place behind the curtain while people mingled at a bar set up at the back.

This final event was a replay on a grander scale of the smaller nomination meetings we'd been having all over the Yukon. Each candidate gave a speech, all the members present voted, then these ballots were combined with the ballots we'd carried back from the communities, and the counting began. By this time I had become comfortable with the idea of myself as the next NDP candidate for Yukon, but I was naturally quite nervous about the outcome. Would I make a good showing? Would it at least be as close as my more optimistic supporters were predicting? Was it possible that I might even win?

When Max Fraser, president of the Yukon NDP, emerged from behind the curtain and announced the results of the initial count, quite a few people were visibly surprised. I was narrowly in the lead 256 to 236. This was starting to be fun, but a long night lay ahead since it seemed to take forever to tally each count. To cover my tension, I chatted with anyone and everyone

in range. The people who'd worked on the campaign were buoy-
ant; they knew we'd put on a great effort and turned a few heads.
But in the back of my mind I kept wondering if I'd find myself
drumming up consulting contracts the next day while people
congratulated me on a "moral victory." Quite frankly, I was tired
of women winning moral victories. I was ready for a real one.

After the second count, I was again narrowly ahead. During
the third count, the tension was rising; with Tom Burke and Robb
Ellwood both out, the race was now between me and Maurice. I
remained outwardly calm as Max got up on the stage and walked
to the microphone to announce the final tally, but I'm sure I'd
stopped breathing. He was typically deadpan as he read out the
result: 271 votes for Byblow; 284 votes for McLaughlin.

Parts of the crowd erupted into wild cheers, but many people
in the party establishment sat stunned. One of my supporters
remembers watching Tony Penikett, the Yukon government
leader. In her words, "to say that his jaw dropped would be an
understatement." He (along with many others) was upset because he believed I didn't have a hope of winning the by-election. Tony and I can laugh about this now; as one of the people
who had urged me to run in the first place, he'd been caught in
a trap partly of his own making.

It's always exciting when the underdog snatches the bone.
For me, however, the excitement of winning the nomination was
combined with something deeper than the satisfaction that came
from proving the doubters wrong. Once again, just as at the
University of Western Ontario in 1964, I'd exceeded some
people's low expectations and overcome my own self-doubts. It
was as if I'd studied hard and earned another degree; it was a
very good feeling.

• • •

Jumping into the unknown seems to have been something of a
habit in my life. My decision to run for the nomination certainly
qualifies, but one of my greatest leaps was my move to the Yukon

in the spring of 1979. At that time I was living in Toronto and working as the executive director of the Canadian Mental Health Association of Metropolitan Toronto, a non-profit agency that promoted education and prevention in the area of mental health. I liked my job and enjoyed the city, but I didn't want to get too comfortable. I noticed how many people around me were locked into possessions and mortgages, trapped in a lifestyle they didn't find satisfying. My few possessions were beginning to feel like so many nails in my coffin, and I realized I wanted to take the lid off — to cut free.

Fortunately, I had reached a point in my life where I had responsibilities to no one but myself. My two children, Tracy and David, were both grown and on their own. Tracy, who to my initial dismay had imitated her mother and married at eighteen, was living in Toronto and starting a family. (Despite my parental misgivings, she remains happily married to this day.) At last word, David, a perennial free spirit who kept in touch only sporadically, was working in the construction industry in British Columbia. My only remaining "family" responsibility, an elderly friend whom I had looked after for a number of years, had recently died. And my most recent romantic relationship had ended amicably.

There were two options. Either I would go to the University of Toronto School of Medicine and try for a Ph.D. in community health planning — by this time I had earned a master's degree in social work — or I would follow a long-held dream and head for the North. My application to the University of Toronto had, in fact, been accepted. But in the end, the lure of the North won out: I decided that the Yukon would be my Ph.D.

My choice of Whitehorse was completely unscientific. I knew no one there, and I had no job prospects. But when I looked at the map, I could see that the Yukon capital was near mountains, while Yellowknife, in the Northwest Territories, was not. I've always wanted to live near mountains; it was as simple as that. Whitehorse would be my destination.

When my Toronto friends learned what I planned to do, many of them were flabbergasted. "Why the Yukon?" they asked. I told them I was attracted to the North because I saw it as a different culture, a new world to experience. I suppose, like many people, I had romantic notions that it was some sort of last frontier. But I'd also acquired a taste for different places and different ways in the mid-1960s when my husband and I spent three years teaching in Ghana, West Africa.

I bought a Chevy truck, a maroon half-ton pick-up, and sold almost everything I owned, including all my furniture. I did keep four paintings and a six-foot-tall carving of an African woman carrying a baby, which I had bought in Ghana and simply couldn't part with. I also took my television set, some blankets, dishes, and several trunks full of books and clothes. All my worldly goods were stowed in that truck.

Although Whitehorse was my final goal, I planned to take my time in getting there. It was May, a glorious time to travel across Canada, and I spent a couple of months making my way west, then north. I stayed for a while with my mother in Regina and visited various friends and relatives along the way. My mother recalls that she was convinced I wouldn't last in the Yukon: like her, I hate the cold. Fortunately, mothers aren't always right.

My memories of this trip are stored as a series of vivid images rather than stories: the ocean-like vistas of the north shore of Lake Superior; the wonderful bronze buffaloes inside the entrance to the Manitoba Legislature; the drama of prairie storm clouds gathering on the horizon; the rich yellow of canola fields stretching off into the distance; the turquoise green of glacier-fed lakes in the Rockies; the cathedral-like atmosphere of B.C.'s old-growth rainforests. The sense of total freedom, of having no responsibilities, was absolutely intoxicating. I stayed mostly in campgrounds. Once in a while, I'd check into an inexpensive hotel and have a hot shower and a restaurant meal. Otherwise I'd cook on my camp stove and sleep in my truck, which had a cover on the back to protect my belongings and left just enough room for me and my sleeping bag.

By June, I had reached British Columbia. After travelling to Victoria and exploring the lower mainland, I spent a couple of weeks with my friend Katie Hayhurst in the coastal town of Bella

Coola, where she and her husband ran a Sierra Club lodge. Then I headed northeast to the Alaska Highway and my new home. I spent my first night in the Yukon near Swift River, a small community just across the border from B.C. As I was cooking dinner over my camp stove, I was totally engulfed in mosquitoes and finally forced to take refuge in my truck. It was a suitable introduction to Yukon wildlife.

Whitehorse, which sits on the banks of the Yukon River, was then a town of about 16,000. Because it is such a small place, where everybody knows everyone else, I quickly discovered a happy coincidence. My son had left British Columbia and moved to the territory as well. This didn't come as a complete surprise: as an eighteen-year-old, David had been on a long canoe trip in the Yukon and fallen in love with the North. But I had no idea he had decided to make Whitehorse his home.

Until I found a place of my own, I stayed with friends of my son's. Since I was in no hurry to settle in and since we hadn't seen each other in quite a while, David and I decided to take a trip together to Alaska. When we returned to Whitehorse several weeks later, I started to look for a job — no easy task. Eventually, in October, I found a part-time post doing research for the Yukon Department of Health and Human Resources, which was working on improving the Yukon's child welfare legislation. Since I still had time on my hands, I also volunteered with a brand-new outfit called the Yukon Educational Theatre. I worked several days a week at Health and Human Resources; nights I became an actor — or at least I tried.

Yukon Educational Theatre was a theatre company with a social purpose. It had been founded by a talented local actor and writer named Chris Dray and a local judge, Barry Stuart, who wanted to use community theatre to educate people about the perils of alcohol, a factor in most criminal offences in the territory. Acting itself wasn't new to me — I'd been in plays on and off over the years — but I had never before been part of a collective creation. Under Chris's direction, we improvised a series of skits called the *Bad Old Booze Blues Show*. One of the characters I developed was a lady named Fingers, who would steal even the local RCMP cruiser once she got into the sauce. Chris polished the skits into a script, which we rehearsed and took on the road.

The experience was as much an education for me as for our audiences since this was my first real contact with the Yukon's rural communities and their problems. What surprised and delighted me was how involved people became in our performances — sometimes talking back to our characters and occasionally walking up on stage to join the action. It was a foretaste of the Yukon's lively community life and the intensity of Yukoners' engagement with the world around them.

There is still a sense of the frontier about the territory, even though the main roads are paved and there's a satellite dish out behind many a trapper's cabin. The gold rush days are long past, but a certain spirit of adventure remains. Although some Yukoners have come to escape the South, many are lured by the romance of the North. Others are descendants of people who have lived on the land for 20,000 years and know its stories by heart. Perhaps because the people are few and the spaces vast, the Yukon has more than its share of unusual individuals. It's not completely far-fetched to imagine a modern Yukoner carrying a piano on his back across the Chilkoot Pass, as happened during the gold rush of 1897, or riding from Whitehorse to Dawson City in midwinter in an open horse-drawn sleigh, as Laura Berton (Pierre's mother) describes in her memoir, *I Married the Klondike*.

A typical small rural community shows physically the historic divisions of Yukon society. Although people of aboriginal ancestry make up one-third of the total population, most of them live in the rural areas. On one side of the road are the native houses; the other side is where the "white people" live. Until recently the aboriginal side of the road was much poorer, and it was rare to find indoor plumbing, but that situation is changing rapidly. And the two solitudes are starting to talk to each other. When I first arrived in the Yukon, it was common to find non-natives who'd lived in the territory all their lives and had never exchanged a word with an Indian. This is much rarer now.

As I've come to call the Yukon home, I've come to think of it as a kind of microcosm of Canada. Like Canada, it has a mix of relatively recent immigrants — Greeks, Italians, Latin Americans, Vietnamese boat people, and so on — and people who've been here much longer. It has a small but vital francophone population. And it has a significant aboriginal population, which means we are learning to confront not just racism but deep historical grievances, including the suppression of languages and long-unresolved land claims. We live next door to an American state, Alaska, which has ten times the population and ten times the economic weight. The Yukon's economy is still primarily resource based, so we are struggling to diversify. And because the northern environment is so fragile, we deal in a very urgent way with the supposed dichotomy between encouraging economic development and preserving the environment. What is different is the scale and visibility of social processes. Because the population of the territory is so small, the fault lines are more evident than in more populous areas, the problems thrown into greater relief — although they are almost always at least as difficult to solve as elsewhere.

The Yukon is also a good place to gain some perspective on the rest of the country. In part I attribute this to the Yukoner's sense of being on the margin, of being an outsider. Actually, in the Yukon we refer to every place else as "outside." Certainly we have a very strong sense of not being listened to, of being ignored when the big decisions are made. Perhaps this helps explain my attraction to the place; I've always felt something of an outsider myself.

• • •

There were only ten weeks between my early May 1987 nomination victory and the late July by-election. At the start of this second and more rigorous campaign, it looked like a tight three-way race. The edge belonged to David Leverton, the young Tory who hoped to inherit Erik Nielsen's loyal following. The Liberal candidate also looked strong. He was Dr. Donald Branigan, the longtime mayor of Whitehorse, whose holistic medical practice had given him a high profile in the communities as well as in the capital. Don and I both hoped Leverton would be hurt by the unpopularity of the Mulroney government and by resentment that Erik Nielsen had neglected the riding in recent years. As it turned out, he inflicted the worst damage on himself.

Early in the campaign, Leverton tried to defuse the most difficult issue facing him, the recently negotiated Meech Lake Accord on the Constitution. Although he toed the party line and endorsed the Accord, he argued that it was of little concern to Yukoners — a stance that alienated many of his potential supporters. Meech was extremely unpopular in the Yukon because the territorial governments had not been part of its negotiation and because of two of its provisions. The first of these required the unanimous consent of all ten provinces before a territory could become a province, which meant, in effect, that the Yukon and the Northwest Territories would almost certainly never achieve provincehood. The other gave the provinces the right to unilaterally extend their borders, which would allow a province to annex part of a territory without the consent of the residents. (The anti-Meech sentiment in the Yukon was emphatically not anti-Quebec. If anything, as perpetual outsiders in Confederation, Yukoners tend to identify with Quebec's sense of alienation.)

While Leverton attempted to downplay Meech, both Don Branigan and I came out against it. I felt very strongly that despite the fact that Ed Broadbent and the federal caucus had decided to support the deal, I could not. As a Yukoner, I couldn't support something that completely excluded Yukoners from determining their own future. Throughout the campaign I repeatedly argued that the deal had to be reopened and that the territorial governments must from now on be guaranteed a seat at the constitutional table. I also talked about my other objections to Meech, notably the fact that it left out aboriginal peoples and that it had nothing to say about the rights of women.

Apart from the Meech Lake Accord, the main issue in the Yukon that summer was representation. People hadn't seen much of Erik Nielsen in recent years and many were fed up. The crowning touch had come after he resigned as MP, when he refused to grant interviews to the local media. People wanted to be sure that the next MP would tend the riding well. Like most other Canadians, they were also pretty cynical about politicians and politics in general.

I lost count of the number of people who said to me during the campaign, "If you get elected, you'll become corrupted. You'll go down to Ottawa and you'll behave just like the rest of them." I don't think they thought I was going to take bribes, but rather that I would disappear into the system, that I'd become arrogant and lose touch, that I'd forget about the people who'd elected me. This feeling went beyond any specific anger at Nielsen to the deep sense Yukoners have of being disregarded, marginalized, left out of the big decisions. Meech Lake was just the latest example.

I felt entirely comfortable promising that people would see a lot of me between elections, not just during the campaign, that I wouldn't become a remote and inaccessible figure — this is the kind of connected politics I really believe in. And I know people liked what I was saying, but there was another factor: they knew that with a general election coming soon, they could throw me out if they didn't like the way I handled myself. I'm sure this awareness made many of them more willing to take a chance on me.

Campaigning is always hard work. Campaigning in the Yukon is made harder by the great distances involved. But it was summer, and the weather was beautiful so I wasn't complaining. Quite often, when I knocked on doors people weren't home. In June and July, with the sun still shining at midnight, many people grab the chance to be out of doors — hiking or fishing or canoeing or just out "on the land." But many of those who were home gave me an earful about the arrogant Ottawa government.

One of the most revealing remarks was said to me more than once and invariably by a woman. I'd be standing at her door or sitting in her kitchen sipping tea and she would say to me, "But if you go to Ottawa, will they listen to you?" I think what she was really saying was, "Nobody listens to me."

Many of the women I met didn't believe that I would be taken seriously in politics, that any woman's voice would be heard in

that very male world. Sometimes a woman would protest that she
didn't know anything about politics, yet as we talked she would
come to realize that the cost of groceries, the kind of schooling
her children received, the quality of health care available in her
community, and many other supposedly "domestic" matters were
in fact political problems about which she was very well informed. These conversations taught me how much the word
"politics" needs to be demystified — how we have to make
politics real and immediate, something that relates directly to
everyday life. If I needed any further rationale for running, these
women gave it to me.

Politics in the Yukon is very personal. Of course people feel
quite strongly about certain issues, but they are really voting as
much for the candidate they like and trust as for the party or its
policies. There was some resistance to the fact that I was a
woman, but very little of it to my face. Besides, I could always
remind people that the Yukon had once before elected a
woman — Martha Louise Black, who in 1935 became only the
second woman ever elected to the House of Commons. Despite
the Yukon's reputation as the last frontier, nobody ever pulled
a shotgun and drove me off the property, although I'm not sure
I would have been surprised if they had.

As election day approached, the local pundits considered the
race too close to call. And it turned out they were right. In the
end, I won over Don Branigan by 332 votes out of a total of 9,843
votes cast. David Leverton was another 500 votes behind. In
Whitehorse I polled just slightly behind the better-known
Branigan and won on my strength in the communities. Now what
had seemed far-fetched was a reality. I was the new member of
parliament for the Yukon, an idea that was still going to take
some getting used to.

• • •

After the victory celebration that evening at the Yukon Indian
Centre in Whitehorse, I had a good night's sleep, then spent the

morning at home making phone calls and receiving visitors. Ed
Broadbent, who'd failed to reach me the night before, finally got
through, clearly overjoyed that our party had swept all three of
the by-elections in the country that day and delighted to have
two women — myself and Marion Dewar, the former mayor of
Ottawa — joining the caucus along with Jack Harris of St.
John's, Newfoundland.

That afternoon I held a meeting at my bungalow in
Whitehorse with the key people who'd worked on the campaign.
Although the feeling of euphoria lingered, we didn't sit around
the living room congratulating ourselves. Determined to prove to
Yukoners that they had voted for the right person, we discussed
ways to follow through on my campaign promise to represent the
territory well and to keep up strong lines of communication. We
came up with the idea that I should write a weekly column for
the *Whitehorse Star* and the *Yukon News* (my *Star* column continues to this day). We also talked about practical matters, such
as finding a constituency office and hiring a constituency assistant. Beyond these tasks, Ottawa loomed.

After everyone had left, I sat alone awhile with my thoughts.
The past few months had been a blur of activity. Since early April
I had been campaigning non-stop, with almost no time to pause
and reflect. Now I looked inside myself and asked why I had
really wanted to embark on this new adventure. Yes, it was an
exciting challenge. Yes, I felt I could be an effective representative of the Yukon. I was certainly looking forward to grappling
with the issues of the day and learning to become the best MP I
could be. But beyond these things, what were my underlying
reasons for getting into electoral politics?

My political philosophy can be put very simply: I believe
there is such a thing as the public interest and that to work on
behalf of that public interest the government must strike a
balance between those who have and those who have not. I also
believe in using government to bring people who are outside the
system of decision making — people who feel they are excluded
or on the margins — into a revitalized system. In fact, it is
precisely these people who will accomplish that revitalization,

by bringing fresh insight to the main tasks of government, which
are to redress social injustice, help create economic opportunity,
and redistribute wealth and power more fairly.

I'm sometimes criticized for using words like "empower" and
"inclusive" — criticism that puzzles me as much as the words
and the ideas behind them seem to puzzle my critics. Maybe it's
because the message is so unfamiliar. The message is this: only
by granting a meaningful share of power to the people who've
been left out of its operations and rewards — left out on the basis
of their gender, their race, their "disability," their sexual orientation, their poverty — will we move towards a fairer, more just
society. This is not "woolly-mindedness." Inequality and injustice are recipes for economic decline and social disintegration.
We can see this truth all over the world, from South Africa to
Northern Ireland to Yugoslavia.

The other criticism I sometimes hear is that I am idealistic.
I see nothing wrong with ideals; perhaps they seem strange
because so few politicians nowadays pay them more than lip
service. I also happen to be quite realistic and practical about
what a single politician — even a party leader — can achieve.
Rarely does a system change from the inside; rather, change
comes because pressure builds on the outside. When that pressure becomes great enough, those who have power in our society
find they must begin to share it.

That's one of the reasons I have no problem with the "special
interest groups" that come in for so much disapproval. There
have always been interest groups — the church, business, farmers, workers — but now there are more groups and they are often
better organized. Some of them are very vocal and sometimes
they make the political process seem messy, but they are simply
representing people that used to be silent. Those who see this as
a problem have a shallow concept of democracy. I believe that
the more "interests" brought into the decision-making process,
the better the end result.

I often hear Canadians say that the country has no leadership. The real problem is that we've got the wrong kind of
leadership, a bullying leadership that doesn't listen to anyone

beyond the core of traditional power holders who serve no one's interests but their own. I want to lead in a different way: by listening carefully and helping pull open the doors to power.

•   •   •

The days following my by-election win were tinged with anxiety and excitement as I got organized for my new life and dealt with a thousand details. Leaving home is never easy, and I knew I would badly miss the Yukon and the regular contact with my close network of friends. At least the problem of finding a constituency assistant soon solved itself when Sarah Steele, who'd worked on the campaign from the beginning, agreed to give up her job with the Yukon's Addiction and Drug Services, taking a cut in pay to work with me.

The next problem was finding a place for Sarah to work. Shortly after the by-election, I was walking past the "log skyscrapers" in downtown Whitehorse when I noticed that one of them was for rent. These log buildings — one two storeys, the other three storeys — are Whitehorse landmarks. The two-storey was available and it was the right size, accessible, central, and known to everyone. I rented it on the spot. Abe Lincoln was born in a log cabin and ended up as president of the United States; I may not have been born in a log cabin, but I've ended up in one.

I had little time to help Sarah move in. I received word that parliament was being recalled on August 11 to deal with a perceived refugee crisis sparked by the landing of a boatload of Sikh refugees on the East Coast. In a few days I would board a plane for Vancouver, where I would catch another plane to Ottawa. Even sooner than I'd expected this new chapter of my life was beginning.

There's a method used in teaching group dynamics in which you ask people to write down their understanding of the adage "A rolling stone gathers no moss." There is no right or wrong answer. The two usual interpretations identify two very different

personality types. Many people, maybe most, interpret this saying to mean that it's best to stay in one place and put down roots.
Others interpret it as meaning you've got to keep moving and
growing or you'll become stale. I guess I'm one of the others.

CHAPTER   TWO

THE   MEN'S   CLUB

THE DAY I ARRIVED on Parliament Hill, I walked alone in brilliant sunshine past the eternal flame and up the steps under the Peace Tower to the main entrance of the Centre Block. I was thinking about some of the people who had walked up these steps before me: pioneer women in politics such as Agnes Macphail, Grace MacInnis, and Judy LaMarsh — and the founders of the CCF and the NDP, people such as J.S. Woodsworth, M.J. Coldwell, Tommy Douglas, David Lewis, and Stanley Knowles. Suddenly the responsibility I'd taken on seemed even greater.

The last time I had entered the pillared neo-Gothic foyer, with its vaulted ceiling and inlaid marble floors, was thirty-five years earlier. Then, at age fifteen, I'd been with a girlfriend who had invited me to share her prize for winning a high school essay contest — a trip to Ottawa as guest of the local MP, Paul Martin, Sr. We stayed in style at the Château Laurier, dined in what seemed unimaginable elegance in the hotel dining room, and met

Mr. Martin briefly in his office, where he shook our hands and posed for a photograph. In those days I would have laughed outright at the notion that I might ever come to Ottawa as anything other than a tourist.

When one of the uniformed guards approached me, I told him what the party Whip had instructed me to say. "I'd like to see the sergeant at arms to get my identification pin." I was promptly ushered into an office where a woman was working at a desk. I smiled, told her my name, and stated my business. The woman searched through a typed list, studying it for a long time. Finally she looked up and said, "I'm really sorry, but I can't find your name anywhere." I replied, "Oh well, it's probably because I've just been elected in a by-election." "Oh dear," she said, "I thought you were a spouse. I've been looking at the wrong list!" At the time, I thought the incident was funny, but it proved to be a portent that I had entered an alien world.

When a woman enters the House of Commons, she enters what in significant ways is an old-fashioned men's club. There are all sorts of reminders — some subtle, some not so subtle — that this is not a woman's place. The first and most obvious is simple numbers. In 1987, with the addition of Marion Dewar and me, there were 29 women out of a total of 282 members of parliament, or 10.3 percent. (After the 1988 election, the figures improved slightly. As of this writing, there are 40 women out of 295 MPs, or 13.7 percent.) When you stand up in the House to speak, you look out over a sea of blue and grey — the men in their club uniform, the business suit. Here and there will be a splash of colour: the women. When you walk into your first committee meeting, chances are you'll be the only woman.

Although Marion Dewar and I were welcomed warmly into the NDP caucus, we both observed how quickly Jack Harris, who had won the by-election in St. John's East, was accepted as "one of the boys" while we, and the other women, remained in some ways very much apart. Within days, it seemed, Jack was off to have a drink with the Speaker or with the caucus Whip or out on the town with a group of male MPs. Marion and I found this amusing rather than irritating, but we were fully aware that, intentionally or not, we were being relegated to an expected position — on the sidelines — a position neither of us had any intention of occupying.

The parliamentary men's club is organized, in part, around social drinking — although this is changing. I seldom drink — not out of any prudery; I have simply never developed a taste for alcohol. And I don't want to sit in somebody's office until two in the morning drinking beer and spinning yarns. It is just not the way most women socialize, let alone lay the groundwork for serious decisions. I long ago determined that if politics meant going out drinking with the boys every night, it just wasn't for me. But the fact is, Marion and I weren't invited. Maybe the men thought we weren't interested. Or maybe it didn't enter their heads that being outside the club was a political disadvantage for us. Or maybe they were just more comfortable doing things the way they'd always been done.

Rosemary Brown, in her autobiography, *Being Brown*, describes what it was like as a new member of the British Columbia legislature in 1972 — the first black woman ever elected to any Canadian legislative assembly. One bald fact seemed to stand for the larger situation: "All the washrooms [in the legislative building in Victoria] meant for the use of elected members had been built with urinals in them. In the particular washroom being used by female politicians and staff, the urinal had been concealed behind a temporary box-like wood structure — a clear indication that our legislative forefathers had not conceived the possibility of women one day serving as elected members in that building, and that our presence there is still accompanied by the hope that our sojourn will be temporary." I didn't have to cope with that particular problem in the House of Commons in Ottawa fifteen years later, but the place was no less steeped in the assumption that women were interlopers.

The most visible manifestation of the male culture is the behaviour in the House of Commons itself. I remember how amazed Marion and I were when we sat through our first Question Period. The posturing, the banging on desks, and the shouting made us think of school kids. And like children in a school yard,

the men seemed to be constantly jockeying for territory and domi-
nance. More than once, while observing them at their worst, I've
recalled an episode of the television sitcom "Murphy Brown," when
several of Murphy's colleagues were locked in a very competitive
male argument. When she'd finally had enough, Murphy said,
"Why don't you just drop your pants and I'll get a ruler?"

Don't get me wrong. I enjoy the give and take of a good
parliamentary debate. I relish the combination of genuine pas-
sion and keen intellect that many members bring to the discussion of serious issues. Unfortunately, unless you watch the
Parliamentary channel beyond Question Period, you will know
little or nothing of these proceedings, since the press seldom
reports them.

As for Question Period, the abuse that is shouted back and
forth, the heckling and the histrionics strike me and my women
colleagues as silly and childish, sometimes wounding, and
always counter-productive. These performances get in the way
of rational problem solving, and make the House ridiculous in
the eyes of Canadian citizens.

The worst heckling is directed by men at other men, but the
women come in for a special brand of nastiness. Many people
recall the occasion in May 1982 when NDP member Margaret
Mitchell rose in the House to speak on the issue of violence
against women, specifically about a parliamentary report indicating that one out of every ten husbands beats his wife and does
it often. At least one MP made a joke of it, shouting, "I don't beat
my wife," and the House erupted in derisive laughter. Ironic,
isn't it, that they were being abusive of a woman trying to speak
about the difficult issue of wife abuse?

Not long ago a Tory MP referred to a female Liberal member
as a slut, which is a much more sexual and belittling slur than
a guy calling another guy a bastard. On another occasion a
female member of our caucus was called a fishwife. It has been
ruled unparliamentary to refer to a member as "scarcely entitled
to be a gentleman" since 1876, but words such as "slut" and
"fishwife" have not yet been included in the list of unparliamentary language.

Some of us have begun to work on making the House more civilized. Recently NDP MP Joy Langan distributed buttons to members of our caucus bearing the letters HWD — "Heckle With Dignity." It is a subtle but serious announcement that we mean to change things. But I've no doubt this will be a long, slow process.

It all makes me wonder how far we've really come since Agnes Macphail, the first woman ever elected to parliament, took her seat in the House in 1921. In 1949, reflecting back on her career as a member of parliament and then Ontario MPP, she wrote, "I couldn't open my mouth to say the simplest thing without it appearing in the papers. I was a curiosity, a freak. And you know the way the world treats freaks." Women in parliament are no longer curiosities, but they are still far too rare a species.

•   •   •

During my first weeks in Ottawa, however, I knew little of the slings and arrows facing women who crash the men's club of parliament. I was faced with more urgent practical matters, such as hiring a staff and setting up an office. In addition, I needed to find a place to live and to buy some clothes, since after eight years in the informal atmosphere of the Yukon my wardrobe held few items suitable for my new job. I think I had one pair of decent shoes and a pair of dress-up slacks — and maybe a skirt or two. That was it.

Looking for an apartment at the end of a long day was both tiring and discouraging. Fortunately a longtime friend from my days in Toronto, Jane Condon, now lived in Ottawa. She offered to drive me around to look at possible places. One beautiful summer night that first week after we'd done our rounds, she took me down Sussex Drive to a lovely little park overlooking the Ottawa River. It was a rare moment of peace. As we gazed out over the river towards the Gatineau Hills in Quebec, I suddenly noticed unusual lights flashing in the sky. We watched them flickering and playing for a few moments before I realized what they were: northern lights. I remember Jane kidding me that it was some kind of omen. At any rate, it certainly brought back memories of home and the people whose belief in me I so much wanted to live up to.

That was one of the few occasions I had to catch my breath during those first days, for I was immediately plunged into the pressurized world that MPs inhabit when the House is in session. The party Whip assigns your office — mine was in the Confederation Building, a block west of the House of Commons — and the leader assigns what are known as critic areas or shadow cabinet responsibilities — mine were northern development and tourism. These are the policy areas I would be responsible for and ask questions about in the House. After that a new MP is pretty much on her own, learning her portfolios, boning up on parliamentary procedure, and figuring out how the place works. It's akin to learning a foreign language by total immersion.

The Commons sits every weekday and sometimes into the evening. Wednesday morning is given over to the weekly caucus meeting. As well, there are endless other meetings to attend — of parliamentary committees, with constituents, with other members of the caucus. If I wanted to ask a question in the House, I would attend the 9 a.m. meeting of the caucus executive to make my pitch. As all this was going on at full speed, I still had to get my office in gear.

Soon after I arrived, I was extremely lucky to find a wise veteran of the Hill to take charge. Bernice Rambert, former Trinidadian businesswoman extraordinaire, had been working for members of parliament on and off since 1969 and knew how to harass the appropriate departments for everything from furniture to paper clips — and get them. Thanks to her, my office was functioning in less than a week. Shortly after Bernice took things in hand, I hired Janice Tripp, who became my executive assistant — doing research, helping write speeches, and handling casework for the constituency. Her long experience, first working for Tommy Douglas just before he retired and later for Howard Pawley in Manitoba when he was premier, proved invaluable. The third staff position was divided between two people, Sarah Davis, a lawyer on maternity leave and looking for a part-time job, and Ben Cashore, then in his early twenties and finishing his master's degree in political economy. I was fortunate to have such a crackerjack staff. And as a rookie MP, I needed all the help I could get.

A new member of parliament is bound to make some mistakes, and sure enough I embarrassed myself the first time I got up to speak in the House of Commons only a few days after my arrival on the Hill. New members are encouraged to take the plunge as soon as possible, usually by making a sixty-second statement during the first fifteen minutes of Question Period. I was given a statement prepared by the caucus research staff, something to do with David Crombie's responsibilities as secretary of state.

Everything went fine until I reached a place in the text where the minister was referred to by name. Although I didn't know it then, parliamentary rules dictate that a member is never referred to directly by name but only by his or her constituency. The text in front of me read "David Crombie," instead of "the honourable member for Rosedale" — and that's what I read out.

Instantly, the House erupted into jeers and catcalls. As I slumped back into my seat, thoroughly mortified, it seemed as if every Liberal and Tory MP in the place was shouting and screaming with glee. It was something like hazing in a boys' boarding school, a way of putting the new member in her place.

My maiden speech, on August 20, during debate on the proposed National Transportation Act, a bill to deregulate air and rail transport, went considerably better. (I remember being struck at the time by the incongruity of the term "maiden." As a mother and grandmother, I certainly didn't qualify. And the term is even odder when applied to a man. Let's put it this way: when I rose to give my speech, there were very few maidens present.) Traditionally in a maiden speech, the member is given great latitude to stray from the topic under debate and talk at length about her or his constituency. But knowing how dependent the Yukon is on regulated transportation, I wanted to oppose the bill from a territorial perspective, arguing that its passage could greatly damage the Yukon economy.

Afterwards Ed Broadbent and many of my caucus colleagues congratulated me for speaking well; they had been through it themselves and knew how difficult it is to stand up for the first time and address the House. The speech made no headlines, except perhaps in the *Whitehorse Star* and the *Yukon News* — but then few maiden speeches are noted by anyone outside an MP's home riding.

The tasks I found most difficult in those first few months were speaking in the House and putting forth my views in caucus. Like the women I'd talked to during the campaign, some part of me wasn't yet entirely convinced that if I spoke up I'd be listened to. Drawing attention to myself is not something I do with ease, and I'm uncomfortable using the word "I" — which makes writing this book especially ironic. Only gradually did I become more comfortable in my public role. Often I found that after I'd done something new two or three times, I could say to myself: "You can do this pretty well after all. And you'll get better." Then I'd just stop worrying about it. When I doubted myself or my courage failed, I would simply remember, "Audrey, you've got a job to do. Get on with it."

A number of the more experienced caucus members were especially helpful in those early days. Pauline Jewett and Margaret Mitchell were wonderful. Jim Fulton, who relinquished the responsibility for northern development to me, was gracious about the change and helped me learn the ropes. And Neil Young, the MP for Beaches-Woodbine, whose office was right across from mine, was always happy to answer my endless questions.

As for Ed Broadbent, he was a friendly but distant figure. I always sensed his support, but we weren't close. This is hardly surprising: I was a new member and few backbench MPs see much of the leader. However, I came to know his principal secretary, Bill Knight, somewhat better. While I continued to look for an apartment, I'd arranged to use a room in Bill's house. One of his tenants was a woman who wanted to spend a month in the Yukon. So I exchanged my house in Whitehorse for her room in Ottawa.

Bill, who wasn't married at the time, had something of a reputation for his succession of women friends. As a result, there was a subtle undercurrent of amusement in caucus at the fact that I was "living with Bill." During a coffee break in a Wednesday morning caucus meeting after I finally moved into my own apartment, I walked over to Bill, handed him his keys, and announced quite audibly to the room, "Bill, it's all over between us."

The most difficult issue facing the NDP caucus at that time was the Meech Lake Accord, which had been finalized the previous spring. Before I was elected, the caucus had been through a tremendously wrenching internal debate over whether to support Meech. Many MPs, especially those from the west, disliked the deal, primarily for what it didn't contain. But in the end, the caucus had decided to support it — despite its failings — in the interest of bringing Quebec back into the constitutional fold.

I arrived in caucus having campaigned and won in the Yukon in part on a promise to vote against the deal. Since Ed had known this in advance, he had no choice but to let me follow through. Although he never formally gave me permission to break ranks, it was my clear understanding that he would not discipline me for doing so. Nonetheless it gave me a very uncomfortable feeling. My style is always to be part of the team, to co-operate with the group. I became even more uncomfortable when my colleague Ian Waddell, who also voted against the Meech resolution in the House, was punished by being stripped of his critic portfolio.

It was on September 30, during the debate on the Meech Lake resolution, that I rose in the House to explain why I was opposing the Accord. As I would many times subsequently, I explained that my opposition to Meech was not in any way opposition to Quebec's legitimate demands, including the distinct society clause, which I fully supported. My opposition was based on the exclusion of the Yukon — in fact of every Canadian living north of the 60th parallel — from this round of constitution making. As I said that day, "Perhaps it will be the Québécois who understand best what we are saying in the northern territories when we speak of feeling like second-class citizens because we feel that our voices are not being heard and our opinions not respected."

• • •

Despite the effort it took, I made sure I spoke my mind in caucus and stood up in the House when I felt I had something to say. Still, I tended to do more listening than talking during those first months in Ottawa. I saw my election to parliament as a great opportunity to learn. And as someone who'd never held elected office before, I was on a very sharp learning curve.

Of the privileges accorded MPs, free French tutoring is one I believe to be justified — and I took full advantage of it. I tried to schedule an hour of French every day. Luckily I hit it off immediately with my teacher, Assya Wacas, who has continued to tutor me to this day. She's wonderful at her job — enthusiastic and encouraging, yet always demanding. After a few months, I began to make some genuine progress.

Learning a second language is somewhat like climbing a steep mountain interrupted by a series of plateaux. Each time I reached one of those plateaux, I would heave a sigh of relief and think, "Now I'm really getting somewhere." That feeling would last until I encountered a situation where my French wasn't adequate. Then it was on up the cliff face towards the next plateau.

On one occasion when I was about to enter the House, I stopped to talk with a bilingual Tory backbencher from Quebec. We were chatting in French and I was feeling quite pleased with myself; fluent bilingualism seemed just around the corner. Then I reached a point in the conversation when I wanted to say, "I envy you," "Je vous envie." Instead I said, "J'ai envie de vous," which, as my colleague explained once he'd stopped laughing, roughly translates into "I lust after you." Obviously I still had a lot to learn.

During those early months, the first issue I tackled in earnest was one of particular immediacy to my northern constituents. In the spring of 1987, it had been revealed that the United States and Japan were negotiating an agreement to fly plutonium from Europe for use in Japanese nuclear reactors. I was disturbed to learn that Canada hadn't been party to the negotiations, even though the proposed flight route passed over approximately 2,400 kilometres of the Canadian North. Transport would begin sometime in the early 1990s and continue twice monthly for about ten years. Part of the rationale for choosing to fly over the North was that it was considered uninhabited. You can guess how my constituents would react to that assumption.

The government had refused to take any action, preferring to wait to be reassured by the Americans that the flights were safe. It looked like the U.S.-Japanese agreement would be submitted to Congress in September, after which it would be very ticklish politically for Canada to intervene. As a *Globe and Mail* editorial on July 30 put it, "Canada does not seem to care. The federal government is not without options. It can legally refuse the flights. So far it has shown no inclination to do that, or to use its power in the matter to force its way into the negotiations."

Clearly the flights would undermine Canadian sovereignty over the Arctic, but as well they posed a potentially devastating environmental and health hazard — and not just to residents of the North. The plutonium was to be carried as a fine powder in casks designed to protect it from dispersal in the event of a crash on take-off or landing. But any crash over Canada would have been from a very high altitude, the implications of which seemed to have eluded those who had made the safety calculations. If a cask was broken, the tiny particles of plutonium would potentially disperse over hundreds, possibly thousands, of miles, and each speck was capable of causing cancer if inhaled. Furthermore, the plutonium's radioactivity would actually increase for decades as it decayed and would represent a health risk for thousands of years. Even if the possibility of dispersal was proved to be infinitesimally low, in my view no risk of this sort was acceptable.

On August 21, 1987, I stood in the House to ask when the government would demand that Japan and the United States prohibit these flights. I received a typical non-answer: Canada would act only when and if the United States and Japan actually applied to cross Canadian territory. Unsatisfied, I continued to press the issue through the fall and into the following year — for most of my first term in the House. At the same time, I helped organize a North American campaign against the flights. In short, I made it "my" issue.

I consulted with experts, and my staff prepared an information package, which we sent to environmental and peace groups in Canada and the United States and to anyone who asked. I worked with people throughout the North, with U.S. politicians, including the governor of Alaska, with organizations such as the Physicians for Nuclear Responsibility. We organized petitions right across the country opposing the flights.

One of those petitions was in Inuktitut, the Inuit language. When I presented it to the clerk to have it certified for presentation in the House, I was told that it was unacceptable because it wasn't in one of Canada's two official languages. I said, "Fine, I guess I should call up the papers and tell them that the House of Commons won't recognize a petition in one of Canada's aboriginal languages." After some dithering, the petition was accepted, apparently the first one in a language other than French or English to be certified.

Thousands of signatures were collected, and editorial after editorial expressed outrage over the plan. In the face of this broadly based opposition, Japan and the United States backed down, agreeing not to transport plutonium over Canadian territory. Much more than a victory for an individual MP, I see this kind of political action as a classic example of empowerment. It proves that individual voices can be heard if they are well-organized, and that people do have power if they choose to exercise it.

The plutonium issue also demonstrated the potential for a

backbench opposition MP to have a measurable impact on public policy. Being a member of parliament is an opportunity to do useful work for something you believe in, yet far too few back-benchers take full advantage of it. We have staffs and access to the superb research resources of the Library of Parliament. And if we have something important to say, we have a platform on which to say it. It may not always be easy, but a single MP can make a difference.

The NDP, although the perennial third party in federal pol-itics, has had great impact on public policy. Back in 1931, veteran CCF member Abraham Heaps successfully introduced a motion calling for a system of unemployment and disability insurance. Stanley Knowles became the acknowledged expert in the House of Commons on pension issues. More recently, when the government withdrew funding for women's centres across the country, Dawn Black helped bring the issue to national attention (after widespread protests, the funding was restored). And Svend Robinson, through both his personal courage and committed advocacy, has done as much as anyone to further the rights of gay and lesbian Canadians.

● ● ●

I am frequently drawn to issues where opposing camps are locked into extreme positions and have lost the ability to listen to each other. In such situations I attempt to start a dialogue, to bring in some new information and perhaps find some common ground between the two sides. My aim is always to inject balance into the debate. This partly explains why, in early 1988, when I learned that the British government was planning to enact fur-labelling regulations that would adversely affect Yukon trap-pers, I decided to take on the issue.

If you've listened to aboriginal people talk about their rela-tionship with the land and their profound respect for the web of life, it's hard to think of trapping as a brutal, mindless activity. Trapping has been part of the aboriginal way of life since long

before Europeans arrived in North America. And trapping as it
is now practised in the North by both aboriginal and non-aboriginal people is an environmentally sustainable activity that actually works to preserve the wilderness. These days it is not in a
trapper's interest to overtrap, which would only undermine his
or her economic base. Trapping is not just an important local
industry in an area where jobs are scarce; it also provides an
economic rationale for keeping the land wild and unspoiled.

In Britain and Europe the issue was being presented very
simplistically as a matter of cruelty to animals, which I agree is
a serious concern. The specific complaint involved leg-hold
traps — still commonly used for many species — because they
don't kill the animal immediately. Any issue of animal rights is
an emotional one, but in this case the human side of the story
wasn't being heard — including the efforts in Canada to develop
more humane trapping methods.

By mid-May 1988, I had been working for several months
with trappers and aboriginal groups to organize a campaign in
opposition to the proposed British law, which would have required retailers to sew warning labels into products that might
include fur from animals caught in leg-hold traps. We decided
that I might make some impact if I went to London to present the
case personally. (Interestingly, although this trip generated a
small amount of coverage of the issue in the Canadian media,
what got me the most press was the fact that I chose to pay my
air fare and expenses out of my own pocket — a maverick action
for a member of parliament, it seemed.)

I felt a little like a female Don Quixote riding off to do battle
with a whole field of windmills. Here I was, a lone opposition
MP from Canada, taking on the British Tory government and the
powerful anti–fur-trade lobby. The British politicians and bureaucrats must have been bemused to encounter "this woman
from the Yukon" working the corridors of Westminster telling
them more than they really wanted to know about fur trapping.

However, I did get my point across, and I had a chance to
lock minds with some very interesting individuals. I met with
people ranging from Neil Kinnock, leader of the Labour Party,

to Roy McMurtry, then the Canadian High Commissioner in London. Most important, I talked to Alan Clark, Margaret Thatcher's trade minister, who was sponsoring the bill that so many of my constituents would have been hurt by. Repeatedly I made the argument that we should be putting our energy into researching more humane methods of trapping rather than fighting a traditional local industry that employed many who had no other job options. My focus on more humane trapping was an attempt to find some common ground with those who wanted to see all trapping banned, period — to inject dialogue into a polarized stand-off. By the time I left, I hoped that people who'd never thought about trapping from the aboriginal or ecological point of view were now enjoying a fresh perspective.

On June 1, the House of Commons held an emergency debate on the fur-labelling issue. All parties spoke out against the British legislation, sending the loudest possible message to the British government, which dropped the legislation a few weeks later. The debate has since moved to the European parliament, which plans to introduce similar regulations by 1996. If efforts by Canadian researchers continue at their current level, by then we should have developed more humane traps that will make the regulations meaningless.

• • •

I continued to handle northern development and tourism throughout my first brief term in parliament. Later, after the 1988 election, Ed Broadbent asked me to take on the additional responsibility of acting as caucus critic for Revenue Canada. At the time I wondered why he was handing me a job for which I had none of the usual experience. But I realize now that he did me a great favour, and I'm sure it was deliberate. He saw it as a way to expand my knowledge and develop a stronger position from which to move ahead in the caucus and in the party. (If he saw me as a possible candidate to replace him, he certainly gave no indication of this to me.)

My first reaction to this new responsibility was mixed. I looked forward to the challenge, but I assumed that I would find taxation policy pretty dry stuff. That attitude soon changed. I started to realize that how people are taxed is fundamental to how a country is run. In Canada, taxes are intended to serve three basic purposes. First and most obviously, they pay for our public services. Second, taxes can be used to help stabilize the economy, to fuel economic activity during bad times, and to dampen it somewhat when the economy gets overheated. Finally, the tax system is supposedly designed to redistribute income, to move some of the money in the hands of the wealthiest people and most profitable corporations into the hands of the poorest people in our society.

Most Canadians don't object to paying taxes so that governments can provide important services such as medicare, unemployment insurance, workers' compensation, public transit, police, roads, and so on. They understand that these services are best handled by government and that they cost money. What Canadians object to is the unfairness of the tax system, a system that is becoming less fair all the time. Take the most recent and most outrageous example of this trend, the Goods and Services Tax.

As critic for Revenue Canada, I sat on the finance committee when it was conducting hearings to solicit public input into the government's proposed legislation to bring in the GST. Our party's basic objection to the GST was then, as it is today, that it is a regressive tax. A regressive tax is one that requires everyone to pay the same rate regardless of ability to pay. A single mother on welfare pays the same GST on a litre of milk as a lawyer who makes $100,000 a year. A flat-rate tax on consumption, such as the GST, is by definition regressive. And all regressive taxes hurt the poor the most. This is not to say that the tax the GST replaced, the hidden tax on manufactured goods known as the Manufacturers' Sales Tax, was a good tax. It unfairly penalized Canadian manufacturers as well as being just as regressive as the GST. Although it applied to far fewer items, namely goods manufactured in Canada, it was also at a much higher rate, 13.5 percent. The GST simply replaced one bad tax with another.

But the GST is only the tip of the iceberg of tax inequity. Consider these facts. Wealth in Canada is concentrated in amazingly few hands. Of the 500,000 corporations doing business in Canada, 3,316 earn 68 percent of all the profits. Nine families control 46 percent of the shares of the three hundred most important companies on the Toronto Stock Exchange. Yet, between 1982 and 1990, personal income taxes rose 232 percent for the poorest 20 percent of taxpayers while the wealthiest 20 percent paid only 82 percent more.

As I looked more deeply into the Canadian tax structure, I discovered even greater and more serious injustices. Since the 1960s, the tax system has become increasingly regressive. Successive Liberal and Conservative governments have managed to design an incredibly complicated tax system through which the rich get richer and the poor get poorer, all the while paying lip service to the principle of fair taxation.

They have done this in three ways. One has been to shift an increasing proportion of taxation into consumption taxes such as the GST. The second has been to shift the tax burden away from corporations and onto individuals. And the third has been slowly but surely to flatten out the personal income tax rates so that the richest now pay relatively less of their income in the form of taxes and the poorest pay relatively more. There are now only *three* tax brackets; the topmost tax rate is between 45 percent and 50 percent when federal and provincial income taxes are combined. Compare this to the situation in the 1960s when there were *seventeen* rate brackets, and the top combined federal and provincial rate for the top money makers was 80 percent. The richest people in Canada pay much lower taxes now than they did thirty years ago. When you add to this the various tax loopholes enjoyed by the wealthiest individuals and corporations, you get a system that is totally failing to promote economic fairness. In fact, it actively promotes economic inequity. In 1991 more than 7,000 people making more than $50,000 each paid no income tax at all. In 1987, the last year for which figures are available, more than 90,000 profitable Canadian corporations paid no tax on profits of $27 billion thanks to various tax breaks and loopholes.

The argument made by those who favour lower taxes for the wealthy and for corporations is that they will turn around and invest this money in Canada. In fact, statistics show that countries with a tax system that more effectively redistributes income also tend to be the countries with the highest rates of labour productivity and the highest rates of increase in productivity. The United States, which has the least equitable tax system in the developed world, has also had one of the slowest rates of growth in labour productivity in recent years. There's also the myth that countries where taxes are relatively high in relation to Gross Domestic Product do poorly. This is simply not the case. Our total tax revenues equal about 34 percent of GDP, making us a relatively low-tax jurisdiction compared, for example, to the countries of the European Community, where taxes average almost 41 percent of GDP and where some of the most successful countries collect considerably more. Norway collects taxes equal to 46.9 percent of GDP, and Sweden, 55.3 percent. It seems that redistributing income more fairly can actually promote economic health.

A complete overhaul of our tax system is long overdue. The main thrust of this overhaul would be to make the system much more progressive through such measures as repeal of the GST and a reform of income tax rates — more tax brackets with the top rate much higher. We also need to close loopholes for the wealthy and shift more of the tax burden to corporations — possibly in the form of a minimum corporate tax. To quote Neil Brooks, professor of tax law at Osgoode Hall Law School, "Tax reform to raise revenue and remove inequities is not a choice in a democratic society. It is a necessity."

We will design a truly equitable tax system only if we involve many more people in the process. Tax reform can't be left to the lawyers and accountants and politicians — who represent primarily those already at the top. The Ontario Fair Tax commission is leading the way in this more democratic approach, having mobilized a broad constituency of citizens to study and debate tax policy. In the process, it has eliminated much of the mystery and insider jargon from the discussion. I am convinced that the surest route to sound tax reform is to look at the question from the point of view of the people currently most damaged by the system, not those who have the most to gain by leaving it the way it is.

• • •

With a fall election looming, there was no summer recess in 1988, but we did break several times over July and August. I took advantage of these respites to return home and get out and around the territory. In the previous year, I'd managed to get back to the Yukon once or twice a month for as much as a week each time. During those visits I had spent time meeting with people, travelling around the riding, and handling constituency problems. When I'm home, I keep a full schedule. I don't exactly relax, but I definitely recharge.

If I get in on a Friday night, I usually drop my bags at my place on Hoge Street and head down to the bar at the Taku Hotel in downtown Whitehorse — not to drink, but to talk. On Friday nights the Taku is hopping, and I always run into people I know. If someone has a question, say about unemployment insurance, he or she doesn't hesitate to come up to me. I never mind — it's the other reason why I'm there.

My trips home to the Yukon are essential restoratives for heart and soul, a chance to draw on the reservoir of warmth and support of my friends. They're the kind of people who know how to tell the truth about their lives, and also how to listen when I talk about mine. When we get together, I can let my hair — and my defences — down.

Most of my time in the Yukon is taken up with constituency work, an aspect of the job I find very satisfying. I get a great sense of accomplishment from helping an individual with a problem. And that first year people seemed impressed that my office and I were so accessible. We handled hundreds of individual cases and have dealt with up to a thousand per year ever since.

Much of the credit for the immediate success of my Yukon office must go to Sarah Steele, who stayed on as my constituency assistant for my first two years as MP. Like so many Yukoners, Sarah is a self-starter who doesn't need a lot of supervision. She just takes something on and gets it done. She's not afraid to take charge.

I knew she would do a great job, but I worried that our friendship might suffer from the inevitable strains of an employer-employee relationship. Particularly in those first months, I asked a lot of her. After a week in Whitehorse or travelling around the communities, I generally left the constituency office with a big load of casework. I'm obsessive about detail and about follow-up. And I'm very impatient. Once back in Ottawa, I would almost always be on the phone to Sarah the next day to find out if everything on the list had been addressed. This sense of urgency can be hard on the people who work for me. But Sarah cared about the people and their problems as much as I did, which probably helped her survive those times when my demands seemed excessive. Happily our friendship has survived intact.

Much constituency casework involves helping people find their way through the federal bureaucracy — unemployment insurance, tax questions, immigration problems, human rights issues, Indian Affairs, northern development. When an MP and her staff get involved, the problem usually gets to the top of the bureaucratic pile. We don't always win; sometimes the system is right and the individual is wrong. But working with individuals in this way, I've become attuned to the frustration most people have with large bureaucratic systems. It's not that the employees of those government departments are bad or lazy; it's all the hurdles that are put in people's way and the jargon that is incomprehensible to people outside the system. And often, of course, it's just a case of bad government policy.

That first year, Sarah and I were able to help a number of aboriginal people who'd previously felt completely ignored by government. I remember one Indian elder who came to me with a pension problem. Somebody had filled in her Canada Pension Form incorrectly, putting down her guaranteed income supplement of three or four thousand dollars as earned income. As a result, the government had reduced her pension payment by half, taking a huge bite out of her monthly income. We were able to sort out that one so that she received her full pension.

A common pension problem with aboriginal people is that their births were never registered. Many were born in isolated communities or out on the land. As far as the government is concerned, they don't exist. In such a case, someone in my office would have to go through the process of proving that the person did exist and really was sixty-five years of age and did qualify for an old age pension.

I'm proud of what we were able to do that first year and have continued to do since. On several occasions, our office has helped young people start a youth club or a recreation service or get a team organized. When I've been asked to talk to a school class, I've almost never refused. And we've helped launch a number of seniors' projects. Activities such as these aren't part of any job description, but they have everything to do with the way I define the responsibility of a member of parliament.

Last year I helped the local Young New Democrats organize a panel for Equality Day. The panellists included a judge, someone from the native community, a francophone, a representative of the black community, and a lesbian. This was the first time in the history of the Yukon that an openly lesbian or gay person had ever spoken in a public forum, and that single event seemed to overcome an invisible barrier. There is now an association for lesbian and gay people in the Yukon. The credit goes to the woman who had the courage to break the silence and to the others who worked for this change.

Naturally, many constituency issues transcend the problems of specific individuals and are generally much more difficult to resolve. There is still a terrible shortage of adequate housing in the Yukon — especially for aboriginal people. There's an ongoing problem with pollution of the Yukon River, since Whitehorse still has no sewage treatment plant. And there's an unacceptable level of pollution in Lake Laberge, where Sam McGee was cremated, according to the famous poem by Robert W. Service. Whatever else is going on, these things are never far from my mind as problems I want to help solve.

• • •

In early October of 1988, when Brian Mulroney called the federal election, the women in the caucus and in the party had high hopes the NDP would elect more women to parliament than ever before. Our leader and our party had never been more popular, and many fine women candidates had come forward. We were to be sorely disappointed.

Looking back, it's easy to second-guess the national campaign, as many people subsequently did, inside and outside our party. Ed and his strategists had set out to deal with many of the issues facing Canadians, not just the U.S.-Canada free trade deal, which our party had vehemently and consistently opposed from the beginning. Their plan was to hit free trade hard and often, but to talk frequently about the many other policies we believed to be important. Early on, this approach seemed to be working. The Liberals under John Turner were making no impression on the electorate, and on October 11 an Environics poll reported that the NDP had moved firmly into second place, with 29 percent of the decided vote to the Liberals' 25. (The Tories stayed well ahead with 42 percent.)

It's difficult now to remember that the 1988 election was about more than free trade. There were four years of neo-conservative Tory policies to talk about, including major moves towards privatization and deregulation and the failure of constitutional reform. But after the English-language television debate, the election was reduced to a two-man contest. A few seconds of television time in a two-hour debate among the three party leaders was used to recast the election into a face-off between John Turner, the defender of Canadian sovereignty, and Brian Mulroney, the man who was going to sell Canada down the river.

On October 24, the day of the debate, I was campaigning in Mayo, a small mining community in the middle of the Yukon, about two hundred kilometres east of Dawson City. Free trade was barely an issue in the Yukon campaign; we were talking about development issues, mining issues, and environmental issues. Above all, the campaign came down once again to the issue of representation: had I done my job or had I been "corrupted" by Ottawa? According to our canvassers, the signs were good, and of course I had no inkling of what was about to take place on national television.

That night I finished campaigning as the debate was ending and got to my hotel room in time to watch the post-debate analysis. The commentators on CBC and CTV seemed to agree that the debate was a three-way draw; I went to bed feeling relieved. We all know how a debate can influence an election, as happened in 1984 when Mulroney skewered Turner on the issue of political patronage.

The next morning, however, it was as though a different debate had taken place. The broadcast media played the same clip over and over again. "I happen to believe you've sold us out," Turner charged. "You do not have a monopoly on patriotism," Mulroney angrily retorted. When the prime minister went on to describe the free trade deal as an act of nation building, Turner countered that it would instead "reduce us I'm sure to a colony of the United States." Those few seconds had been made into the defining moment of the debate and, as it turned out, the turning point of the election. The media spin left Ed Broadbent on the sidelines; the NDP campaign never recovered.

In the Yukon, we were shielded from the impact on the party generally. I received 51 percent of the vote, winning by a margin of more than 2,000 over Tory candidate Charlie Friday. Nationally, despite the perception that Ed's campaign had failed, the NDP collected more seats than ever before in our history, 43, although we were back in third place with 20.4 percent of the vote. Once again we had failed to reach beyond our traditional base of support.

And to my great dismay, representation by NDP women did not increase. Margaret Mitchell and I were re-elected, but Marion Dewar lost narrowly in Hamilton Mountain and Lynn MacDonald was defeated in Toronto's Broadview-Greenwood. The good news was that, although Pauline Jewett had decided not to seek re-election, her old riding, which had been split in two, gave us two new women MPs, Dawn Black from New Westminster-Burnaby, and Joy Langan, from Mission-Coquitlam. And Lynn Hunter had been elected in the B.C. riding of Saanich-Gulf Islands. That left us once again with five NDP women out of a total of 39 in a House of Commons now expanded to 295 seats. (Six months later the number increased to 40 with the election of Reform candidate Deborah Grey in an Alberta by-election.) As I headed back to Ottawa, I wondered when women would ever truly make a breakthrough.

Pauline Jewett used to joke, "When women can fill up a table in the parliamentary dining room, that's when the men will really start to worry." After the 1988 election one table was still full, but just barely. True, we women MPs were making our voices heard in the caucus and in the House, but I for one felt something more had to be done.

As a party, the NDP was already far ahead of the Liberals and Tories in bringing women into positions of power and responsibility. Party rules now required that the national executive, the federal council, and all committees within the party have equal representation from men and women. That left the parliamentary caucus as the last mostly male bastion. I therefore saw electing a woman to the executive as an important symbol. With elections about to be held for a new caucus executive, I talked to my women colleagues about the idea that one of the three caucus executive positions — house leader, caucus chair, or caucus Whip — should be filled by one of the five of us.

I remember sitting around that table in the parliamentary dining room, arguing that NDP women from all over the country had fought for and won support for affirmative action in the non-parliamentary party and that now it was time for us in the caucus to look at ourselves. Not everyone was convinced that this was an opportune moment to rock the boat. And these reservations were reinforced when we discussed the idea with sympathetic members of the caucus. Those urging caution repeated the time-worn phrase that all who work for change hear all too often: "The time isn't right." In this case, the free trade debates were raging late into the night, there were rumours that Ed was going to resign, and the caucus was generally on edge.

But there is never a right time for women unless we make it for ourselves. "We've really got to do this," I said at one point. "As the third party we don't have the power to change the world, but we do have the power to change ourselves." Eventually the doubters agreed.

However, when it came to deciding who would step forward, the other women all declined. Once again, I found myself having to live up to my own rhetoric. I was caught in the logic of my favourite quote from Gandhi: "You must first become what you seek to change." In the end I agreed to seek the position of caucus chair, a job that involves running the weekly caucus meeting, consulting regularly with the leader, and helping plot parliamentary strategy.

Since an opposition party doesn't have many positions of power to award, these elections are taken very seriously within the caucus. (In the other parties, the caucus executive is simply appointed by the leader.) But as it turned out, no opposition to my candidacy materialized. The truth of the matter, I think, is that Ed Broadbent quietly supported me behind the scenes.

I became the first woman chair of the parliamentary caucus of any federal Canadian party. Outside the NDP, this achievement went virtually unnoticed. No one in the press picked it up. Nonetheless, it was a small but concrete step in the right direction.

CHAPTER THREE

LEADERSHIP

POLITICS CAN BE A VERY UNFORGIVING business, never more so than for a leader who is seen to have fallen short. In the immediate aftermath of the November 1988 election, people in the party were angry at what they saw as a botched campaign, and most of their anger was directed at Ed Broadbent. He himself was deeply disappointed that we hadn't done better, especially in Quebec, where despite coming close in two ridings, we'd once again failed to win a seat. Early in the campaign, when we were riding high in the polls, he had addressed a large and enthusiastic rally in Quebec. To the assembled crowd he declared that this was what he had worked for all his political life. He believed that our party was about to make a historic breakthrough. Now, with the NDP once again well back in third place, the rumours began to fly that Ed was about to resign.

I was among those who went to Ed and urged him to stay on as leader. I had enormous respect for him and felt he had the ability to survive this difficult period. Although I hadn't come to know him well during my short time in parliament, I had seen ample evidence of his toughness under fire and his determination to stick to his principles. For example, although there were those who thought his support of the Meech Lake Accord was some sort of pandering to Quebec in order to win seats there, he believed profoundly that the Accord was the best compromise for Canada and was courageous enough to fight for it no matter how bruising the opposition. At the end of our brief chat, he thanked me for my expression of support, but gave no hint whether he would leave or stay.

Ed didn't tell the caucus in advance of his final decision. In fact, he kept all but his immediate family and a few close friends and advisers in suspense. He was to announce his decision at the meeting of the NDP federal council on March 4, 1989, in Toronto. The federal council is the governing body of the federal party between conventions, and it is made up of representatives from each province and territory along with the federal party officers (I was there in my capacity as Yukon representative). These were people who'd worked with Ed for many years, many of them close friends.

When Ed rose to speak that day, the hotel ballroom was packed tight with reporters, camera crews, and party faithful. Apart from his wife, Lucille, few people in the room knew what his decision would be. Some felt it was time for him to move on. Others wanted him to remain and fight another election. Whatever was in his mind, he seemed serene, clearly relishing the drama of the situation. It was one of the best speeches I'd heard him give, a passionate defence of the principles of social democracy on which he'd based his political career. But he saved the punch line until the end, keeping his audience on an emotional tightrope.

When he finally looked into the glare of the camera lights and announced he was resigning, there were loud shouts of "No! No!" and "Stay, Ed, stay!" Many people in the audience, myself included, wiped tears from their eyes. A few were sobbing openly. Even those who believed it was time for him to step down were carried away by the emotion of the moment. Everyone

realized how much he'd done for the party, how much respect
he'd achieved in the country, and what a thoroughly decent
human being he was. It was difficult to imagine the New Democratic Party without Ed Broadbent as its leader.

As the meeting broke up, the minds of the media immediately
turned to the question of who would succeed him. Since November, there had been much speculation about possible contenders. There was talk of Ontario NDP leader Bob Rae or Stephen
Lewis, the former Ontario leader and ambassador to the United
Nations. Bob White, the president of the Canadian Auto Workers, had been mentioned, along with various members of the
federal caucus, among them former B.C. premier Dave Barrett.
Marion Dewar, although she had lost her seat in the election,
seemed another strong potential candidate.

Marion, however, had another individual in mind. Hugh
Winsor, Ottawa correspondent for the *Globe and Mail*, approached her after Ed's speech and asked whether she thought
a woman would run. Her reply? "Audrey McLaughlin just might
do it." Marion hadn't yet mentioned this idea to me, so I was
somewhat surprised when Hugh asked if I was running. I told
him, quite honestly, that I hadn't even considered it. "Well, your
press agent is already at work," he reported.

By the time I got back to my Parliament Hill office, my staff
was buzzing with the news that I was one of the contenders to
succeed Ed; an item had already been broadcast on the local
radio. At that stage I found the whole notion preposterous. I'd
been an MP for less than two years; as far as I was concerned, I
was still learning my job. And the voice in my head was still
quick to say, "You can't do that."

Although I couldn't yet see myself in the role, I did agree
with NDP women across the country: there had to be a credible
woman candidate. In the days following Ed's resignation, there
was much telephoning and talking over lunch as our extended
network conducted an ongoing cross-Canada strategy meeting.
The only subject on the agenda: which woman inside or outside
the caucus should carry the banner?

My choice was Marion Dewar: former mayor of Ottawa, former

president of the national party, former member of parliament. But Marion felt the fact she had failed to hold her seat in the 1988 election disqualified her, and indeed several people agreed with her. I thought there were a number of highly qualified women who could have run, and I said so. Apart from Marion, there were party president Johanna den Hertog; Rosemary Brown, who'd finished second to Ed in 1975; Pauline Jewett, the former MP and former president of Simon Fraser University; Alexa McDonough, the leader of the Nova Scotia party; and Elizabeth Weir, the New Brunswick leader.

After Alexa and Elizabeth indicated they didn't want to leave their current jobs, a consensus gradually began to build that the candidate should be a current or recent caucus member, someone familiar with the workings of parliament and the parliamentary party. (I wonder if this wasn't an example of the old syndrome that a woman in the same job has to be twice as good as a man. Certainly no one had objected to Stephen Lewis as a candidate on the grounds that he hadn't sat in a legislature for years, or to Bob White, who'd never sat in a legislature, period. For that matter, Brian Mulroney became Tory leader without ever having been elected to anything since model parliament when he was in college.) Dawn Black, Lynn Hunter, and Joy Langan were all newly elected and removed themselves from consideration; Margaret Mitchell wasn't willing to take it on. And both Pauline Jewett and Marion Dewar wanted me to run.

Marion, a very tenacious woman, kicked her machine into gear. Suddenly I was getting calls of support and encouragement from all over the country. One of the first people who urged me to take the idea seriously was Tim Wood, who'd been working as Ed's press secretary when I first came to Ottawa. It was flattering; certainly I was feeling the pressure to say yes. But I took my time in reaching a decision.

A leadership campaign would be challenging enough, but what if I won? This time I didn't need anyone to tell me that the unexpected might happen. Did I really want to take on this difficult and demanding job — the long hours, the criticism, the lack of privacy, the isolation? Did I want to deal with the complexities of the national party and the caucus and endure the endless travel? In early April, I told everyone that I wasn't going to make any decision until the middle of May. Then I systematically consulted as many people as I could. I asked their advice and their assessments of the pros and cons. I met with people in my riding. I met with people in the party. I discussed what I might or might not have to offer as leader, what kind of leader was needed, and what goals that person should have.

Above all, I talked to the women of the party. Each province and territory has a Participation of Women committee, a group whose job is to encourage more women to get involved in the party and to run for office. Each of these committees sends a representative to the federal committee that promotes women's participation in the party. All the reps on the federal committee urged me to run. My female caucus colleagues, Dawn Black, Joy Langan, Lynn Hunter, and Margaret Mitchell, did the same, as did several male MPs, including Svend Robinson, John Brewin, and Ross Harvey. In fact, my discussions with people all across the country told me that if I ran and ran hard I did have a chance of winning.

One of my first concerns was that if I won the leadership, I wouldn't be able to properly represent my constituency. But most of my supporters in the Yukon were enthusiastic. Essentially they told me, "If you decide to run, we'll do everything we can to help you win." I assured them that I would do my best to maintain a strong commitment to my riding, even though I knew how difficult this would be.

Through April and into May I agonized about what to do. I was concerned about my limited parliamentary experience, about my unfamiliarity with some of the issues, about my lack of polish as a public speaker. I was especially concerned about my fledgling fluency in French since I believed that any national leader must be able to function well in both official languages. Whenever I expressed these doubts to Marion Dewar, she would look me in the eye and say, with typical optimism, "You'll just learn."

In the end it came down not to whether I could do the job,

but to what I could bring to it. Marion was right: I could learn to manage in French, I could learn to handle a media scrum, and I could master difficult policy areas. I also figured I could use my skill at working with groups to lead an effective caucus. So the real question became whether the party would be better off with me as leader than with anyone else who was likely to run.

It's difficult to write about this without sounding self-serving. But the truth is that the more I thought about it, the more convinced I became that my unconventional path had prepared me very well for the leadership. I'd lived several lives: wife and mother; graduate student; social worker; manager of a social agency; small businesswoman. I'd worked with people of many different backgrounds in many parts of Canada and in several parts of the developing world. I'd travelled widely. Through it all, I'd acquired a sense of empathy for people of every race, creed, and condition, an understanding that transcends anything you can learn in school or out of books. And I felt a deep commitment to Canada and to making it a fairer, more egalitarian and prosperous society. Could either of the other parties' leaders claim as much?

Mine would certainly be a profile very different from that of the standard political leader. And not merely because I was a woman — although that alone would send an important signal. Brian Mulroney and Jean Chrétien are both lawyers who have spent most, if not all, of their lives in pursuit of political power. For them, winning power and holding onto it have been the point. Power does not appeal to me except as a means to an end.

In the final analysis, I realized I wanted to play a role in changing the political culture of the party and of the country. I wanted to see a major shift towards leaders and elected politicians who are representative of the population as a whole, rather than the elites, and who bring a much wider range of experiences to political office. I wanted to air out those smoke-filled backrooms. If there was anything worth giving up my personal life for, surely it was this.

Yes, I had good reasons to run for the leadership. That left me with one final question: Do I dare? And just as I had when I first decided to run for parliament, I visualized sitting in that rocking chair asking myself what if and why not. Put into that perspective, even the worst that might lie ahead began to seem exciting.

• • •

On May 24, 1989, I called a press conference at the National Press Theatre on Wellington Street, across from the House of Commons. Apart from the assembled journalists, a small group of supporters was there to cheer me on: Marion Dewar, Pauline Jewett, Svend Robinson, Margaret Mitchell, Dawn Black, Joy Langan, Ross Harvey, and John Brewin. (Four out of what would ultimately be a field of seven announced their leadership bids before me — B.C. MP Ian Waddell; Saskatchewan MP Simon de Jong; Windsor, Ontario, MP Steven Langdon; and B.C. school-teacher Roger Lagassé. MP Howard McCurdy, also from the Windsor area, joined the race in late June.)

I made my announcement, explained why I was running, and then fielded questions from the reporters. Afterwards I turned to Svend Robinson and asked him how he thought the press conference had gone. He seemed a little taken aback. "Don't you know?" he replied. "It went fine." I explained I had nothing to compare it to since it was the first press conference I'd ever given in the press theatre. I'll never forget the look of astonishment on his face. Perhaps even he, one of my strongest supporters, had forgotten just how new I was to the world of electoral politics.

As in the Yukon, once I decided to run, I ran to win. There is no point in making the effort as a noble or symbolic gesture; victory was my goal, not glory. I was facing a leadership campaign that was unusual — and unusually taxing — because of its length. Ed Broadbent resigned in early March, but the convention was not to begin until November 30. The rationale was in part to give prospective candidates ample time to sound out support and make up their minds. But those of us who declared by May then faced a campaign of six months' duration.

In some ways the extra time worked to my advantage. Except for Roger, I was the least known of the candidates. So while the campaign entered the summer doldrums, I went on the road to meet as many potential delegates as possible. During June, July, and early August, I travelled continuously and visited every region of the country.

The typical setting for these meetings was the crowded living room of someone's house, or perhaps a local union hall. After I'd made a few remarks and invited questions, the meeting would break for coffee and informal conversation. This kind of relaxed occasion is one I very much enjoy.

In those early days I was trying to establish my campaign as offering something fresh, something original. When I met with prospective delegates I would talk about my vision of a more open party and a more inclusive, consultative way of operating. In terms of policy, there was very little to distinguish the candidates from each other. Leadership campaigns ultimately come down to questions of style as much as substance — although style is substance in some cases. I was trying to communicate an approach to politics that would bring new people into the party and into the decision-making process, a "style" that would actually mean a new way of doing things.

Meanwhile, back in Ottawa, my tour was being orchestrated by Valerie Preston, who'd agreed to act as campaign manager. For the first five months Val was the only paid staff person working on my leadership bid. We simply couldn't afford any others. The campaign would eventually spend $129,000, a comparatively small sum beside the hundreds of thousands of dollars — even millions — spent by recent leadership contenders in other parties. Almost all of that money went to paying for my travel, for basics such as brochures and other materials, and for the organization of the final phase of the campaign, especially the convention.

Apart from her function as part-time tour director, Val reached out across the country to build a national organization of dedicated volunteers. She was superbly suited for this role, having served during the previous four years as the federal party's women's co-ordinator. As a result, Val knew many of the influential women in the NDP and had strong connections with all the provincial and territorial organizations. She knew many of the men, too, having worked as executive director for Allan Blakeney when he was premier of Saskatchewan, and, having run various campaigns in her home province of Saskatchewan, she possessed solid organizing skills. She would need them, since a national campaign almost inevitably becomes a many-headed monster.

Tessa Hebb, a Nova Scotia native, former federal candidate, and member of the party's national executive, as well as its representative on the Socialist International, chaired the campaign strategy committee, a gradually expanding group that reflected the increasing depth and diversity of our organization. At our early sessions, the people who sat around the table with Tessa and Val Preston were Marion Dewar, who also took on the job of fund raising, Svend Robinson and Margaret Mitchell, Elizabeth Weir, and former Saskatchewan cabinet minister Doug McArthur. As the campaign progressed, this circle expanded to include people such as Carol Phillips, Bob White's assistant at the Canadian Auto Workers, along with key organizers working in the various regions. In the end, the weekly meetings became weekly conference calls.

Our basic strategy was to forge a coalition between the younger generation of party activists and the more seasoned party stalwarts — the so-called establishment. We would argue that Canadians were ready for a new kind of politics and a different kind of politician — not just a woman leader. Over and over again I used words such as "democratization" and "empowerment" to convey the kind of party I wanted to lead and the kind of politics I wanted to practise. I remember Val saying to me at the beginning of our long marathon that by the finish line she hoped we would have brought together all the elements of the party — men and women, academics and labour activists, farmers and small business owners, young and old — on our campaign team. And ultimately we did just that.

Over the summer, as I criss-crossed the country, our organization gradually coalesced. By late August, we had in place a well-organized, extremely effective grassroots political campaign with volunteer workers in every province and both territories. As the convention drew nearer, we constantly tracked delegates and built support. If political campaigns are won or lost on the ground — and I believe they are — then my victory was due as much to these volunteers as to anything I did or said. No other campaign surpassed the breadth and depth of our organization — or the sheer number of people involved.

As summer wound down, the leadership campaign geared up. But Bob Rae, Stephen Lewis, and Dave Barrett were still undeclared, one way or the other, causing many party members to hold back their support from the rest of the field. However, B.C. MP Nelson Riis and Saskatchewan MP Lorne Nystrom, who had come third in the 1975 leadership convention, had decided not to run. Nelson soon joined our campaign team.

In late August, a series of fifteen all-candidates debates was staged in major centres across Canada. That fall I was on the road as much as I was in Ottawa. In between these command performances, I continued to travel and campaign on my own. At the same time, I attended to my duties as an MP, which now included my responsibilities as Revenue Canada critic as well as handling northern development and looking after my constituency. I'm not quite sure how my staff managed, but they did.

My biggest problem was lack of support from the labour wing of the party. Although I felt I had developed a good understanding of labour issues, had met with many labour leaders across the country, and many rank and file members too, including groups of labour women, very few prominent people had signed on to my side. I could understand why: I have no background in the trade union movement and labour was naturally wary of this unknown quantity. In their eyes, I hadn't paid my dues. Also, many of them were still holding back, hoping that Bob Rae or Stephen Lewis, both with strong ties to labour, would change their minds and enter the race. Some were probably reluctant to see a woman as leader, but in all honesty I don't think sexism was the critical factor — at this point the president of the

Canadian Labour Congress was a woman and many women had risen to high rank within various Canadian unions. Mainly they were waiting to be convinced that I understood their concerns and would represent them well.

No aspirant to the leadership of the New Democratic Party can win without substantial labour support. As any student of our party knows, the NDP was formed in 1961 out of an alliance between the affiliated unions of the Canadian Labour Congress and the Co-operative Commonwealth Federation (CCF), founded in 1933. But our party's labour roots go even deeper than that. The CCF was a socialist party with a strong base in the prairie movement of farmers' co-operatives and in the urban working class. One of the formative events in the history of democratic socialism in Canada was the Winnipeg General Strike of 1919. Among the strike leaders arrested was J. S. Woodsworth, who eventually became the CCF's first leader. Of the 2,500 delegates at the convention, almost a third would come from labour.

Given all this, every appearance I made before a trade union audience was crucial. I was particularly anxious to do well when the MPs in the race were invited to speak to representatives of the United Steelworkers of America on September 18. The audience would consist of about forty of the leaders in the Ontario division of the union, which claimed 160,000 members and would be sending close to two hundred delegates to the convention.

When I arrived at the Steelworkers Hall on Cecil Street in downtown Toronto, I was reasonably confident. I had been well-briefed by Carol Phillips. I knew that the union president, Leo Gerard, and his aide, Michael Lewis (Stephen's younger brother and an important figure in the union's Ontario region), were both leaning towards supporting me. But as I was speaking, I could tell that I might as well have been talking a foreign language. I was not yet fluent in the codes and customs to which a labour audience responds. And they, steeped in a political tradition of fiery rhetoric, perhaps wanted me to move them to tears or sweep them off their feet with my speech. That I failed to do so didn't help our campaign morale, although it made me determined to work even harder at winning labour over.

Shortly after, when I broke my wrist in a fall down the front steps of my apartment building in Ottawa, things seemed to be going from bad to worse. Fortunately I was fitted with a fibreglass cast that allowed me to keep on shaking hands. In the following weeks, I developed the best physiotherapy in the world for a broken wrist: running for leader. Once the cast came off, the wrist was as good as new.

On September 29, Dave Barrett entered the race with the backing of a sizeable contingent of caucus; suddenly the whole complexion of the campaign changed. Until then we'd all been running against one another. Now it seemed that we were all running against Dave. Because of his previous experience as premier of British Columbia, he automatically became the "serious," candidate, the man to beat. Although I didn't necessarily agree that his qualifications were better than mine — just more conventional — that was the way the media saw it.

I relished the opportunity to take Dave on. He is a dynamic speaker and a skilled debater; his high-energy presence greatly enlivened the final two months of the campaign. Furthermore, the other candidates and I were no longer boxing with shadows. Those in the party who had been waiting for a "real" candidate to enter the race — Rae or Lewis or Barrett — need wait no longer, and potential supporters who had been sitting on the fence since May would now be forced to make up their minds.

The most frustrating aspect of the final stage of the campaign was the persistent reporting in the press that I was a "lightweight." Those who couldn't understand what I was trying to say — and that seemed to be most of the media — discounted the messenger. They reported, for example, that my speeches lacked substance. Although this perception wasn't shared by those who really counted, the party members who would be going to the convention, it could have posed a significant threat to the campaign: if an opinion is repeated often enough in the press, it becomes the truth in many people's minds, whether or not it is grounded in fact.

I do take criticism seriously and I try to evaluate it objectively. Accordingly, I sat down with my campaign colleagues and went over all my speeches. Our conclusion was that, if anything, they had *too much* content for political speeches, perhaps they could use some simplifying. I made a practice of talking at length about my economic ideas — about the need for a fairer tax system, about co-operative approaches to economic development, about the economic damage caused by the free trade deal, about the need to integrate environmental thinking into economic planning — but the press had already made up its mind and the negative labelling continued.

Criticism like this inevitably hurts. I would have had to be stone cold dead not to feel it. But I didn't stay awake at night fretting because some reporter decided to give me a hard time. In fact, I was surprised and pleased that I took the criticism so well; it was a healthy sign of maturity, an indication that I was better equipped than I'd feared to handle the job if I won. The criticism I'd heard so far was tame compared to what I would face as leader — or prime minister.

• • •

By the eve of the convention, Dave Barrett and I had each gained the endorsement of more than a quarter of the MPs in the federal caucus. And my labour support was growing, despite Barrett's strong base among the West Coast unions and the fact that much of the Ontario labour contingent was divided between Steven Langdon and Howard McCurdy. Although none of the big names in labour had publicly supported me yet, there were strong signals that Bob White of the CAW and Leo Gerard of the Steelworkers would put on our big yellow and black "Audrey" buttons soon after the delegates arrived in Winnipeg. Whether they would bring the majority of their members with them was another question.

At this point most pundits believed it had come down to a race between McLaughlin and Barrett. The general consensus in the media was that "it's Audrey's to lose." Our delegate tracking indicated that I would lead on the first ballot and that I had enough support as other candidates dropped off to win, but I never believe in polls. Only in results. I never took for granted that I was the front runner. Going in, I thought I had a 50-50 chance.

My only previous experience of an NDP leadership convention had been in 1975 when Rosemary Brown gave the party establishment — and Ed Broadbent — a huge scare, running second on the final ballot with 658 delegates to Ed's 948. As not only the first woman to run for a federal party leadership, but a black immigrant as well, Rosemary was a pioneer in more ways than one. I was a delegate at that convention representing the Toronto riding where I'd been active since joining the NDP in 1970. In 1975, I supported Rosemary, the person who challenged the status quo.

In 1989, many people drew parallels between my candidacy and Rosemary's. There was one obvious similarity: we were both women. And in some ways our campaigns did tap similar reservoirs of disenchantment with the old guard and the established way of doing things in the party. The main difference, as I see it, was the fact that my support bridged the gap between the generations and between the establishment and the up-and-comers. True, I was in many ways an outsider, but many insiders had decided to back me, from veteran MPs and MLAs to provincial and territorial leaders.

It's startling to realize that I was only the third woman to run for the leadership of any federal party. The year after Rosemary Brown came so close, Flora MacDonald made a determined bid for the Conservative leadership. Despite much professed support, she ended up a disappointing sixth on the first ballot at the 1976 Tory convention. Both Brown and MacDonald were widely seen as token women candidates who had no real chance of winning. As Sylvia Bashevkin notes in *Toeing the Lines*, her study of women in Canadian politics, these and other failed attempts by women to win party leadership at the provincial level reflected "a fundamental unease with the prospect of a female party leader."

But the New Democratic Party had genuinely changed between 1975 and 1989. It had become a more egalitarian institution, more reflective of society at large. Roughly 50 percent of the delegates to this convention were women. And despite the media criticism of my speeches, no one relegated me to the status of token. Nonetheless, it remained to be seen to what degree that "fundamental unease" persisted.

• • •

By the time I arrived in Winnipeg on the evening of November 29, most of the delegates had already gathered and excitement was definitely in the air. In our camp there was great optimism tinged with anxiety. We knew that some of my first-ballot support was soft and that I would have to perform well to hold onto all of it. We also knew that no matter how much groundwork and careful planning we had done, conventions have a habit of taking on a life of their own.

Much of the next three days is a blur: an endless shaking of hands, talking to reporters and smiling at cameras, punctuated by a series of command performances — a meeting with one or another delegation wanting to clarify my stand on some issue; the bear-pit session on Thursday; and the big speech on Friday night. Candidates probably know less about what is going on at a convention than almost anyone else — certainly less than the people watching on television. During the three days between my arrival and the balloting, I moved in a kind of suspended animation from one event to another, focusing only on what I had to do and say next.

Occasionally I would exchange a few words with my mother or my daughter, Tracy. Tracy, who was living in Winnipeg with her husband and two children, helped out with the campaign. My mother was a delegate from Regina and often sat with me at the Yukon table. But it wasn't an ideal situation for mother-daughter chitchat. Because of the demands on my time, the three of us spent few private moments together.

Meantime, holed up in a hotel room surrounded by empty cola cans and discarded pizza boxes sat Dave Gotthilf, the pollster and statistical whiz who had designed the questionnaire we'd used to poll the roughly 2,500 delegates before the convention. The information on voting preferences that he had gathered had been entered into a computer data base. Now, as reports came in from the convention floor, Dave was constantly revising the data and producing hourly updates — computerized lists showing how each delegate was likely to vote. This information was then fed back to the campaign troops. The speed and accuracy of this delegate-tracking system would prove crucial during the actual balloting. Each time a candidate dropped off, our team already knew exactly which of his delegates were likely to switch to us — and could then go after them.

As I'm sure my campaign staff would tell you, I can be a difficult person to manage. This stems partly from the fact that I've run a few successful campaigns myself, and partly from the fact that I have strong opinions about what I will and will not do. I insisted on sitting with the Yukon delegation whenever I was in the convention hall instead of up in the bleachers where the media would have had better access. And during the leadership speeches, I was in the hall listening to the other candidates. Apparently this is considered a tactical error: the prevailing wisdom is that if someone gives a scintillating speech just before you go on, your own performance might be negatively affected. I also refused to let my "handlers" set the pace as I moved about the convention floor. To me, it was more important to finish the conversation I was engaged in than to rush on to the next one.

Our team made one strategic decision that ruffled a few feathers. We decided not to have a hospitality suite. Although it is a long-standing tradition to provide a room where delegates can come to drink and be wooed, we decided to send a signal that we weren't going to do politics the old way. If delegates needed to booze and schmooze, they could go elsewhere. Most of the other candidates had rooms set aside for this purpose.

Thursday afternoon, the first day of the convention, brought the first spotlight event — the bear-pit session where the candidates faced the assembled delegates in a free-ranging question-and-answer format. The seven of us sat on the convention stage and fielded whatever questions the delegates threw at us. Once I got over my initial jitters, I began to enjoy myself. I liked the spontaneity and the chance to engage the delegates one on one. And apparently I escaped without getting mauled.

By the end of the day it became clear that our patient work building bridges to the labour contingent had indeed paid off. Leo Gerard of the Steelworkers publicly endorsed me, as did Bob White. When Bob announced his decision, many of the 120 CAW delegates booed. But the two announcements sent a strong signal to trade unionists, many of whom ultimately came to me. By Saturday, the day of balloting, Jeff Rose, president of the Canadian Union of Public Employees, and Gordon Wilson, president of the Ontario Federation of Labour, had also declared their support for my candidacy.

As I sat through the Thursday evening tribute to Ed Broadbent, I wondered what thoughts were running through his head. Despite the praise from speakers such as Shirley Carr, president of the CLC, and Allan Blakeney, his mood must have been bittersweet. In 1987, under his leadership, the NDP had briefly led all three national parties in opinion polls. The 1988 election had seemed an opportunity to win seats in Quebec and to break out of our rut as the perennial third party. But these dreams had not come true. And in another couple of days he would simply be the former leader of the New Democratic Party. It was an appropriate lesson in humility for prospective leaders.

Apart from the balloting itself, by far the most difficult and emotional part of the convention was the floor debate on the Meech Lake resolution on Friday. The resolution was a compromise between those close to Ed Broadbent, who wanted the party to unambiguously reaffirm our support for Meech, and those who wanted to see the deal renegotiated. The compromise wording recognized Quebec as a distinct society and accepted Quebec's other basic constitutional demands, but at the same instructed the party to work "now for changes and improvements" to some of the other provisions in the Accord. These included ending the

requirement for provincial unanimity in future constitutional
changes; safeguards to protect federal spending powers; recognition of the aboriginal right to self-government; and clearer
recognition of sexual equality. Although Ed ended up endorsing
the compromise, I doubt it made him very happy. And it certainly
angered the Quebec delegation. But given the mood of the party
and the very deep flaws in the Meech Accord, I believe it was a
sound resolution.

The most important performance of the campaign came on
Friday night when each of the leadership contenders addressed
the full convention. My usual apprehension before a big speech
only increased as I reworked my remarks. It seemed as if everybody in the campaign wanted a hand in its final drafting. As a
result, the text kept changing up until the eleventh hour. Although the result was a speech written by committee, I thought
it wasn't bad. Perhaps it had less punch, but it spoke to all the
concerns we felt needed to be addressed. I'd rehearsed it carefully and going in I felt reasonably confident.

Instead of making a grand entrance, accompanied by a
splashy floor demonstration with delegates parading around waving signs and chanting "Audrey, Audrey, Audrey," as my handlers wanted, I insisted I would simply walk up to the podium
from my seat with the Yukon delegation. We have to get away
from the notion that a leader should be a movie star. We have to
stop turning politicians into icons — who will then, of course,
go on to disappoint us. But on Friday afternoon, only a few hours
before the speeches were to begin, the convention's sound tech-
nician pointed out that we had no theme music. To the folks in
my campaign, that was taking a plain and simple entrance too
far. So David Pepper took charge. An assistant to Svend Robinson, David had helped set up our convention headquarters and
had already attended to an endless string of details. Now he
dashed from the hall to the nearest mall, found a record store
and purchased a likely sounding audio tape. When I walked to
the podium that evening, I heard the stirring strains of Tracy
Chapman's "Talkin' 'Bout A Revolution" for the very first time.
Afterwards we received countless compliments on our "brilliant

strategic choice," which seemed to characterize the spirit of change our campaign was attempting to convey.

So much has been written and said about my convention speech that it is now almost impossible to separate fact from fiction. But one thing is clear: however good or bad it was, Stephen Lewis's negative comments became received wisdom that haunts me to this day.

There is no name in the New Democratic Party more powerful than the name of Lewis. Stephen's father, David, was one of the pioneers of the CCF, one of the chief architects of the NDP, and federal leader from 1971 to 1975. He is remembered as a keen intellect and a great debater. Stephen followed in his father's footsteps and is probably the most admired NDP orator of his generation. As leader of the Ontario party, he'd come closer than anyone to winning in Ontario (at this point no one guessed Bob Rae had an even better chance). His stint as Canada's ambassador to the United Nations had only increased his stature. It was widely assumed that if he had run for the leadership, he would have won. When Stephen spoke, people listened.

I thought my speech went rather well. I wasn't getting as many standing ovations as had Dave Barrett, but down on the floor my supporters — who placed even more stock in my "performance" than I did — were relieved. Tessa Hebb recalls catching Svend Robinson's eye as I was speaking and nodding at him as if to say, "Everything is fine." Their reaction has been echoed by almost everyone I've talked to since; the speech was fine — not brilliant, but not terrible. Many of those watching on television had an even more favourable reaction. Although Mordecai Richler, who was covering the convention for *Saturday Night*, wasn't overly impressed, when he called his wife who'd been watching at home, she felt that I had come over "extremely well, fresh, even sparkly."

I had barely finished speaking before Stephen Lewis, who was working as a commentator for CBC, pronounced my speech "pedestrian" and commented that I should "fire the speech writer." (We laughed at that one later since it would have meant firing virtually the entire campaign team, including myself.)

Almost immediately the news rippled across the convention floor: Stephen had panned my speech.

Fortunately, I didn't find out about his reaction until much later. After the speech I returned to my seat with the Yukon delegation, beyond the range of roving journalists, and listened to the remaining speakers. Once Ed Broadbent had given his passionate and gracious farewell speech, I went straight back to my hotel. I wanted to get a good night's sleep before the balloting. Regardless of the outcome, I knew that Saturday would be a very long day.

Unknown to me, my campaign team had gone into crisis management mode. The key organizers huddled in our headquarters at the convention centre, trying to figure out how to counteract Lewis's negative comments. It was clear we had to do something to regain the momentum. The strategy decided on was simple: to get up early and not stop campaigning until the last vote was cast — to behave as if nothing had happened. Meanwhile many of Barrett's supporters, sensing victory, partied into the wee hours.

When the first delegates arrived at the Winnipeg Convention Centre the next morning, they were handed a copy of the morning edition of our convention newspaper. And when they stepped off the escalators to enter the hall, they were met by some of my most prominent backers: Marion Dewar, Alexa McDonough, Carol Phillips, and Nelson Riis. The campaign never faltered.

That afternoon as the balloting began, there was an excruciating climate of suspense in the hall. Had Barrett's strong speech gained him followers? Had Stephen's review driven first ballot support from me to other candidates? There was a feeling that the convention was truly up for grabs — and so it proved over the next five and a half hours as fortunes shifted and emotions ran high.

When Johanna den Hertog, party president and chair of the convention, arrived on the podium to announce the results of the first ballot, I felt remarkably calm. I knew I'd done all I could. Besides, I didn't know the precise number of votes we were anticipating. I hadn't asked and no one had told me. I only knew that I was expected to be in the lead.

Which I was, but barely. At 646 votes to Dave Barrett's 566, I held a margin of only 80. And Steven Langdon, who'd given probably the best speech of any of us, was in third place with a surprisingly strong 351. Only later did I learn that our workers had been expecting well over seven hundred votes on this first ballot, and many of them were now shocked and worried. (The only silver lining was the fact that Barrett's vote had come in right where our tracking had predicted it would; those who had deserted me — temporarily, we hoped — had moved mostly to Langdon.) What had seemed like an almost sure thing now looked in danger of slipping away. Everything would depend on our ability to hold the lead on the second ballot. If not, all bets were off. Val Preston turned to our floor manager, Bob Dewar (Marion's son), and sighed. "It's going to be an awfully long day."

It was now that all the preparation and planning proved its value. Our volunteers, armed with walkie-talkies and the latest delegate-tracking information from Dave Gotthilf, fanned out across the floor to persuade the released delegates to come to me on the next ballot. They had only fifteen minutes before the second ballot would be announced and they used every second of it.

The fifty-three delegates who'd supported seventh-place finisher Roger Lagassé were now free to move. To this number were added Ian Waddell's 213 votes, after he announced he was withdrawing voluntarily and walked over to fellow British Columbian Dave Barrett. Howard McCurdy, who'd come in a disappointing fifth with only 256 votes, moved over to fellow Windsor-area MP Steven Langdon. No one came to me. Clearly the momentum was now with Dave.

When a reporter asked if I was considering throwing my support to another candidate, I simply said that I had the lead and expected to keep it. The question was not who would be the king maker but "who would be the queen maker."

Throughout the afternoon, Stanley Knowles sat beside me in the bleachers. The support of this legendary elder of the party meant more than I can say. Also, despite the stroke he'd suffered a few years earlier, his old political instincts came to the fore. After each ballot, he had every spin on every number calculated — what it would mean if McCurdy moved here or if Waddell did this.

In the wake of the first ballot and subsequent moves, the omens did not look good for McLaughlin, according to the TV pundits. Robin Sears, the deputy campaign manager in the 1988 federal election and a wise politico, told reporters he had been making some calculations and thought it would be very difficult, if not impossible, for me to win now, that he was sure Barrett would ultimately take it. Meanwhile, Peter Mansbridge, anchoring the CBC's television coverage, seemed to agree, saying, "It's awfully hard to draw the scenario where Audrey McLaughlin wins this afternoon."

The number crunchers in my campaign told me later that there was never any chance that Dave could have won the convention, that when you looked at the delegates' second and third choices he simply didn't have the reserve strength to put him over the top. Maybe that's what the computer printouts said, but the dynamic of a convention defies logic. Anything can happen. And besides, there was Steven Langdon to consider. CBC's Mansbridge and his co-anchor, David Halton, had talked convincingly of a "third man scenario," where Langdon would emerge as the compromise candidate — as Joe Clark had at the 1976 Conservative convention.

Everyone knew the second ballot would be crucial. As the results were being announced, it was as if the whole convention hall — reporters and delegates alike — was holding its breath. Johanna read the tallies in alphabetical order: Dave Barrett, 780 — an increase of 214 (would it put him in the lead?); Simon de Jong, 289 — Saskatchewan's favourite son had dropped 26 votes from his showing on the first ballot (he was clearly out of the race); Steven Langdon, 519 — an increase of 168, but not enough (clearly many of McCurdy's 256 first ballot supporters had gone elsewhere); Audrey McLaughlin, 829. By the narrowest of margins I had retained the lead. Dave had garnered 32 percent of second ballot votes cast; I had won 34 percent. The race was still too close to call.

Steven Langdon now had a difficult decision to make. In third place, he could stay in the race for one more ballot at least. But did he have any hope of overtaking the front runners? Since we expected the majority of his supporters to move to me, we hoped he would drop out and make the walk in my direction. But what if Steven was to stay in and Barrett was to move ahead on the next ballot? Might some of my support shift to Steven in an effort to stop Dave? Hoping for a miracle, Steven decided to remain in to the end. When they heard his decision, his supporters started to chant, "We will not be moved."

As campaign workers swarmed over Simon de Jong's now freed delegates, one of the most dramatic moments of the convention occurred. No one was sure what Simon would do. As a westerner, Simon might be expected to give his support to Dave, but our organization had been strong in Saskatchewan and we knew that many of his followers leaned towards us. At this point, Dave, who thought he and Simon had made a deal, started to walk confidently towards Simon's camp, expecting de Jong to meet him half-way. Just as he did so, Simon began to walk towards me.

Reporters swarmed around Simon, asking him why he'd made the decision. Simon replied, "My head told me to go to Dave Barrett, my heart told me to go to Audrey." I've never been sure how happy I was with his reasoning, but I was delighted to have his support. It was the first clear shift in convention momentum in my favour, an event of great psychological significance as our team worked to pry delegates loose from the Langdon camp and persuade Simon's people to move to me. Next we heard that Quebec's sixty-five delegates were leaving Langdon and coming to us. And then Howard McCurdy walked over, which must have shocked Steven. As we embraced, Howard said, "We have to move the party into the future."

While the third ballot was tallied, the two speeches that had been written for me — one for victory, one in case of defeat — suddenly appeared. When I read them through, I concluded they needed serious reworking. However, the convention floor was bedlam, and wherever I went television cameras and reporters were sure to follow.

I turned to Les Campbell, the young Manitoba party activist who had been with me for the past three days, running interference and helping me keep on schedule. "Follow me," I said. Before anyone could catch us, we slipped out the side and I ducked into the women's washroom. Les returned in a matter of minutes with a small group of advisers, then stood guard outside the door to prevent unsuspecting delegates from entering, while I conducted what has come to be known as the washroom caucus. Media hordes were running frantically up and down the corridors shouting, "Where's Audrey? Where's Audrey?" but the candidate had disappeared. At one point as we were reworking the speeches, a woman made it past Les's blockade and came into the washroom. Our presence didn't seem to faze her, but we crammed into one of the stalls to continue our conversation. The scene was hilarious, and despite the pressure of the moment, it lightened my mood considerably.

I made it back into the convention hall just in time for the announcement of the third ballot. Once again I was in the lead; once again Dave was close behind at 947 to my 1,072, a margin of 125. Steven's total had dropped to 393.

The final act of this four-act drama was now set to unfold. First Steven walked over to me, saying to reporters, "I think she has the potential to be an excellent prime minister." I know how hard it must have been, at that moment, to be so gracious. Then Shirley Carr and Nancy Riche, respectively president and vice-president of the Canadian Labour Congress, threw their support to Barrett. If any more proof were needed that I was more than a woman's candidate, this provided it.

As the final ballots were cast and counted, my supporters waved their yellow and black signs and chanted, "Let's make history! Let's make history!" Although everyone around me was now confident I would win, I couldn't allow myself to believe it. I clutched both of my hastily rewritten speeches, still unsure which one I would deliver.

Finally, Johanna den Hertog stood on the platform for the last time holding a white envelope in her hand. The magic number to win was 1,195. Then she spoke. "Dave Barrett" — the pause before her next words seemed a lifetime — "1,072." My supporters exploded into pandemonium. I hugged my mother and daughter, and then Stanley Knowles. Although I was filled with both joy and satisfaction, my reaction to winning was once again mixed, just as it had been the night I won the Yukon by-election in 1987. Side by side with the sense of accomplishment was the sudden weight of great responsibility.

Dave Barrett, magnanimous in defeat, stood smiling on the podium. When the crowd finally quieted, he spoke: "I want to tell the people of Canada that we are a united party," he said. "I want to tell the young people of this nation that there is hope for this country with this party." After thanking his supporters and saluting all the other candidates and their workers, he concluded by moving that "this party, at the largest convention in its history, embarked upon a new course towards the beginning of the next century, is united and unanimous in endorsing Audrey McLaughlin as the new leader." Once again the hall filled with cheers. After more hugs and congratulations, I plunged through the crowd to join the other candidates on the stage. On the way, someone handed me a single red rose.

Ed Broadbent embraced me and grinned, "It's all yours." I handed my mother the rose, moved to the lectern, and waited for the crowd to settle down. I didn't pay the slightest attention to the "washroom caucus" speech.

"This is just the beginning," I said to loud cheers. Then I thanked all the candidates, praised their grassroots campaigns, and commented, "We didn't just choose a leader. We've got a cabinet here to run the next government."

As I switched into French, I began, "Ce soir nous avons choisi un nouveau chef." But when I reached the word "chef," which means leader, I paused. "Chef est masculin, je pense," I said. "Well, we're going to have to find new words to apply to me, perhaps *une nouvelle leader*. We're going to have to change the language."

Before closing I said, "Merci, thank you, and Massi Cho," the Gwitchin (Yukon aboriginal) word for thank you. My final words were addressed to all Canadians: "Come with us, join us. The NDP welcomes you. We're on the move in 1990!"

• • •

After the convention, a woman friend in the Yukon said to me, "I was so glad you didn't cry when you won." Other women have subsequently echoed her remark. I find their reaction very revealing. We are still not used to women as winners in politics. We accept them more easily as winners of beauty pageants or tennis matches or Academy Awards. We expect to see them handed a trophy and a dozen roses, and then to see them break down and weep.

So for all the women who will seek, or have ever sought, political office, I'm very glad I didn't cry. But I look forward to the day when it won't matter one way or the other. Maybe that day came a little closer because of the events of December 2, 1989.

CHAPTER FOUR

ANOTHER BEGINNING

AFTER THE DELEGATES ASSEMBLED in the Winnipeg Convention Centre had joined in singing the old union anthem, "Solidarity Forever," and then "O Canada," the hall began to empty. My first thought as I left the podium was how the defeated candidates and their supporters were coping. Despite the ritual expressions of unity and support, I knew that the men who'd lost were hurting — it was only natural. I also knew that the many delegates who had supported them felt disappointment and in some cases anger.

In particular I was worried about the implications of the labour split; I knew I had not been the choice of many rank and file union members, some of whom felt betrayed and abandoned by leaders such as Bob White, Leo Gerard, and others who had endorsed me. I was well aware that many of the union delegates had not agreed with their leaders' choice. And the majority of West Coast labour delegates, who had voted for Dave, viewed me with suspicion and hostility. Clearly there was a gulf to be bridged.

On Sunday afternoon, in my farewell speech to the delegates, I attempted to rise above whatever bitterness remained by addressing the future. "This weekend we made some history and in three years we're going to make history as the first NDP government in Ottawa." Brave words. The words a new leader is expected to utter. But I put much less stock in words than in actions. A divisive convention and a divided party do not spell a leadership honeymoon or easy electoral gains. Despite all my attempts to talk about new directions, the political pundits were pronouncing us the party of old ideas, as if we had been left behind by the death of communism and the ascendancy of Brian Mulroney's neo-conservative agenda. Bringing my wounded party together and defining the NDP's program for the nineties would be no small undertaking.

• • •

The simple fact that a woman with my background and eclectic experience was now the leader of a federal party was a revolution in itself. When I was growing up in southwestern Ontario during and after the Second World War, there were few signs to suggest that someone like me could ever achieve so much or move so far.

I was born on November 7, 1936, in the village of Dutton, Ontario, just north of Wallacetown in the middle of Dunwich Township, Elgin County. Both my mother's and my father's forebears helped settle this flat and mostly fertile farming area on the north shore of Lake Erie, about fifty kilometres southwest of London. In the late thirties, it was a world still very much like the one described by John Kenneth Galbraith in his memoir of the area, *The Scotch*, a tightly knit, ingrown farming society with rigid social codes.

My mother's parents left Dutton around the turn of the century to homestead in Saskatchewan, part of the wave of prairie settlement following the completion of the Canadian Pacific Railway. My mother, Margaret Clark, and her eight sisters and one brother were born on a dirt-poor prairie farm and into a life

of constant struggle and occasional hunger. After my grandmother died, my grandfather couldn't cope with such a big
family. So my mother, then in her early teens, was sent along
with one of her sisters to Dutton to be raised by my great-grandmother Campbell — her mother's mother. She grew up on the
same Dunwich Township farm where her mother had been born
and raised.

My father, William Brown, was a Dutton town boy, but his
life was no easier than my mother's. He too had come from a large
family — thirteen brothers and sisters — and he too had lost a
parent: his father died when he was still quite young. In those
days, before any kind of social welfare, single parents depended
on their children to help keep the wolf from the door. My father
went to work while he was still a teenager, and he never stopped
working until he had a stroke in his sixties.

Although my parents left Dutton after I was born, we returned
often to visit relatives. I have warm memories of the threshing
bees, when all the local farmers would co-operate to bring in the
harvest. These hard-working people, whose worlds seldom exceeded the boundaries of a few square miles, had a sense of
community we often miss today.

When I was tiny, we used to visit my great-grandmother
Campbell, the family matriarch, who still lived on the original
farm. Her husband had died when their eldest child was twelve,
and she in her early thirties, leaving her to run the farm and raise
six children on her own. My mother remembers her never at
rest — always cleaning, cooking, making her own soap, curing
her own ham. She must have been a woman of iron. By the time
I knew her she was in her eighties, but still cut an imposing
figure.

I have one especially vivid image of my great-grandmother,
sitting in a rocking chair in the farmhouse kitchen next to the
old woodstove. She is wearing what she always wore — a great
floor-length black dress — and her collie lies at her feet. She
takes a drink from the cup of tea in her hand and sets it down.
Then the dog takes a drink from the same cup. Then my great-
grandmother. Then the dog. And so on. Naturally I found this

ritual rivetting: it would never have been permitted in my mother's household.

Money was never plentiful in my family, but it was particularly scarce immediately after I was born. At the time of my birth, my mother was diagnosed with breast cancer, and she had to remain in hospital for several months for treatment. It took ten lean years before my family was able to pay off the medical bills in those pre-medicare days.

While my mother was recuperating, I was looked after by friends of my parents, the Newkirks, who lived in Port Stanley on the shore of Lake Erie. I'm sure a psychologist might try to read something traumatic into this separation from my mother so soon after birth, but I never lacked for the kind of nurturing an infant needs. My father lived nearby and worked as a junior clerk in the office of the Shell Oil Company in town. And the Newkirks, who had no children of their own, treated me like a daughter. I always referred to them as my aunt and uncle; they became my second family.

After my mother recovered, she joined us in Port Stanley, where we lived for about five years before moving to Windsor. My mother says I was a shy and introverted child, that I kept my thoughts and feelings very much to myself. Sometimes she found this frustrating. If I came home from a birthday party, for instance, and she asked me what I'd eaten, my typical reply would apparently have been, "Food." Or if she asked me what I had learned at school that day, I'd say, "Nothing much." If something was bothering me, it would often be weeks before I would mention it.

It's funny what one remembers and what one doesn't. When we were living in Windsor, I developed a fantasy about running away to some exotic foreign land, and I spent a lot of time concocting elaborate plans of escape. I don't think I was unhappy at home; I simply wanted to have an adventure. One day at age eight or nine, I hopped on a bus and headed downtown. I have no idea where I planned to go or how I planned to get there, unless I thought of Detroit as Shangri-La. At any rate, the bus driver knew my mother and recognized me, so I didn't get very far. Since I was absolutely forbidden to go downtown alone, I'm sure I was punished, though it's the escapade rather than the consequences I recall.

I may have been shy with adults, but I had no shortage of friends. One of our favourite games was "church" and I always got to play the minister. The mock congregation would sit dutifully while I delivered the sermon — I wish all my audiences these days were as attentive. I was also something of a teller of tall tales back then — I liked to romanticize and embroider. I clearly remember telling my friends that my mother was part Indian, which of course meant that I was part Indian, too — different and exotic.

My mother and father had their problems, like most married couples, but I remember them as loving parents. They both had an innate sense of decency and fairness that they passed on to me — not through any deliberate teaching, but through the example of their actions. They were both involved in the community. My father in particular was very active in the local service clubs.

Although I thought of my parents as ordinary people, I can see that my mother was in some ways rather unusual for her time. She had no formal education beyond high school, so she educated herself. After we moved to Essex, Ontario, a small farming community just east of Windsor, she took a part-time job as the area correspondent for the *Windsor Star*, reporting on local events and writing the occasional feature article. She also developed her artistic talent, which she expressed through lovely landscapes and flower paintings. When I was a teenager, she ran for Essex town council and won, the first woman ever to do so.

I seem to have inherited my mother's restless energy. She too is a doer, not a sitter. She never looked back or dwelt on her misfortunes even after my father's stroke, which left him an invalid for the last ten years of his life. Those were hard years for my mother — working in a dental office to pay the bills and nursing her husband. After my father died, she moved to Regina to work with one of her sisters and made her living using her artistic talent to create designs for my aunt's craft business. She always developed her talents beyond the limitations of her time and place.

Only last summer I went with Steven Langdon, who represents the riding of Essex-Windsor, to visit the area where I spent my teenage years. The soil is rich, and it remains a prolific area for farming and market gardening — although a recent period of drought has put many farms at risk, a sadly familiar story these days in Canada. On that trip we visited a large dairy farm, a father and son operation. The senior of the two remembered my dad, who as the credit manager of the local farmers' co-operative had helped many farms avoid bankruptcy. "There's a lot of farmers around here who wouldn't be farming today if it hadn't been for Bill Brown," he told me.

My early high school years were happy ones. I was a loner but I wasn't lonely. My first day in grade nine, I met the girl who would become my best friend during the years I lived in Essex — Gayle Annett. The students were seated alphabetically starting at the front of the row, so Audrey Brown ended up sitting directly behind Gayle Annett. Most of the kids in our class were from the surrounding farms, but Gayle and I both lived in town, making it natural for our friendship to grow. We had other things in common, too: we were both only children; we were both young for grade nine, having skipped a year in elementary school; and we both liked sports.

Our favourite sport was basketball. The girls' team became our major extra-curricular activity. What with practices after school and out-of-town games, we were kept busy. In March 1952, when I was sixteen, our team reached the regional play-offs in London, which meant travelling by bus to the city and staying overnight in a hotel.

Although we ended up winning the championship over teams from Meaford and Waterford, I remember the trip for another reason. There was one black girl on our team, Freda Walls. When the team bus arrived at the hotel in London where we'd made reservations, the manager informed our coach, Miss Murphy, that the black girl wasn't welcome. The team could stay at the hotel, but Freda couldn't. (It's amazing to think that this wasn't very long ago, the early 1950s.)

Miss Murphy gathered the whole team together and said, "Girls, we've got to make a decision here. You can all stay at this hotel and I'll take Freda to another hotel, or we'll all leave and stay someplace else." She was very astute; she left the decision up to the group. And of course, we all voted to go to another hotel with Freda. I've always remembered Miss Murphy's wisdom, her lesson that day about racial discrimination and tolerance. She also provided me with my first concrete example of the consultative process, of reaching a decision by consensus.

When I wasn't playing basketball or sitting through the Saturday afternoon double feature at the Rialto Theatre or hanging out at the Deluxe Restaurant on Main Street with Gayle, I read. Almost from the time I learned the alphabet, I've devoured books. This may have something to do with being an only child — with no brothers or sisters, books can become your closest companions. I read all the usual things girls read in those days: Nancy Drew and *Little Women* and the Just Mary stories — almost anything I could get my hands on.

In my teenage years, I was drawn to biographies and autobiographies. Two that particularly impressed me then were about George Washington Carver and Albert Schweitzer. Carver was the black American scientist who became famous for his agricultural research into peanuts. But it was his work to promote the interests of African-Americans that left the strongest imprint on me. Schweitzer's work as a medical missionary in West Africa and his profoundly humanistic philosophy also made a deep impression. There is a scene in his memoirs in which he recounts being asked why he persists in this apparently impossible task — there are so many sick people and no hope that he can cure them all. Schweitzer replies, "Well, it's similar to pebbles on a beach. You'll never pick up all the pebbles, but if you picked up six a day, you could eventually build something very beautiful."

Almost every summer into my early teens, I would spend time

with my "Aunt and Uncle" Newkirk in their big old house in Port Stanley, a lively summer resort whose Stork Club attracted all the big-name big bands. As I grew older, I stayed in Essex during the summer and worked at various jobs — anything that was going, from picking fruit and vegetables for one of the local market gardeners to working in a canning factory. At different times I found work as a waitress and as a clerk in a dime store.

My later high school years were not particularly happy. I was a gawky teenager and considered myself unattractive, an opinion reinforced by the fact that I wasn't popular with the boys. As a result of my general unhappiness, my grades were slipping and the school guidance counsellor was disapproving. Eventually she called my parents in for a meeting. As I sat in silent humiliation, she launched into a speech about how I should be ashamed of my poor showing. I suppose she was trying to brow-beat me into doing better, but instead of building up my confidence she made me feel utterly worthless. By the end of the session, both my mother and I were in tears. Of course, this didn't work either. I continued to do poorly and did not complete all my grade thirteen credits — there just didn't seem to be any point.

After this I started to wonder whether people in authority always knew what they were doing. I began to question the assumption that those in positions of power automatically deserved my respect. The counsellor didn't; I was in no doubt about that. I never looked up to authority figures in quite the same way again.

In 1954, nursing and teaching seemed to be the only professions open to women. Gayle decided she wanted to be a teacher and was accepted at the teacher's college in London, Ontario. I wanted to be a nurse, but at sixteen I was too young to apply to nursing school so had to settle for the home economics course at the Ontario Agricultural College at Guelph. I chose Guelph at the urging of friends of my parents; both had attended the school and felt it would broaden my horizons. After completing the one-year course, I worked as a junior dietician at Victoria General Hospital in London until I married Don McLaughlin.

My mother says she had no qualms about my leaving home at age sixteen. It was far more important to her that I continue my education, something she had been unable to do. I know she has watched my life since then with surprise and pleasure. She says she sees in mine the more adventurous course she might have taken had her circumstances been different. But when I won the leadership of the New Democratic Party in December 1989, I'd arrived at a place beyond her wildest imaginings. Or mine.

● ● ●

On Monday, December 4, 1989, as the convention delegates dispersed to their homes and jobs, I sat in an office in downtown Winnipeg making phone calls across the country. These were phone calls of congratulation and condolence in about equal measure, talking to the people who'd helped me and the others who hadn't and speaking to each of the defeated leadership candidates.

Tuesday I was back in Ottawa, accompanied by Ginny Devine, who had agreed to act as my interim chief of staff during the first few weeks of the transition. Ginny had held many jobs with the Manitoba party, including acting as Howard Pawley's principal secretary when he was premier. I was greatly relieved to have her with me, even if only briefly. In a couple of weeks, John Walsh, an equally experienced politico I'd first met when he worked as Tony Penikett's principal secretary in the Yukon, would replace her. Together they would help me through my first month in the job while I looked for more permanent staff.

The leadership convention had taken place while parliament was in session, so I was permitted no grace period to ease gradually into my new responsibilities, no chance to rest and collect my thoughts. It was a little like stepping off one fast-moving train and onto another. It seemed that every journalist in the country wanted an interview. Virtually every MP in the caucus wanted to talk to me about his or her critic responsibility. I had to prepare for Question Period every day and be briefed on the breaking issues. And through it all I was determined to keep up my daily hour of French. Ginny now says that she was worried I was trying to do too much. But I was more concerned about her, since she was five months pregnant and working the same long hours. She says that when she left the office about ten each night, she often felt "ready to call an ambulance." Happily for me, my energy seldom wilted.

For the first few days, we operated out of my MP's office in the Centre Block, which I'd moved to after becoming caucus chair. Ed naturally needed some time to clear out his office and say good-bye to those who had worked with him for so long. From the moment I won the convention, Ed's staff was technically working for me. This would take some adjusting to, since I'd abruptly gone from a staff of four to a staff of approximately sixty.

On December 6, the House of Commons temporarily suspended its normal acrimony in order to welcome me as leader. Ed sat beside me at the front desk reserved for the NDP leader; the press and public galleries were full and the House was packed. Both Brian Mulroney and outgoing Liberal leader John Turner were witty and congratulatory, although neither could resist a few pointed remarks. Turner made a joking reference to Ed Broadbent's prediction during the 1988 election that Canada was about to become a two-party system, Tories and NDP. "Whenever the NDP is ready to close up shop and join us, we can begin talks," he said. And Mulroney made an ironic reference to my predecessor as Yukon MP, Erik Nielsen, whose departure had ruffled a few Tory feathers: "Whatever our differences may be in the future, I hope that the new leader keeps in mind that the honourable member for the Yukon, whoever he or she is over the years, always has a special place in my heart."

I replied in kind. "I would like to say to the prime minister that I am glad that members from the Yukon have a special place in his heart. I assure him that he will have a special line in my book." Everyone on both sides of the House understood that I was referring to Nielsen's recently published memoir, *The House*

Is Not a Home, in which he had roasted his former Tory colleagues as mercilessly as his former political foes.

I then spoke more seriously, talking of "the dignity with which all leaders in this House have acted," and saluting the defeated leadership candidates. Finally I paid special tribute to the leader I was replacing, deliberately breaking with parliamentary decorum forbidding any reference to an MP by name. "The Honourable Ed Broadbent has brought great honour to this House through his career, and not only to the New Democratic Party but to us all. He is a politician who is respected, who speaks his mind, who stands up for what he believes." No one treated my departure from the rules as a gaffe this time.

I closed by saying, "I look forward to working with you. I am sure that this gracious moment will continue through the next — three-quarters of an hour!"

My good mood that day did not last long. Only a few hours after I had spoken in the House, Marc Lépine gunned down fourteen women engineering students in a classroom at the Ecole Polytechnique at the University of Montreal, wounding thirteen others in the rampage. It is difficult to express the mixture of rage and sadness that filled me when I heard the news, but my emotions didn't prevent me from grasping the larger symbolism of the event. Those women were killed because they had dared to trespass in a traditional male preserve. Through no fault of their own, they became the victims of one man's hatred of all women who strive for equality. The killer may have been mad, but his anger — and his need to express that anger through violence — is shared by many who are all too sane.

And so, tragically, my next words in the House of Commons were words of mourning, as the next day I rose to deplore the event that has come to be known as the Montreal Massacre. "Those lost lives were our future; young minds who were attending school to acquire an education to work in their community, to share their abilities with their friends and families; young minds who wanted to contribute to Canada, and I guess young hearts that wanted to love. We will never know what gifts of joy or of laughter were extinguished by this act of horror."

It wasn't easy to shake off the strong feelings engendered by this tragedy, but I simply threw myself back into work with even more intensity.

• • •

Among the many jobs assigned to a party leader is "leading" the parliamentary caucus. In fact, the head of a third party in the House of Commons has very little power beyond the power of persuasion and the power of example. Apart from the assignment of critic responsibilities, there are no perks or privileges to dispense — no fancy offices or government departments to run. I likened my caucus to a group of forty-two small businesspeople whose first responsibility was not to me but to their businesses — their constituencies. No successful politician can afford to ignore his or her riding for long.

At the same time, I knew that many in the media and in the party were saying that I had won the leadership primarily because I was a woman, that I was an "interim" leader, a caretaker who would see the party through the next election before handing things over to another, better leader, presumably a man. I found such sentiments insulting to me and to women politicians in general, and I was determined to prove them wrong.

In those first weeks, I did what I could to bring the caucus back together. I invited each of the defeated candidates to dinner. All accepted save Dave Barrett, who simply told me, "I'm not ready yet." About a year later, he and his wife, Shirley, had me over for dinner, perhaps his way of saying he was ready to forgive and forget. He has been a valued colleague throughout my time as leader.

I also met individually with each member of my caucus — in their offices — to discuss his or her role. This proved a logistical nightmare that had Ginny tearing her hair out. Given all the demands on my time, it seemed crazy to her that I would go traipsing all over the Hill to see members of caucus at their convenience, but for me it was simply a fundamental matter of respect. After I had met with them all, Ginny and I carefully analyzed the skills and talents available and assigned shadow responsibilities on this basis.

By refusing to distribute the caucus critic jobs according to some policy of punishment and reward, I hoped to establish from the outset that I would hold no grudges and play no favourites. Sometimes this meant making overtures to someone whom a more traditional leader might have sought to ignore or isolate. My aim was to include everyone. I don't know any other way to operate.

Given the size of our caucus — forty-three members as compared to the Liberals' eighty-three — I concluded that some sort of reorganization was in order. It seemed futile to attempt to mimic the official opposition and its shadow cabinet. We simply didn't have the resources. The answer, I concluded, was to operate in a smarter, more co-operative fashion, one that would organize our human resources and knowledge in a more effective way. Eventually my advisers and I worked out a system of caucus teams: groupings of critic areas with overlapping concerns. There is now a finance team, an economic policy and fair taxation team, a labour team, a constitution and justice team, an environment team, a social policy and anti-poverty team, a regional and rural development team, and an international affairs team. The international affairs committee, for example, includes the critics for external affairs, immigration, defence, and the Canadian International Development Agency, the government's main dispenser of foreign aid. The idea was to get people working together on broader issues. On the whole, these teams have turned out to be highly successful and have improved the communication and sharing of information between policy areas. We've seen a real cross-fertilization of ideas.

After almost three years as leader, I think I can say that my approach has proved its merit. Despite occasional problems, I believe the caucus now works more co-operatively than before. Recently, when several members broke ranks and voted for the government's constitutional referendum legislation, the crisis quickly waned. (It was more of a crisis in the media than in the caucus.) I didn't see this "rebellion" as a challenge to my authority or a threat to my leadership. The main point is that, through many difficult times, we have almost always emerged from the caucus room to speak with one voice.

In caucus, I prefer to listen first and talk later, rather than stating my views and waiting for the group to come around to my way of seeing things. I try to make sure I'm well informed, that on a difficult issue I have talked to people outside the hothouse of the parliamentary party. Usually I will have phoned people right across the country and gauged their sense of how the issue is breaking in their area. Then I'm in a position to help shape the discussion in caucus and to correct statements such as "In Saskatchewan everyone is ready to resign over this one." When I hear a remark like that, I'm often able to say, "Well, I just spoke to so-and-so in Regina and he doesn't see it quite that way. Let me tell you what he said." My position is seldom engraved in stone except on a matter I regard as one of basic principle.

When you spend as much time in Ottawa as MPs do, it is easy to lose your sense of perspective. Not long ago in caucus, Vic Althouse, who represents the Saskatchewan riding of Macken-zie, used an apt metaphor to describe a federal politician's preoccupations. He said, "If you think of Canada as a doughnut, we spend about 90 percent of our time concentrating on the hole in the middle." Ottawa is where the government is and where the national media focus their attention. But in reality, the majority of Canadians don't share this focus. They don't read the *Globe and Mail*; they watch local television and read local newspapers. We MPs must keep going back into our communities to stay in touch with the everyday realities of the people we represent. Sometimes in the glare of the television lights on the brink of some new "national" crisis, this is easy to forget.

• • •

One of the most vivid examples of this kind of Ottawa-centred thinking is the issue of MPs' pensions. When I was first elected, I hadn't even enquired about the House of Commons pension plan and was therefore completely taken aback when I discovered how generous MPs' pensions are. Under the current system, any MP, regardless of age, automatically qualifies for a pension after six years and can begin collecting it immediately. Thus an MP elected at age twenty-one who is defeated at age twenty-seven can collect $23,390 a year for the rest of his or her life, regardless of what else he or she does next. After fifteen years of service, an MP becomes eligible for a full pension, which amounts to 75 percent of his or her salary.

This arrangement struck me as wrong. I realize members of parliament have an unstable job situation and often give up large salaries when they enter political life. But this pension set-up was much more generous than anything in the private sector. After becoming leader, I tried repeatedly to persuade someone in my caucus to take the issue on, but no one would touch it. In the end, I decided I would have to take it on myself.

Not until two years after I became leader did the opportunity appear. In February 1992 the government introduced a bill that made revisions to pensions for both civil servants and MPs. Given the depth of the recession, parliamentary pensions were even more difficult to justify. As Canadians were being asked to tighten their belts, I felt MPs should be making some sacrifices, too. So I rose in the House and suggested that MPs' pensions be reformed, calling for an independent commission to review the pension scheme and make a recommendation to parliament.

Predictably, the government and most opposition members opposed any changes, many taking the familiar patronizing line that I simply didn't know what I was talking about. However, the press and the public reaction was so overwhelmingly positive that the Tories reluctantly agreed to refer the whole matter to a committee independent of the House of Commons that will recommend changes to the plan. It's a good example of what happens when the people who live outside the doughnut hole raise their voices loudly enough to be heard.

• • •

As I discovered during the months following my convention win, a leader becomes a collective property. It seemed almost everyone was offering advice on how I might be "improved." A great many people's hopes were now invested in my success as the new NDP leader, and the first woman to be leader. Some wanted their support for me during the leadership campaign to be vindicated. Others simply wanted me to do well so that the party would do well. All this was natural. However, one aspect of this well-meaning counsel drove me mad: the persistent suggestions that I change my image.

One of the first recommendations was that I do something about my teeth — they were too crooked. Another theme was that my eyebrows were too dark. Some people wanted me to change my hair. A lot of people didn't like my clothes — all those bright colours I enjoy wearing. And many people wanted me to change my speaking style. I began to joke that if I acted on all the advice I heard I might as well go on to change my party, my gender, and my job. Of course I was willing to learn and change where it mattered, but I wasn't going to alter my image to suit the wisdom of the moment. Supposedly I'd been elected leader because of who I was; now I was being told to be someone else.

The campaign for a new, improved Audrey reached its peak when a group of party people organized a support dinner and overnight retreat in my honour. "Support" turned out to mean a long discussion about all the things I could do differently and better. I remember thinking to myself, "I'm never going to put myself in this position again."

I comforted myself with the knowledge that this sort of thing is an automatic reaction to almost any new leader. When Mike Harcourt first gained the British Columbia leadership, he was criticized mercilessly for his supposed lacklustre style. And people forget that Ed Broadbent heard a constant litany of complaints in the party and the press when he first became leader: he was dull, he was bland, his hair was too long, and his suits didn't fit; he couldn't speak a sentence without turning it into a paragraph. Partly he improved with experience and partly people simply got to know him and to trust him.

In fact, to me, one of the main reasons Ed became and remained such a popular leader — ultimately the most person-ally popular of the three federal leaders of this time according to the opinion polls — was that the person the public saw and the person he really was were one and the same. He had become smoother and more confident in the job, but more importantly, there was no incongruence between the public Ed Broadbent and the personal Ed. The same couldn't be said of the other federal leaders. John Turner managed to lose his nervous cough and improve his TV performance, but that wasn't the problem. I don't think people ever believed the person they saw was the real John Turner. They certainly don't feel that the man they see on TV these days, either oozing charm or waxing with righteous indignation, is the real Brian Mulroney. And now they seem to have tired of Jean Chrétien's formerly winsome act as the down-home "p'tit gar" from Shawinigan.

While all new leaders must expect criticism and advice, there is an extra dimension to it when that leader is a woman. How often have you read a newspaper report about a male politician that began like this? "Brian Mulroney, wearing a dark blue suit tailored by Armani, a cream coloured shirt by Dior and a silk tie from Pierre Cardin, visited Calgary today." That sort of coverage is common for women in public life.

My favourite example of this nonsense was the recent occasion when two Tory women cabinet ministers showed up at the same function wearing the same outfit. This event caused a minor sensation in the media. Whatever for? The papers could as easily have run the following headline: "Two Hundred and Fifty Male MPs Appear in Commons Wearing Same Dark Blue Suit!"

Of all the people helping keep my feet on the ground and my courage up in those exciting but difficult early days, Marion Dewar proved especially invaluable. Without her urging, I likely would never have run for the leadership in the first place. Now that I'd won, she undoubtedly felt some responsibility to make sure that I survived, but it went far beyond that. If I had a cold, Marion would show up on the doorstep with fresh orange juice. If I had a problem with the caucus, Marion had a solution. If I despaired of ever becoming truly fluent in French, Marion would repeat her favourite line, "You'll learn." She is without question

one of the most sensitive, compassionate, and nurturing people
I know.

• • •

To a great many Canadians, Question Period seems irrelevant, a
piece of absurdist theatre that further alienates the populace
from its politicians. Sadly, however, this is virtually the only part
of parliament's proceedings that is regularly covered by the
media. When you see a leader on the evening news, it is either
a clip from Question Period or from the media scrum afterwards.
As I've said, I didn't like the childish competitiveness of this
forum, but I knew it was important to perform well. I worked hard
on preparing the questions I would ask and improving my delivery.

Once in a while Question Period does serve its original
purpose, namely to provide a daily opportunity for the parliamentary opposition to hold the government accountable for its
actions. (Imagine if the president of the United States had to
regularly appear before Congress and explain what he was
doing.) And occasionally an opposition leader comes up with a
question that really does leave the government gasping for air.
You can always tell when you've dropped one of these bomb-
shells because the House goes dead silent.

I was able to deliver a great one right after the government
appointed the so-called GST senators — eight extra Tory senators that gave them a majority in the Senate, where the Liberals
were threatening to block the GST legislation. The government
had neglected to note that in appointing James Ross of Freder-
icton, it had contravened a section of the Constitution that states
that no province can have fewer Commons seats than senators.
With Ross's appointment, New Brunswick had eleven senators,
but only ten MPs. When I pointed this out in Question Period,
you could have heard a pin drop. The party later took the matter
to court, but before it could be resolved, one of New Brunswick's
eleven senators died.

Neither Brian Mulroney nor his ministers seemed quite sure how to handle a woman leader in the House. For a time the Tories assigned Joe Clark to heckle me (this stopped once he took on the constitutional brief and he required a nicer image). However, I soon adopted a technique every mother learns: selective hearing. When your kids are driving you nuts, you learn to block them out; it works very well with the hecklers during Question Period.

The men just don't seem comfortable yelling at a woman who won't yell back at them — such behaviour would appear overly aggressive. So when I ask a difficult question — about the jobs lost under free trade, or the increase in child poverty, or the erosion of health care standards — they often resort to a patronizing, dismissive tone. The prime minister is especially prone to this, as in, "The honourable member for the Yukon clearly doesn't understand this complicated issue," or "If only she was aware of the facts." I don't think this tactic fools anyone, but I suppose it's easier than answering the question.

In early January, Sharon Vance arrived in Ottawa to act as my interim principal secretary until April. Although I would have loved her to take on the job permanently, she wasn't prepared to leave Montreal for good. She had previously worked in Svend Robinson's office, as Ed Broadbent's executive assistant, and as Dave Barrett's caucus secretary when he was B.C. premier — among other jobs. I had first met her in the Yukon in 1985 when she headed up Tony Penikett's transition team after the NDP won the territorial election, but she is best known in the party as a "wagon master" — a specialist in organizing and running the leader's tour during an election campaign. She had worked in this role for many of the NDP leaders across the country. In sum, she had unparalleled connections throughout the party — and knew virtually every member of my caucus.

Sharon's experience and savvy helped me navigate successfully through those difficult early months as I learned to work with the parliamentary caucus and the federal party, which have entirely separate governing structures. As leader I knew I was responsible to the individual members of the party as much as to the members of my caucus; I saw it as part of my job to consult as widely as possible. Together Sharon and I prepared a list of fifty or sixty key people I should be phoning regularly, to touch base, to seek advice, and to keep them informed. It's fortunate I like to talk on the phone because I have to do it endlessly. It may be the only thing Brian Mulroney and I have in common.

In late January, the government introduced its legislation to bring in the GST. In mid-February, after the bill had passed second reading — approval in principle — it went to the Standing Committee on Finance for final study. This was where we decided to make a last-ditch stand against what we regarded as an outrageously bad tax.

After some deliberation, I assigned Dave Barrett and John Rodriguez to sit on the committee. Both have a great sense of drama and are experts at garnering publicity. They are also indefatigable public speakers and were knowledgeable about tax issues. In an effort to embarrass the government into reconsidering, they launched a filibuster of the committee hearings into the GST bill. At one point, when the two of them vowed to keep the committee talking all night, Rodriguez showed up with his pillow and toothbrush.

Although the media loved their performance and acknowledged it with much editorial space, some members of the caucus did not. They argued that our approach should be more serious and dignified. Furthermore, there were many in the party and in the press who tried to suggest that by giving Barrett and Rodriguez free rein I was showing "weak leadership" on this issue. Two members of the caucus were stealing the limelight that should be the leader's. This argument neglected to note the fact that I continued to take the lead on the issue during Question Period in the House.

Despite the criticism, I held firm. I was convinced that Barrett and Rodriguez were being effective, which is what mattered, and I said so. To me, leadership is not about how much attention you can draw to yourself but how you can draw the best out of the people on your team.

• • •

My first spring as leader I had to grapple with one of the more venerated traditions of the parliamentary men's club — the annual Press Club Dinner. This is an occasion when each of the three party leaders along with the governor general gets up in front of a crowd of journalists to make fun of himself or herself for twenty minutes or so. The event is of no significance to the rest of the country, yet in Ottawa it has been until recently something on the order of a religious ritual, an example of just how clubby and in-grown the world of Ottawa politics can become.

I have no problem making fun of myself. (In fact I've been told I can be self-deprecating to a fault.) But I had serious reservations about doing it as part of this particular club rite. First of all, I objected to the amount of a leader's time and of the people's money that goes into turning leaders into stand-up comedians. Second, I didn't like the symbolism of a woman leader performing this ritualistic self-putdown in front of an audience that is still overwhelmingly male.

I knew, however, that a refusal to appear at my first Press Club Dinner would be deemed an act of cowardice and do me no good in my dealings with the press. There is definitely an element of blackmail here: no leader wants to be the one who "can't take the heat." And I have a big problem with being seen to lack guts. It was also a classic woman's conundrum: to play along would be to accept the rules of a very male game and then score points for showing I could "take it like a man." To opt out would be to seem like a "poor sport" and add to my outsider status by spurning the only game in town for reasons that would be impossible to explain. Damned if you do, damned if you don't. After some soul searching, I decided to attend the dinner.

We figured that if I was going to do it, I should do it right, so we hired feminist comedian Nancy White to help write the material. The preparation process proved quite therapeutic. My speech writer, Paul Degenstein, who crafted the final product, says he had never seen me laugh so hard. But I wasn't looking forward to the show I would have to give.

You have to picture the scene. The setting is the Parliamentary Dining Room in the Centre Block — white tablecloths, polished silver, crystal and china. The dress is formal, black tie for the men and, for the few women, formal evening dresses. The place is packed and hot. By the time dinner is over and the foolery is set to begin, many, if not the majority of those present, have already had more than enough to drink.

The audience is a mix of media types and politicians since each member of the press gallery can invite an MP as guest. You can sense the MPs' anxiety: Will my leader give a "winning" performance? On the surface, it's all in good fun, but underneath it's deeply competitive. And even though the event is officially off the record, you can be sure that the performances will be reviewed in the papers the following day.

I wasn't far into my speech before I knew that the jokes that had us howling with laughter back in the office weren't going over too well with this audience. Maybe part of the problem was that I was poking a little fun at them, not just at myself. That wasn't the way the game was supposed to be played. Somewhere near the half-way point, the heckling began. Soon dinner rolls as well as insults were being hurled in my direction. When I finally sat down, it was to a mixture of boos, catcalls, and mild applause.

When it was over, I was more convinced than ever that the whole event was not only distasteful, but obsolete. The next day I wasn't too happy about my decision to play along with the game, especially when I saw Paul Degenstein's face. The word was out that Audrey had bombed, and Paul was feeling awful — as if somehow this was his fault. I went up to him, put my hands on his shoulders, and told him, "You know, I don't care what happened and I don't want you to feel bad. Preparing that speech was the most fun I've had since becoming leader. That alone made it worth it."

Actually, I'm quite sure the other leaders found it almost as unpleasant as I did, but as men it must be even harder for them to contemplate breaking the tradition. (I believe Trudeau once refused to attend, one year when he was particularly annoyed with the press.) At my second dinner in the spring of 1991, I watched the prime minister tell jokes about being drunk and about having troubles in his marriage as Mila smiled and appeared to look on approvingly. This was at a time when the press was full of rumours that he'd fallen off the wagon and that his marriage was in trouble. I had no idea whether he'd been drinking or whether the marriage problems were real — and I didn't want to know — but surely this performance must have been embarrassing for him and hurtful to her. This wasn't humour; this was humiliation.

That second year, I settled on what seemed a tolerable compromise. I accepted the invitation but decided to keep my performance short. Paul and I spent a few hours in preparation, then I got up and spoke for about five minutes — maybe less. I simply said how great it was to be there, told a joke in English and one in French, and then sat down. This year I declined to attend, instead spending the weekend in Regina with my mother, who was recuperating from surgery for lung cancer. For whatever reason, the event was subsequently postponed.

• • •

In early April, Sharon Vance headed back to Montreal, turning the job of principal secretary over to Les Campbell from Manitoba, who had been my convention shadow. Les had worked in Howard Pawley's cabinet office during the latter days of his administration in Manitoba, then served as a key aide to the new leader, Gary Doer. He helped see the party through the dark days when it dropped to third place and helped orchestrate its resurgence to official opposition status in 1990. Now he had signed on for more ups and downs. Although we didn't know it when he arrived on the Hill, the year ahead would bring the acrimonious death of Meech, the ugly stand-off at Oka, and the Gulf War.

The Liberal leadership campaign was in the spotlight, so media eyes were averted from parliament, making it even more difficult than usual to promote national debate on the issues. The latest Gallup Poll showed NDP support at 24 percent, down from 28 percent in December. Reviews of my first months as leader weren't glowing, but I was hardly expecting raves after so little time. And I could take some satisfaction in what I had been able to accomplish. The team that is with me now would soon be in place. The important work of policy renewal was under way. I could also point to a breakthrough in Quebec the previous February, when Phil Edmonston took the riding of Chambly and became the first-ever NDP member of parliament from that province. Perhaps most important of all, my efforts to heal the wounds and pull the party together seemed to be working. I'd begun to put my leadership talk about consultation and inclusion into concrete action.

I felt I was beginning to make points that some people were hearing. Not yet perhaps in the press, but certainly in much of the party and parts of the general populace away from the self-obsessed political centre. True, I'd spent my first five months doing more listening than talking. But when you listen to people, it's amazing what you can learn. When you act on what you've learned, it's amazing what you can change.

CHAPTER   FIVE

STALEMATE AND STAND-OFF

FOR ANY FEDERAL LEADER the constitution is a treacherous issue. In an interview with political journalist Graham Fraser, I once compared it to a field of steel-jawed leg-hold traps. No matter how carefully you cross the field, you're almost sure to be caught in one of them. Each new round of constitutional negotiations arouses conflicts of ideology and regional interest. Within a federal caucus that generally means fractious debates and wounded sensibilities.

I learned this only too well during my first six months as leader, which coincided with the dying days of the Meech Lake Accord. My position on Meech remained a combination of support for the clauses that recognized Quebec's needs and opposition to its exclusion of other regions and groups. I left the Winnipeg convention with a mandate to work for changes, but in reality, as leader of an opposition party I was in no real position to do so. Parliament had already passed the Meech Lake resolution in the fall of 1987, just after I was first elected. I could speak out against the provisions I didn't like and about the need to design a more open process next time, but unless the government chose to reopen the issue, it was out of my hands.

This situation changed — albeit briefly — on March 21, 1990, when New Brunswick premier Frank McKenna proposed a companion resolution that would be ratified by all the provinces along with the Meech Lake Accord. If accepted, this add-on resolution would have addressed many of the deficiencies of the Accord; most importantly, it would eliminate the unanimous consent requirement for the creation of new provinces and guarantee that aboriginal issues would be at the top of the agenda during the next round of constitutional talks.

The next day the prime minister appointed a parliamentary committee, to be chaired by Quebec MP Jean Charest, to consider the New Brunswick resolution and recommend a revised draft to parliament. I saw the committee process as an opportunity to reach a reasonable compromise that would prevent the Accord from dying, leaving Quebec once more on the outside. And the caucus agreed. We decided to work hard to see that the final report addressed as many of our concerns about the original Accord as possible. Our decision was based on the assumption that the committee's work was to be more than window dressing.

During the next month, the committee travelled across the country and heard from 160 witnesses in a series of public hearings, the first genuine public consultation in the entire Meech process. There followed several weeks of deliberations as a compromise text was hammered out and many debates in caucus about where to insist on stronger wording, where to give way. Our representatives on the committee, Svend Robinson and Lorne Nystrom, successfully argued for a number of improvements, especially for aboriginal people.

On May 17, the committee delivered its report to parliament. It expanded somewhat on the original New Brunswick resolution, adding to or clarifying McKenna's original list. For instance, it included an amendment indicating that the distinct society clause did not confer new legislative powers on any province. It also proposed the addition of a "Canada Clause" that included explicit recognition for aboriginal people. The result wasn't perfect, but we could live with it.

Unfortunately, Mulroney dropped the report like a hot potato when Premier Robert Bourassa rejected it. Lucien Bouchard, Mulroney's Quebec lieutenant, resigned from the cabinet in protest, saying the companion resolution effectively wiped out Quebec's gains. I truly believe Bourassa and Bouchard were wrong, that the committee had come up with a compromise proposal that gave all parties room to manoeuvre and provided grounds to start talking again. But we never had a chance to find out. Instead, the prime minister reverted to one of his favourite pastimes — making deals behind closed doors.

On June 3, 1990, the ten premiers and the prime minister met in Ottawa for one last attempt to reach a compromise that would permit the ratification of the original Meech Lake Accord — reducing the Charest Report to an exercise in futility. With the deal due to expire on June 23, Mulroney adopted a tactic that had worked well for him in his days as a labour lawyer: negotiation by exhaustion. As the week wore on and the premiers wore down, he apparently believed they would be forced into some kind of agreement — if nothing else so they could go home for a good night's sleep. This may or may not be an effective method of negotiation, but it's a terrible way to amend a constitution.

Mulroney later boasted that during that week in June he had "rolled the dice" and won, a comment that infuriated many Canadians both inside politics and out. (Not only that, but he turned out to be wrong.) His gamble originated with the way Meech Lake was negotiated in 1986 and 1987. It had been agreed in secret and presented to the Canadian public as a done deal, a "seamless web" that could not be altered by so much as a single strand. In early 1990, as the web was unravelling, the prime minister and his advisers adopted a high-stakes strategy: they argued that to reject Meech was to reject Quebec; to reject Quebec was to risk breaking up Canada. Having abandoned the Charest Committee proposals before they had been given a chance, Mulroney was again threatening us with a "take it or leave it" ultimatum. In my view, to deliberately create such a crisis was unforgivable. By painting the situation in such terms, he guaranteed that the failure of Meech could only be interpreted as a slap in the face of Quebec. We are still paying the price for Quebec's resulting sense of humiliation and betrayal.

As an opposition leader, I played no direct role in the final secret negotiations during those seven days in June. Like other Canadians, I was relegated to the role of anxious spectator. The only NDP leader in the country who had any influence on the final outcome was Manitoba leader Gary Doer. Since Tory premier Gary Filmon led a minority government, Doer's caucus had a real say in the process — as Manitoba MLA Elijah Harper would soon prove. However, I did manage to build one small, mostly symbolic, bridge between the premiers and the aboriginal leaders, who were bitter at their exclusion from this constitutional round.

During the talks, access to information was strictly controlled and selectively distributed. The Ottawa Conference Centre, where the meetings were taking place, might be imagined as a series of concentric circles. At the centre were the ten premiers, the prime minister, and Senator Lowell Murray, the minister responsible for the Constitution — the only people in the negotiating room. The next circle consisted of those advising the negotiators — federal bureaucrats, provincial ministers, and various constitutional experts. More distant still were the federal and provincial opposition leaders, along with various other interested parties such as the MPs who had served on the Charest committee. Many of those from out of town passed the time in the conference centre lounge, drinking coffee and waiting for the occasional word on the progress of the negotiations. The next circle consisted of the media, whose only information came from their twice-daily press briefings — one in the morning and one late at night — and from the snippets they could glean from those with more privileged access. That left the Canadian public — as usual — in the outermost circle of all, at several removes from what was really going on.

The full absurdity of this set-up hit home midway through

the week. I had made a daily habit of dropping by the conference centre lounge to chat with people like Gary Doer and Ontario NDP leader Bob Rae, to learn how the talks were going. On this particular morning, Ovide Mercredi, a vice-chief of the Assembly of First Nations, appeared while I was there. Not many people knew him then; Georges Erasmus was still the grand chief of the AFN and Ovide one of his deputies. Since the aboriginal leaders were entirely excluded from the Conference Centre, Ovide had had to borrow someone's pass just to get inside the door. He told me the AFN had set up their headquarters in the Westin Hotel across the street and asked me if I would join Gary Doer and Manitoba Liberal leader Sharon Carstairs in briefing his people on the day's developments. I gladly agreed.

But the more I thought about it, the more this situation struck me as intolerable. Here were the representatives of Canada's aboriginal people — who ought to have been sitting in the same room with the premiers — completely excluded even from information about the talks. The least I could do was try to get them more direct access to the people who did know.

I called Paul Tellier, the Clerk of the Privy Council, one of the inner circle of advisers. "This is ridiculous," I said to him. "I shouldn't be briefing the native leaders, you should." He agreed to see what he could do.

Shortly after I arrived at the Westin where the native leaders were waiting, the phone rang. It was Tellier to say he had clearance to brief the AFN himself. This small concession turned out to be more significant than it looked. As a result, aboriginal leaders were far better informed than they would have been and better able to publicize the fact that the premiers were ignoring aboriginal concerns.

The story may be a minor footnote to the more important events of that week, but it points out the exclusionary nature of the Meech Lake process and the traditional notions of power in which all of Ottawa is steeped: those who have information guard it jealously and dole it out stingily.

On the evening of June 9, at 10:30 p.m., after a week of negotiating, the haggard premiers filed into the Centennial

Room of the Ottawa Conference Centre. Against all odds, Mulroney's strategy of negotiation by exhaustion and emotional blackmail appeared to have worked. And yet there was an air of unreality about the whole proceeding. I watched and listened intently as each premier spoke. Although the prime minister proclaimed that it was "a happy day for Canada," it soon became clear that he had not achieved quite the miracle for which he was claiming credit. When Clyde Wells spoke, his words, for those who actually listened to them, were ominous: "I will take this proposal back — and this is what I have committed to do and this is what my signature means, and it means only that." He was not committing himself to active support for the deal. He would submit the Accord to his cabinet and his caucus, who would then decide whether to call a free vote in the Newfoundland legislature or a provincial referendum. It was plain to me that the so-called deal was not a deal at all, but in the climate of euphoria created by the politicians, and echoed by the media, few took note of this reality.

In the end it was NDP MLA Elijah Harper, the lone aboriginal member of the Manitoba legislature, as much as Clyde Wells, who killed the deal. But Harper had become something of a folk hero, so the government's strategy was to isolate Wells and paint him as the villain. This became apparent on the night of June 22, after both the Manitoba and Newfoundland legislatures had adjourned without voting on the Accord, and Lowell Murray called an impromptu press conference.

Les Campbell and I were watching television in my Centre Block office when Murray began to speak. "Premier Wells's decision to break his commitment has dashed the one remaining hope to have Meech Lake succeed," he declared. This despite the fact that earlier in the day the federal government had offered to extend the Meech Lake deadline if Newfoundland endorsed the deal, an attempt to put further pressure on Wells. Apparently this tactic had backfired. As I listened to Murray trying to assign the blame elsewhere, I grew more and more angry. I had no admiration for the performance of Wells, who had tended to characterize himself as the only person of principle at the table, but I couldn't let the government line go unanswered. It was clearly a distortion of the truth.

Murray was speaking in the central lobby of the House of Commons. My office is on the fifth floor, at the west end of the Centre Block, three floors above. That weekend, the Liberals were in Calgary choosing a new leader, so the place was unusually empty, even for a summer recess. The hallways echoed eerily with our footsteps as Les and I hurried down them, hoping to reach the lobby before Murray finished speaking.

Although the lobby was crowded with reporters and cameramen and bathed in television lights, it too had a ghostly air, with Murray's voice booming over loudspeakers and bouncing off the vaulted ceiling. I stood where the cameramen and reporters could see me, so they would keep shooting once Murray finished. But the instant he was through, the House of Commons staff whisked away the microphone and loudspeakers. Just as quickly, someone from the CBC set up a microphone for me.

I said that the government should be ashamed of itself for blaming other people for this failure when it was no one's fault but its own, and I blasted those who would not accept their responsibility in the matter. The deal, I said, was a victim of the flawed process by which it was born, not of one or another person's intransigence. I called for a more open process, saying that parliament must establish a standing committee on the Constitution and that its first order of business should be to develop new ways of constitutional reform, including a constituent assembly where all Canadians can be involved in the process.

This was a call I and others would repeat often in the months to come, but it was certainly not a new idea. David Lewis and F.R. Scott had called for just such an assembly forty-three years earlier in their book *Make This Your Canada*. It was an idea derided at first by most politicians in other parties and by the constitutional pros, but it has gradually gained credence. Unfortunately, although we bargained for and won a series of constitutional conferences during the next round, old-style politics prevailed and we did not achieve a constituent assembly.

• • •

I feel passionate about the importance of "process" and the perils of exclusion, partly because of all that I experienced during my years as a social worker in Toronto in the 1970s.

In the summer of 1967, following the three years I and my family spent in Ghana, we returned to Canada and settled in Toronto. I found myself with no clear idea of what to do next; I knew only that I was going to get a job. My children — Tracy was now eleven and David, thirteen — were both at school all day, so there was no need for me to stay home. The more I pondered my future, the more I was drawn to the idea of social work. First, I worked as a volunteer with the Family Services Association, an agency that provided counselling to both parents and children in conflicted families. I acted as chauffeur, provided childcare, and simply made friends with some of the clients. I was impressed with the agency and with the commitment of its staff of social workers.

In the spring of 1968, I applied to enter the diploma program in social work at Ryerson Polytechnical Institute in Toronto. When Ryerson looked at my educational history, they advised me to apply to the master's program in social work at the University of Toronto, an idea that had never occurred to me.

The initial response from the U of T was less than encouraging. The faculty of social work was suspicious of my degree from Western because I'd earned it by correspondence. I thought their reaction ought to have been just the opposite: here's a woman who has managed to graduate with an A average while raising two small children and running a farming business. Instead they questioned whether a former "part-time" student could handle the course.

A few weeks earlier, I hadn't even dared think I was good enough to enter a post-graduate program. But now that I'd found the courage to apply, no one was going to tell me I couldn't handle it. I persevered and was accepted, but I did lose part of the battle: I had hoped to attend part time so I could spend more time with my children; the university insisted I become a full-time student.

Until then I had had an image of the University of Toronto as a huddled group of nineteenth-century buildings peeking out from under Queen Victoria's voluminous black dress — smothered by a stodgy, nineteenth-century sensibility. Their response to my application only reinforced this image of self-important stuffiness. But the school of social work turned out to be anything but stuffy.

That fall of 1968 was a time of political activism and intellectual ferment on campus. Until then, the "radical sixties" had pretty much passed me by. Although I didn't become directly involved in student activism, it was impossible not to be infected by the spirit of change. In the department of social work, this translated into the sense that social workers really could make a difference to society.

My classmates were a mixture of mature students, like myself, and recent graduates. Although the different ages mingled and got along well, there were inevitable social divisions. The single women all looked forward to the weekend as time for fun. Those of us who were married went home and did a week's worth of housework in two days: we looked forward to Monday when we could get back to school.

One of my professors was Alan Borovoy, who had recently become the general counsel of the Canadian Civil Liberties Association. Since I took my studies seriously, I was upset near the end of the semester when I learned that Professor Borovoy had lost my term paper. He was apologetic and offered to give me a B, but I wasn't satisfied. "Why don't you give me an A?" I remember asking him. "Why do you assume mediocrity? Why don't you assume excellence?" We got into quite a debate about it, but I got the B.

As part of our first-year requirement, every student in the master's program did a field placement. Mine was at the Vanier

Reformatory for Women in Brampton, just outside Toronto, where I assisted the social workers involved in counselling the women serving time there. Vanier is a medium-security prison for short-term female offenders — up to two years less a day. Contrary to the Hollywood image of prisons, it was quite a pleasant place. The women lived in cottages spread over spacious grounds and there was a genuine attempt by the staff to prepare them to return to society better able to cope.

My experience at Vanier made me question society's harsh and arbitrary definition of good and evil. It is true that the women had committed criminal offences, that they'd used drugs or abandoned their children or committed acts of vandalism. But, in spite of it all, they weren't necessarily inherently bad people. Their crimes often grew out of serious social ills: many had suffered real poverty or been abused.

At Vanier I learned a great deal about the pain some people live with. A few of the women there, who had previously committed more serious crimes and done time at the maximum-security prison in Kingston, were truly tortured personalities. I won't ever forget those who were known as slashers. They were covered with scars from having cut themselves over and over again and had to be kept away from any sharp object. Such self-hate is tragic.

Although the staff at Vanier tried to help, they had little success with aboriginal women, whose offences were often alcohol-related, which meant their stay at Vanier might last as little as a few weeks. The shortness of their stay wasn't the problem: it was more a question of cultural ignorance. Although most of the native women spoke English, their assumptions and experiences were totally alien. As a result, the social workers often simply gave up and left them to sit stoically through their sentences, whether six weeks or six months.

Furthermore, some of the crimes Vanier residents had committed weren't crimes at all in my book. One woman had been jailed for attempting to commit suicide, which was still a criminal offence in those days. She needed counselling and support, not incarceration. Another woman had been convicted of helping someone procure an abortion. I remember asking myself, "Is this what jails are for?"

In the spring of 1970, I graduated with a master's degree in social work and landed a job with the Children's Aid Society of Metropolitan Toronto (CAS). Those were the days — they now seem like ancient history — when jobs were easy to find if you had a post-graduate degree. I started out as a caseworker assigned to investigate complaints of child neglect or child abuse.

This was a wrenching, emotionally draining responsibility. I sometimes joke bitterly that my job in those days was to knock on a stranger's door and say, "Hi, I hear you beat your kids." (I've found knocking on doors very hard ever since.) My visit would normally be prompted by a complaint — often from a school where someone had noticed suspicious burns or bruises on one of the students. Some of the situations I went into were potentially violent — someone once pulled a knife on me — so every once in a while I was forced to bring the police with me.

It was up to me to decide whether the complaint had any basis. Could those cigarette burns possibly have been accidental? Were those bruises caused by falling down stairs, as the father or mother claimed? If there was clear evidence of abuse, I would take the child into "protective custody" as a ward of the CAS, after which he or she would often end up in a foster home. There were some wonderful foster parents who took in difficult kids and loved them back to health, of course, but many children were passed through a series of foster homes and group homes and ended up emotionally damaged for life.

I found the sexual abuse cases particularly grim. I remember one involving a middle-class family in the suburbs with two beautiful little girls aged five and seven. I was sure the mother knew what was happening but, as so often happens, couldn't or wouldn't intervene. The father was not a monster but a very sad and confused man. Even so, there was nothing I could do except take his daughters out of the home. As I drove them away from their nice, neat house, with the bicycle lying on the perfectly mown lawn and the station wagon in the driveway, I tried to reassure the girls that everything would be fine. They sat quietly:

they didn't ask questions and they didn't cry. Their silence made it even harder for me.

At the school of social work we were taught not to get emotionally involved with clients, but I soon abandoned that "professional" code. I came to see myself as simply a human being working within an imperfect system, trying to make things a little bit better. Sometimes I cried alongside the people I worked with and sometimes I got angry. If helping a mother do the dishes and the housework seemed more useful than trying to counsel her, then that's what I would do.

The teenagers I counselled were the toughest. Usually they were sent to see me because of unruliness in school, trouble with the law, or serious family strife. Often their acts of rebellion seemed trivial. In those days parents and schools still insisted on fighting with kids over such terrible acts as wearing blue jeans or long hair. The futility of it taught me one enduring lesson: if you fritter away your energy on inconsequentials, you will probably never get to the fundamentals.

I developed a technique that almost infallibly brought these "unruly rebels" down to basics. Typically they would arrive in my office sending off sparks of anger and resentment, then slouch sullenly in the chair. Instead of responding to this overt challenge, I would look them in the eye and ask them to tell me something good about themselves. More often than not they would break into tears and open up. They were so used to people seeing only the bad in them — another lesson I've taken to heart.

I came to know many poor women, some of them single mothers, some whose husbands had abandoned them, some whose husbands abused them as well as their children. When I look back, three things stand out about these women. First of all, few people in their lives had ever talked to them like adults. How sad that one of the first people to do this was a social worker. Second, for the vast majority their main problem was that they didn't have enough money. It was as simple as that. Third, despite the obstacles, these women were survivors. Many were stronger than I'll ever be.

Sometimes, however, their difficulties became too much for

them. I remember one day visiting a woman whose husband had recently left her. She had three children, and the welfare money wasn't enough to make ends meet. Her children were constantly in trouble at school and with the law. When I arrived in her apartment that day, I found her in hysterics because she'd run out of laundry detergent and couldn't afford to buy any more. The trigger was trivial; her distress was profound.

One of the most intolerable aspects of the child welfare system in those days was its built-in incentives for parents to give up custody of their children. In the case of a psychologically disturbed child, for instance, parents had to pay the full cost of treatment in a residential facility. But if they gave up custody, the CAS would pay. It didn't make sense.

My experience as a social worker was the key to my politicization. Although as a caseworker I could help some individuals, I could do nothing to address the underlying social ills that had created their problems in the first place. It was like helping a victim who'd been knocked down by a truck, when it was the truck that needed repair. There was a discomforting element of social control in what I was doing, as well: I was helping keep the lid on a potentially unruly minority so that they were barely able to hang on, but not to get ahead. I came to see my job as helping fundamentally functional people cope with a dysfunctional system.

Given my sense of hopelessness at what I was doing, I jumped at the opportunity to join an experimental program in community social work set up by the CAS. I saw it as an opportunity to get involved in community advocacy, to actually help people challenge the system and begin to change it.

The ten of us in the new program were called community workers. Although we still did casework, our primary mandate was prevention. Each of us was assigned to an area — usually including a heavy concentration of public housing — where the incidence of child welfare problems was high. My area was Lawrence Heights, a public housing development near Bathurst Street and Lawrence Avenue in North Toronto. Our energies went into making connections with other social agencies and with groups in the community — local police, teachers, tenants' groups, parents' groups, and so on. We also established support groups for young people who'd been regularly in trouble.

This kind of community development inevitably evolved into community advocacy. We worked with parents who had complaints about how their kids were being treated at school but were afraid — or simply didn't know how — to challenge the system. We worked with tenants who had complaints against their landlords. We didn't try to solve their problems — we helped them organize and get results for themselves, which gave them a sense of power, often for the first time in their lives.

Every couple of weeks, when our team met at the CAS headquarters on Charles Street to unwind and debrief, we shared our excitement at the impact we seemed to be having. All of us remember these meetings with fondness, part of a very special time in our lives. Despite the fact we were working many more hours than we were being paid for, we had the sense that we were making a difference.

Dave Wright, a founding member of the group who is now the director of the Visiting Homemakers Association of Metro Toronto, describes the time as a little bit like being in a war: we were in the trenches. Sometimes we took big risks. There were times when we tried to keep a child at home and worked with the parents to solve the underlying problems when formerly we would have put the child into protective custody. We all lived in fear of waking up one morning to read that a child whose parents we'd taken a chance on had been injured. What's more, we were constantly battling an agency bureaucracy that felt threatened by our independent ways and wanted to rein us in. But, as Dave says now, "Those were the most satisfying two years of my entire career. I've never had that sort of working relationship with people."

I agree about the people; our group became very close. There were three or four women among the ten, and the group was a model of men and women working together as equals. Last year, another group member, Jane Kerrigan, who became a lawyer and now represents children in child custody cases, organized a reunion in a Toronto restaurant. We picked up as if twenty years had not flown by. The main difference between then and now was that our optimism has been replaced with a sense of frustration and anger that, for those with no power, little has changed.

This was also when I first became involved with the New Democratic Party. I began to see that, although we were able to effect some changes in our small communities, achieving more sweeping societal changes meant attacking the system on a grander scale. I examined the policies of the three main parties and concluded that only the New Democrats came close to believing what I believed. I joined the party and became active in the North York riding where I was living, which was represented provincially by NDP veteran Fred Young. That's when I got my first taste of political campaigning and the enormous work involved for all the volunteers behind the scenes.

At one Ontario convention, Fred introduced me to Stephen Lewis, who had become the provincial NDP leader in 1970. "Here's a woman you should meet because she would make a great candidate," Fred said. I smiled. Stephen smiled. I'm sure we were both thinking the same thing: isn't Fred polite.

I had enormous respect for Fred Young. Here was a former United Church minister whose life showed the Christian ethic in action. He worked hard for his constituents and was unfailingly kind and thoughtful. I never saw him motivated by the desire for prestige or power. His stock phrase was "How can I help?" Long before the word came into popular use, he understood the importance of empowerment.

• • •

In the summer of 1990, one group of Canadians, held powerless for far too long, rose up in a protest both frightening and cathartic. I am referring, of course, to the dramatic events at Oka, Quebec, on the Ottawa River west of Montreal. I shared with many Canadians a sense that the Oka stand-off should never have reached the point of violence, that it was allowed to escalate in unacceptable ways. But underlying the flashpoint were all the unresolved historic grievances of the original inhabitants of this country.

Until July 11, most Canadians who had heard of Oka knew it only as the town where a famous cheese is made by Trappist monks. Early that morning, however, officers from the Sûreté du Québec (SQ) approached a barricade erected across the entrance to a pine grove by the Mohawks of nearby Kanesatake; for the Mohawks, the grove was a sacred piece of land that included an ancestral burial ground. The grove was part of land long claimed by the local Mohawks, but it was about to be "redeveloped" by the expansion of the town's golf course from nine holes to eighteen. Despite calls for negotiation from Quebec's minister of Indian Affairs, John Ciaccia, Mayor Ouellette and the Oka town council had been granted an order from the Quebec Superior Court to have the defensive barricade removed. When the Mohawks wouldn't budge, the provincial police were called in.

Officers of the SQ fired tear gas and ordered the defenders, including women and children, to abandon the barricade. There were cursory negotiations in which both sides refused to compromise: the Mohawks said they would not move and the police said their orders were to dismantle the barricade. The police and their bulldozer began to advance, firing tear gas and concussion grenades. Although no one knows who fired first, a gun battle ensued, and Corporal Marcel Lemay of the SQ was mortally wounded. The police retreated. Corporal Lemay had been killed by a bullet type used by both sides. The same day, Mohawks from the Kahnawake reserve just across the St. Lawrence River from Montreal blockaded the Mercier Bridge in solidarity with the Oka protest.

When I heard the news I couldn't believe this was happening in Canada. My second reaction was anger that the situation had been allowed to get so out of hand. Corporal Lemay's death was tragically unnecessary. A young man, a husband and father, had been cut down — for what? A golf course. This was some kind of madness.

Since early March, when the barricade went up, my office

had been watching developments at Oka with increasing concern. We knew this was only the latest in a series of incidents involving the Mohawk community, whose claim to ancestral land had never been recognized by the federal government. Oka had been a crisis waiting to happen. At its root was an unresolved dispute that dated back to before the British conquest. Since the 1970s, the Mohawks of Kanesatake have had two land claims rejected by the federal Department of Indian Affairs, the more recent in 1986. After that setback, a framework agreement for the creation of a reserve was turned down by all three levels of government. The dispute over the golf course began back in March 1989, when the expansion project was first announced. (The Mohawks read about it in the local paper.) In the year leading up to the violence, despite further attempts to have the land claim addressed, nothing was done.

The day after the first violence, I was outraged to learn that Sûreté du Québec officers were preventing food from reaching the Mohawks and restricting movement in and out of Oka. This action punished the majority of the 1,500 Mohawk residents who had nothing to do with the barricade. More important, it was a violation of basic human rights.

I could not believe that in Canada we had stooped to using food as a weapon against our own citizens. Even when the international community imposes sanctions, food and medicine are normally let through. My response had nothing to do with my being a party leader: I decided to buy food and take it to Oka.

I realized that such an action might be seen as support for the Mohawk warriors. I hold no particular brief for the warriors — I don't condone anyone who uses violence as a means, however justified the end — but I simply had to do something. I also knew that my action would be seen as a political ploy, an attempt to grab headlines. But I couldn't allow such misinterpretations to deter me.

My office spoke with the band office in Kanesatake. Ellen Gabriel, one of the chief representatives of the Mohawk community, told us they were setting up a food bank in a gym on the reserve and welcomed our contribution. She advised us to approach by a back way where we would be likely to meet fewer police and no reporters. I bought milk, bread, fruit, vegetables, canned food, and diapers — enough to fill a rented van.

When my office informed the Quebec government of our plan, Sam Elkas, the Quebec minister of public security, warned us that he could not guarantee our safety. Nonetheless, on the early afternoon of July 13, two days after the shooting of Corporal Lemay, we set off for Oka in two vehicles. With me in the van were a couple of staff members and a young Mohawk from Kanesatake who wanted to return home; perhaps we could get him through the blockade. My principal secretary, Les Campbell, and my director of communications, Michael Balagus, were our advance scouts, in another vehicle.

It was a beautiful summer afternoon. As we drove along Route 344, on the Quebec shore of the Ottawa River, we couldn't help feeling a sense of anticipation. We had no idea what lay ahead or whether we could get through the police lines.

Les and Michael encountered no problems until they were almost to Kanesatake. There they ran smack into the SQ barricade at the western end of the blockaded stretch of highway, about five kilometres from the main stand-off.

The police had not been warned we were coming, and they weren't happy to see two staff members from Audrey McLaughlin's office. They already had a small crisis on their hands. A young reporter from the *Montreal Gazette* named Peter Kuitenbrouwer had emerged from Mohawk-held territory and started down the hill towards the police encampment. He had heard I was coming and hiked from the main barricade in pursuit of a scoop. As he approached, he was swarmed by SQ officers.

Les and Michael, also surrounded, attempted vainly to negotiate with the police to let us through with the food. Finally the policemen let Les and Michael out of the car and the three of us attempted to reason with the commanding officer. As we were talking, we heard someone shouting my name. It was only then that we became aware of the dishevelled young man struggling with police on the other side of the roadblock. Kuitenbrouwer had seen us and was calling for help. "I'm being detained by the SQ," he shouted. "I'm a *Gazette* reporter; they have no right to hold me!"

It was clear that the police were not going to let our van into Oka. At least I was able to persuade them to let us take the reporter off their hands. Peter was enormously relieved.

We were not the only people trying to pass the police road-block that day. A number of Quebecers concerned about the food embargo had also brought groceries for the Mohawks. As we were about to leave, several approached us and asked if we would try to take their gifts into Oka. We obliged, since we had decided to make a second attempt.

At Peter's suggestion, we backtracked to Carillon, crossed by ferry to the other side of the Ottawa River, and headed for Hudson, the town opposite Oka. From there we hoped to take another ferry across and enter Kanesatake. If nothing else, we would get Peter back to his car and his colleagues. And our Mohawk friend might find a way to get back into his community.

By the time we reached Hudson, it was dusk. Although the ferry captain advised us not to board, we insisted. Once again I heard the words "We cannot guarantee your safety," which made me even more determined. I joined Les and Michael in the car, as did Peter and our Mohawk passenger. When we reached the ferry wharf, in the centre of town, we were met by equally determined members of the Sûreté du Québec. They allowed the car to disembark, but not the van. As dusk turned to darkness, the ferry returned to Hudson and the food went back with it.

Les and Michael and I found ourselves stranded in the floodlit parking lot near a deserted hot dog stand, surrounded by a high wire-mesh fence, virtual prisoners of the Quebec police. At least Peter Kuitenbrouwer and the young Mohawk had slipped into the darkness — Peter to alert the media forces at the main barricade, the Mohawk to join his friends and family inside Kanesatake.

Men in combat-style garb and carrying rifles were every-where — inside the parking lot compound and outside, patrol-ling the streets of the town. This image of Oka as an armed camp simply didn't compute. I had lived through a coup in Ghana, travelled through the Middle East and Latin America, and walked the Green Line in Cypress, so I was no stranger to guns and soldiers. But this was Canada.

Adding to the surreal feeling was the flicker of candles about a hundred metres away, a vigil of Mohawks and pro-Mohawk villagers, come to protest the police occupation and the siege of Kanesatake.

A few reporters arrived. This was the first press conference I have ever given through a wire-mesh fence — and I hope the last. After I explained why I had come to Oka, I learned that John Ciaccia, the Quebec minister of Indian Affairs, had emerged from behind the barricades where he was negotiating with the Mohawk representatives. He was apparently coming to meet with me.

A few minutes later, Ciaccia's limousine pulled into the parking lot, escorted by more police. He invited me into the car and we talked for half an hour. He was truly distressed and eager to find a way to break the impasse. When the barricade had gone up, he had urged the town not to demand that the police move in, hoping to negotiate a settlement. Now he was operating in a much more difficult and volatile situation.

I asked Ciaccia to instruct the police to let me bring the van back across the river so I could at least leave the food. He was apologetic, but said there was nothing he could do. He seemed unwilling or unable to take on the police. In essence, his message was: I'm powerless here and I advise you to go home. The police were in charge, not the minister.

We were the only passengers on the last ferry to leave Oka that night. Darkness soon swallowed the lights behind us. I had been prevented from entering a town in my own country, a fact that shocked and angered me. And I had failed to get food into Oka. Exhaustion only deepened my frustration and disappointment.

The next day we learned of a restaurant west of Oka where people were dropping off food for the community. Apparently the Mohawks could make it through woods and across fields during the night, pick up the groceries, and smuggle them into Kanesatake. So we took the van and left it there.

In the following days, as the stand-off continued, I and others called for the federal government to get involved in the negotiations, but Tom Siddon, the federal minister of Indian Affairs, refused outright, saying the crisis was a provincial affair. Brian Mulroney remained silent, holed up at his Harrington Lake retreat and apparently still nursing his wounds following the death of Meech. Rumours that the army would be called in stoked the tension. An explosion seemed possible at any moment.

Some native leaders deplored the Mohawk warriors' willingness to resort to violence, but for many native people across the country, whose frustrations had been building for a long time, the Oka barricade became a symbol of resistance. However extreme their actions, the Mohawks at Oka had finally said enough is enough. Aboriginal people in other parts of Canada staged demonstrations in sympathy.

As feelings escalated among the First Nations, Mohawk Chief Joe Norton called a meeting of chiefs from across Canada. It was to be held at his reserve, Kahnawake, just south of Montreal, where his people continued their blockade of the Mercier Bridge. A few days before the meeting, Chief Norton asked me to address the assembly. I considered this a great honour, since no other federal leader had been shown so much trust.

Because of the Mercier Bridge barricade, the only way to reach the area of the reserve where the meeting was being held was by boat. When we informed the Quebec authorities of our plans to attend, they urged us not to go and told us they would take no responsibility for our safety. In fact, they tried to prevent the Mohawks from ferrying people across to the reserve for the meeting. In response, the reserve mobilized a flotilla of small boats to transport visitors. The disembarkation points were constantly changed to confuse the police.

When our boat docked, we were met by a small crowd of reporters and TV cameras — clearly the police had been thwarted. There was a brief media scrum, then we were driven to the meeting. When we entered the crowded hall, someone was speaking. Almost three hundred chiefs and elders had gathered at Kahnawake that day. Chief Norton, sitting with others at a large square table at the front, noticed my arrival and motioned me to join him. I walked through the long rows of chairs, nodding and smiling at the many people I knew.

When my turn came to speak, I measured my words and spoke as calmly as I could. "This is not the time for old-style politics based on winners and losers," I began. "Resolving this crisis will take a new approach based on consensus and courage." I proposed a five point plan: 1) that an immediate schedule of negotiations involving Indian Affairs Minister Tom Siddon, the Mohawks, and the Quebec government be fixed; 2) that the Town of Oka announce a freeze on all development affecting disputed lands; 3) that all police withdraw from Kanesatake and Kahnawake; 4) that the Mohawks dismantle the barricades at the Mercier Bridge; 5) and that they dismantle the barricades at Oka.

I then spoke about the larger issue, calling for the immediate establishment of an Aboriginal Lands Claims Commission by an act of parliament. I envisaged this commission as being co-chaired by one aboriginal and one non-aboriginal person and having clear authority to negotiate claims, subject to final parliamentary approval.

After my speech I stayed for an hour or so, listening to other speakers and talking to native leaders. When I emerged, Les Campbell was waiting with the news that we were going on to Oka. During the day he had been regularly in touch with Ellen Gabriel in Kanesatake. She had put Les in touch with the SQ officer in charge of the whole operation and he had told Les, "If you can get here today, we'll let you by."

A couple of hours later, having recrossed the St. Lawrence to Montreal and headed west along Route 344, we again approached a police roadblock — this time on the eastern outskirts of the town near the monastery. The officers had not been warned of our arrival, but they radioed headquarters and received clearance to let us through.

We had to pass through several other roadblocks. The streets were deserted. Oka was empty, like a ghost town, except for the ever-present police. About a block beyond the ferry dock, an officer waved us to a halt and motioned for us to park at a closed gas station. We walked the final blocks, past army-style tents where off-duty policemen lounged, past the empty Oka golf course and finally to the police barricade. We encountered not a single townsperson. It was like walking from the real world into a movie.

The police barricade of sandbags sat at the foot of a hill. At the top, a quarter mile away, was the Mohawk barrier of squashed cars and logs, where the stand-off had started. As we approached, we could see about fifteen officers pointing semi-automatic rifles up the hill. They paid no attention to us as we started up the incline.

It is a strange feeling to have guns pointing at you from two directions. I wasn't scared, but I can't say I was exactly relaxed either. It was eerily quiet until we had almost reached the top. Suddenly the media contingent encamped on the Mohawk side of the barricade realized what was happening and rushed to get pictures. The masked Mohawk warriors in their camouflage outfits with their heavy rifles seemed as surprised as anyone by our appearance. To pass the barricade, we had to walk along the ditch beside the road. Finally we had reached Kanesatake.

After talking to the press people behind the barricade, we cooled our heels until someone came to take us into town. I spent the next couple of hours at the recreation centre, which had been converted into a food bank, helping unpack and organize the many stores that had been received. Then we met with Ellen Gabriel and several other local leaders at a nearby restaurant. I promised I would do everything I could to persuade Tom Siddon to get the federal government involved. I was deeply impressed by the dignity and commitment of the people I talked with.

What did my actions at Oka accomplish? As expected, some observers labelled my attempt to take food through the blockade as either hopelessly naive or a base attempt at publicity mongering. Others took a different view, including Carol Goar in the

Toronto Star, who called our mission "the one political act capable of cutting through all the competing versions of the truth at Oka and establishing a simple fact. State authorities were denying the Mohawks food." But for me there was more to it. As the first federal leader to visit the Mohawks behind the barricades, I wanted to demonstrate that at least one federal politician was willing to listen to what they had to say, to discuss peaceful options.

I was also trying to make Canadians aware that the story had more than two sides, that it was not a simple case of warriors versus police. There were different factions within the Mohawk community and even among the warriors themselves. Many people in Oka sympathized with the Mohawks and worked to make sure that food got through. I thought it was important for people to remember that the Mohawks had legitimate grievances, which would have to be dealt with once the immediate crisis was over. Inevitably, however, the press tended to paint the stand-off in primary colours. It was war — a showdown where one side would win and one lose. This approach played into the hands of those in the Quebec government and the police who saw only an armed insurrection that had to be put down by force.

On August 9, the day after Prime Minister Mulroney announced that the Canadian army would move in to replace the police at Oka, I gave the keynote address at a meeting of the World Council of Indigenous Peoples in Tromso, Norway. A few days earlier I had attended a gathering of indigenous women from around the world, where I heard powerful stories of oppression — of beatings, imprisonment, rape, and torture. Here were women from South and Central America whose lives were in danger every day. Some of them had had to be smuggled out of their countries to attend the conference. This helped put the crisis at Oka in perspective, but it did not diminish its seriousness.

When I heard that the army had been called in, I was deeply shocked. In my speech I called on the Canadian government to reject the use of arms as a means of resolving the stand-off. The world knows Canada as a nation of peacekeepers, yet our government was deploying troops against our own citizens. (Ultimately, on September 1, the troops were ordered to take the last step: move in and clear the barricades, by force if necessary. Fortunately, no further lives were lost.)

A number of Mohawks attended the conference in Norway. That day they held a press conference denouncing the government's actions. Afterwards, I sat with them in a restaurant as they poured out their fears and cried for their friends and families. The tears I shed were not only for the people directly involved, but for Canada itself. How could my country have come to this?

• • •

The Oka crisis has become a symbol of justice denied to aboriginal people. It has come to represent in microcosm just how poorly federal policy serves Canada's First Nations in matters ranging from policing to land rights to social and economic policy, and how easily violence and bloodshed can erupt if native people are kept from controlling their own lives and destinies.

The grievances of the First Nations didn't begin with Confederation. Native people signed the original treaties with the Crown on the understanding that they were sharing the land, not giving it away. At Canada's founding in 1867, however, First Nations were not invited to participate in the process of creating a new country. For the next 125 years, Indian reserves were treated for all practical purposes as colonies of Canada and native people as second-class citizens. The residential school system uprooted native children from their homes, and its teachers worked to eradicate indigenous culture and language. It was not until 1960 that status Indians gained the right to vote in federal elections. Until recently, a native woman who married a non-native man lost her Indian status. Indians who fought in World War II or joined the professions as lawyers or doctors likewise lost their Indian status. The list of injustices goes on.

Unsettled land claims remain at the root of much of the

tension between native people and the rest of Canadian society. Aboriginal people have been complaining for years that the process for settling claims is a large part of the problem. They have pointed out that the Department of Indian Affairs and Northern Development is unable to impartially assess a claim's validity because of conflict of interest. The department decides both which claims will be heard and how much money claimants will get to prepare their cases. It also acts on behalf of the federal government in negotiating a final compensation agreement, in effect defending the government against the demands of aboriginal people. No wonder some claims have been under negotiation for more than fifteen years, and some native groups have resorted to the courts and to non-violent forms of protest in an attempt to get their long-standing claims addressed. Since Oka, I have argued that an independent land claims commission with enough power to speedily settle the hundreds of outstanding claims under federal jurisdiction is long overdue.

The other crucial step towards empowering native people is recognition of the inherent right to self-government in the Constitution. The word inherent simply recognizes that aboriginal people were never conquered and that their right to govern themselves predates the arrival of the colonizers from Europe. The other historic fact that must be recognized in the provision for self-government is that the First Nations have always comprised many distinct cultures and lived in many different circumstances. They are not now and never have been homogeneous. Once inherent self-government is accepted as a basic principle, each group must be able to negotiate the form of self-determination appropriate to its traditions, circumstances, and current aspirations. This would allow aboriginal Canadians to establish their place in Confederation as equal partners, not colonized, second-class citizens.

Many people worry about what self-government could mean in practice. It will vary. It will take a very different form for aboriginal people in urban areas than for those living on reserves. Although the details can be worked out only with individual aboriginal groups themselves, the process must entail the establishment of a distinct level of government within the Canadian federation. Native people would have exclusive jurisdiction over their people and their lands in some areas, while federal, provincial, and territorial governments would have exclusive jurisdiction in other areas. The federal Indian Act and the Department of Indian Affairs would be replaced by a system in which native people would have the authority to make laws to govern their own lands and peoples.

There will likely be some areas of shared jurisdiction, probably including health care, education, and the justice system. Over the past ten years, experts and royal commissions have been almost unanimous in recommending more native control over native justice. This will mean amending the criminal code and working out to what degree a native community will operate its own police force, courts, and corrections system. Given the many different types of self-government that will undoubtedly evolve, it is impossible — and counter-productive — to try to define in the Constitution precisely what self-government means. Self-government can only be worked out over time with the First Nations themselves.

The fear that self-government will lead to the establishment of independent sovereign states is surely ill-founded. Ovide Mercredi, Grand Chief of the Assembly of First Nations, has stated, "The First Nations are not a threat to Canada. We do not preach separatism. This is our country, from north to south and east to west. It is the only homeland we have. We did not come from anywhere else; we have nowhere else to return to and we have no divided loyalties. . . .

"One point we tried to drive home time and again during the First Ministers Conferences on Aboriginal Constitutional Matters between 1982 and 1987 was that, in seeking explicit recognition of our self-government in the Canadian Constitution, we were not advocating the dismemberment of our country; rather we envisaged the sharing of this land and its bountiful resources based on mutual respect and co-existence of jurisdictions, and based on the recognition of our inherent rights and our distinct societies in Canada."

Beyond the principle, what about the cost of self-government? The real concern should be the cost of *not* moving in this direction. The scarring poverty and economic underdevelopment that has long plagued most aboriginal communities costs millions in government assistance and is unmeasurable in lost economic potential and human suffering. Self-government is not an end in itself, but a step towards empowering aboriginal people to take control, not only of services such as policing and education and job training but of their economic futures. Investment in the sustainable economic development of aboriginal communities is an investment in a healthier Canadian economy.

Already native people are taking economic power into their own hands. There are successful native trust companies, credit unions, development corporations, and thousands of small and medium-sized businesses owned and operated by aboriginal people. These entrepreneurs are helping to fashion vibrant local economies that respond to local needs and promote community stability. (In many cases, they also provide useful models of environmentally sustainable development for the rest of us.) Such success stories point the way towards a meaningful transition to aboriginal self-government: native-run societies that generate both wealth and self-respect.

Part of the reason for these successes is that aboriginal control of investment capital is becoming increasingly widespread. The Peace Hills Trust, wholly owned by the Samson Indian Band of Hobbema, Alberta, was the first native-owned trust company and is the largest in Canada, with branches in Edmonton and Winnipeg. And the Kitsaki Development Corporation, founded by the La Ronge Indian Band in northern Saskatchewan in the early 1980s, has revitalized that reserve's economy. It has founded eight businesses, often as joint ventures with outside companies, including an insurance company and a highly profitable trucking company. These and the many other examples of native economic empowerment suggest the enormous potential of self-government to transform aboriginal societies.

Working out the details of self-government won't be easy. Five hundred years of colonialism doesn't disappear overnight. On both sides it will require every ounce of spiritual and intellectual strength we can muster. But it must be done.

• • •

Since I moved to the Yukon in 1979, I have been lucky enough to spend a lot of time in aboriginal communities. I have discovered a complex culture and a rich tradition of oral history, and learned much more than I can put into words.

For one thing, aboriginal people have evolved a completely consensual form of decision making. I have sat for many hours with a group of native elders during what sometimes seemed to me directionless conversation. Although I have long advocated decisions by consensus, I wasn't prepared for this remarkable commitment to hearing everyone's point of view. Nor do I always fully understand exactly how the consensus, when it is finally reached, has been achieved.

For me, an often impatient, goal-oriented person, working with native people has meant learning to let go of expectations about structure, of my need to know where the process is heading. I've discovered that just because I can't perceive the structure doesn't mean it isn't there.

It is often difficult for non-aboriginal people to enter into this different cultural universe, even those who are "experts" on native people. A while ago I attended an archaeological conference in Haines Junction, Yukon. The people running the conference were in some ways very knowledgeable about Yukon Indians, but they didn't really understand how aboriginal people operate. In particular, they didn't understand how and why they tell stories.

The organizers asked one of the native elders to tell the story of Skookum Jim, whom she had known when he was still alive. Skookum Jim was an Indian who had participated in the original gold discovery on Bonanza Creek in 1896 that led to the great

Yukon gold rush. The elder began a long and complicated tale —
it was difficult to discern that what she was saying had anything
to do with Skookum Jim at all. It seemed to be about genealogy
and family history. In "European" terms, there was no story line.
I could see the organizers of the conference becoming more and
more uncomfortable. This woman wasn't sticking to their schedule, nor did she seem to be sticking to her topic. Finally, one of
them broke in, suggested that it was time for lunch, and asked
if she could come back after the meal and finish her story. You
simply don't interrupt an elder when she is talking; it's disre-
spectful. And she wasn't having any of it. "No," she said. "I
haven't finished my story yet. You paper people don't understand."

I loved the term she used to categorize the archaeologists —
paper people. No matter how learned they supposedly were about
her culture, they couldn't let go of their conditioning. Their
books got in their way. They let her finish — and indeed she did
eventually get around to Skookum Jim. There is a flow and a
structure to a native story that non-natives cannot always understand. Hers was an intricate tapestry, not a single thread.

One of the most renowned of the Yukon storytellers was an
elder named Angela Sidney. When I met her, she was probably
in her eighties. The last time I visited her, I sat in her tiny house
in Carcross and we looked at a book about the fiftieth anniversary of the Alaska Highway. Her memories went back almost to
the time of the gold rush, long before anyone had even thought
about building the highway. She had grown up in a Yukon where
white people were few and Indian society carried on in the old
ways.

The whole time we sat and talked, perhaps an hour, she held
my hand. Her face, with its deeply etched lines, was very
beautiful, and her words, though simple, held profound truths.

She said to me, "You have a big responsibility and you must
listen to the elders." She didn't necessarily mean I was supposed
to listen to her. She meant for me to listen to the wisdom of my
own elders and of the aboriginal elders — to listen to the past.

A week later she died. When I heard the news I was at the

Dawson City Music Festival with my friend Harriet Davidson, who didn't know Angela but had heard me speak of her. We had just emerged from an evening concert given by the Winnipeg pop group the Crash Test Dummies. Although it was past midnight, we decided to drive back to attend the funeral. It would take seven hours, but being July it would be light the whole way. When we reached my house in Whitehorse, we showered and changed our clothes, then hopped back in the car to drive another hour to Carcross.

There is something about the setting of Carcross that I find particularly uplifting. It makes me think of Machu Picchu in Peru, the wonderful ruined Inca city, one of the most spiritual places I've ever been. Although the snow-covered Yukon mountains are nothing like the green mountains at Machu Picchu, they affect me in a similar way. Years ago when the Dalai Lama saw these same Yukon peaks he said they reminded him of certain holy mountains in Tibet. I have never felt this otherworldly quality more than on the day of Angela Sidney's funeral.

The weather was cold and rainy, but the community centre in Carcross was packed with mourners. The whole town was there along with Angela's friends and relatives from far and wide. Late in life she had become a Yukon celebrity and been awarded the Order of Canada. She was one of the last speakers of the Tagish language, which virtually died with her. But above all she had touched many people in her life. Although many of those present were "important," such as the Yukon's chief judge and the premier, I doubt any were there from a sense of official duty.

The funeral service was a fascinating blend of religious influences, primarily Bahai, a faith embraced by many of her younger relatives, and Christianity. She herself had been eclectic in her observance, part Anglican, part Bahai, and part traditional native spirituality. To her the boundaries between religions had ceased to count for much and I think the service would have pleased her. A number of prayers and passages of Bahai scripture were read and the Lord's Prayer recited. Then the eulogy was given by Julie Cruickshank, an anthropologist who had become very close to Angela while recording her stories.

With my mother and father the year I turned two.

Audrey, aged four.

With Happy and Fern Newkirk, during a summer visit to Port Stanley, Ontario, when I was seven years old.

My mother celebrates her election as the first woman to serve on the Essex, Ontario, town council.

The Essex High School basketball team that won the regional championship in 1952. I'm in the back row, second from the right; Gayle Annett is in the front row middle, holding the ball. (COURTESY GAYLE ANNETT)

Best friends: Gayle and I appear ready to take on the world as we prepared to leave home for the first time in the fall of 1953. (COURTESY GAYLE ANNETT)

Graduation photo from the Home Economics program at Guelph's Macdonald Hall, 1955.

Family Christmas in Wroxeter, Ontario, 1962.

With my mother and father the day I received my B.A. from the University of Western Ontario, 1964.

Before I left Toronto for the Yukon in 1979, Lotta Dempsey interviewed me for the Toronto Star and ran this photo of the subject behind the wheel of her truck. (CANAPRESS PHOTO SERVICE)

All my possessions were in the maroon pick-up that took me across Canada and finally to Whitehorse.

Members of the tenacious team who helped me win the NDP nomination in 1987 pose in front of my Whitehorse home. Back row, left to right: Diane Olsen, Margaret Joe, Jon Leah Hopkins, Sid Scramstead, Paula Pasquale, Lynn Gaudet, me. Front row: Linda Netro, Lucy Van Oldenbarneveld, Janeane MacGillvray, Jennifer Mauro, Rene Carlson.

With my son David and my mother, awaiting the results of the count at the old Yukon Indian Centre, the night of the 1987 by-election.

Raising our hands in victory, July 20, 1987; I am the member of Parliament for the Yukon.

Our log skyscraper constituency office in Whitehorse.

One of the fun parts of being an MP- Indian Days at Brooks Brook in June 1988.

In July 1988, Ed Broadbent visited the Yukon to mark the first anniversary of my by-election win.

Arriving in Winnipeg for the December 1989 leadership convention. Les Campbell is beside me; behind us, left to right: Steve Lee, Katheryn Debree, Dawn Black.

After the second ballot, both Simon de Jong (centre) and Howard McCurdy walked over to give me their support. We knew then that the momentum was shifting our way. (CANAPRESS PHOTO SERVICE)

The moment of victory. Left to right: Nelson Riis, my daughter Tracy, my mother, and beside me, Stanley Knowles. Just behind us is soon-to-be-elected Quebec MP Phil Edmonston. (PHOTO FEATURES)

On December 6, 1989, I made my first statement in the House as New Democratic Party leader. (CANAPRESS PHOTO SERVICE)

On the Sunday following my leadership win, I held my first media "scrum"- a ritual I would have to learn to handle in my new job. (CANAPRESS PHOTO SERVICE)

In April 1990, Canadian Labour Congress President Shirley Carr and I carried a coffin onto Parliament Hill to protest the government's GST legislation. Dissident Tory David Kilgour is the fellow with the hat. (CANAPRESS PHOTO SERVICE)

Christmas 1989: four generations gathered to celebrate an exciting year: grandmother and great-grandmother flank my daughter Tracy and my granddaughter Kelly.

With gandson Derek.

During the spring of 1991 I went on a cross-country speaking tour to discuss our party's ideas for amending the constitution, including the need for a social charter. On April 11, I addressed the Steelworkers in Toronto. (CANAPRESS PHOTO SERVICE)

A treasured photo of some of my women NDP colleagues: friends, mentors, and fellow caucus members: left to right: Dawn Black, Rosemary Brown, me, Lynn Hunter, Joy Langan, Marion Dewar, the late Pauline Jewett, and Margaret Mitchell.

By the time we reached the graveyard, a wooded spot up on a hill, it had stopped raining but the sky was still grey and the air misty. It was the burial place of many of the old gold miners and of Skookum Jim himself. Matthew Fred, a high elder of Angela's Tlingit clan in Angoon, Alaska, now spoke, mostly in the Tlingit language. Then her coffin was lowered into the grave as people wept.

Following the burial her friends and relatives returned to the community centre for a potlach, a formal feast arranged and paid for by the other Tlingit clans. (A year later, Angela's clan would repay this courtesy by holding another potlach in their honour.) After dinner, there were ritual dances and songs. Various people spoke about Angela's life and accomplishments. I remember particularly Matthew Fred talking about the history of her Deishitan clan, and of each of her many children and grandchildren. He spoke of her life, of how she had travelled all over the world telling stories, and of how she had influenced others to take pride in their native heritage. I was especially moved when Matthew reminded the assembly that Angela's spirit would now be dispersed to every corner of Tlingit land.

Then Matthew said, "Well, we've buried Mrs. Sidney. Now it's time to get on with life, so we're all going to tell jokes." He told funny stories about Angela's adventures during her world travels; others simply told jokes. That day tears and laughter flowed in equal measure. It was like nothing I'd ever experienced. It was as though her spirit were still living in that room. I'll always consider Angela Sidney's funeral to have been a very special gift.

WAR   OR   PEACE ?

EVERY ONCE IN A WHILE, a truly testing issue comes along. The Constitution has been one; the Gulf War was another. The subject of war raises strong emotions, of course, and within the New Democratic Party there are profound differences of opinion about when, if ever, armed action is appropriate. Nor is there a party policy that says we will oppose war under any circumstances. In 1939, the CCF voted in favour of the declaration of war against Germany, but J. S. Woodsworth — a staunch pacifist — resigned as leader rather than vote with his caucus. The Gulf War was a far less clear-cut issue than Hitler's acts of aggression, but again the time had come — after all the study and consultation and the many debates in caucus — to take a stand. The one we took wasn't easy, but I believe it was right.

The events that led to war began on August 2, 1990, when Iraqi president Saddam Hussein invaded Kuwait, swiftly occupying the entire country. On August 6, the United Nations Security Council voted to impose mandatory sanctions against

Iraq. On August 8, President Bush announced that he was drawing "a line in the sand" and began the deployment of a huge force of American troops to the Gulf, purportedly for the defence of Saudi Arabia against an attack from Iraq. This turned out to be the first step towards what became a U.S.-led military alliance endorsed by the United Nations but not flying the U.N. flag or having a U.N. command structure. On August 10, Prime Minister Mulroney declared that Canada's initial contribution to these allied forces would be two destroyers and a supply ship. "Our naval forces," he said, "will assist in the deterrence of further aggression." Canada would help make sure that sanctions worked.

The caucus quickly reached a consensus on what our response to these early events should be. We condemned the Iraqi invasion and supported the use of sanctions to force Saddam Hussein to withdraw from Kuwait. In the next few weeks, as the sanctions took effect, blocking virtually all trade with Iraq, we believed it was only a matter of time before Hussein would be compelled to come to the bargaining table.

At first the American administration appeared to agree. In August President Bush argued that "economic sanctions in this instance, if fully enforced, can be very, very effective. Nobody can stand up forever to total economic deprivation." That fall, Secretary of Defense Richard Cheney reported that "the sanctions and embargo are beginning to have an impact." Soon he was informing us that the Iraqi army would begin to run short of spare parts by Easter. His predictions were echoed by CIA head William Webster, who announced that the Iraqi air force would be in trouble within three to six months. In nine months, Hussein's whole armed forces would be desperately short of materiel.

But as the weeks passed, the American build-up in the Gulf went far beyond the numbers necessary for the defence of Saudi Arabia — eventually reaching more than 400,000 troops. And the rhetoric changed. Increasingly it became apparent that George Bush and many in his administration saw a so-called shooting war as an option, possibly even a desirable one. Some strategists argued it would allow the United States to cripple Iraq militarily and readjust the balance of power in the Middle East to American advantage. There was also a purely political consideration noted by some members of the press: a short, successful war would make the president into a political hero, which then seemed likely to guarantee his re-election in 1992.

A related factor also seemed to be at work: the president's desire, even need, to look tough. This temptation is not exclusive to male politicians — witness Margaret Thatcher and the Falklands war — but Bush had long been saddled with a media image as something of a "wimp." He began to characterize the conflict in personal terms, as a fight between him and the Iraqi dictator. He always called Hussein by his first name, using such street-gang phrases as Saddam is "going to get his ass kicked." This was not the behaviour of a man who genuinely wanted to give peace a chance. Deliberately or not, he left little room for a political settlement.

For me, one of the most frustrating aspects of this whole episode was the way Canadian foreign policy simply became knee-jerk support of the U.S. administration. The closer George Bush moved to war, the more bellicose Mulroney and the Tories became. On November 29, Canada co-sponsored and voted for Security Council Resolution 678, which set January 15, 1991, as the deadline after which the U.S.-led alliance could use "all necessary means" to force Iraq out of Kuwait. That same day the Tories introduced a motion in the House in support of this resolution, a motion our party unanimously opposed.

Once Bush's deadline had been set, the temperature of the Gulf War debate rose steadily. Until then our caucus had held firm in its support of sanctions and a diplomatic solution, but now some members began to waver. If Bush went to war and Canada followed, should we support or oppose this action?

In December and early January, I too was wrestling with the contradictory claims and counter-claims. Back then, no one knew whether Hussein's threats were more than bravado. What if he could survive the embargo indefinitely as the American administration was now suggesting? Perhaps the military threat really was as grave as Bush and others now were saying. Maybe Hussein would have an atomic bomb within a year. Maybe he would let his people starve rather than abandon Kuwait. I had to wonder, however, why Hussein had become such an overwhelming military threat only after he invaded Kuwait. The United States and other western countries had contributed massively to his military arsenal; the Americans had backed him in his war with Iran, during which an estimated one million people were killed. Until the eve of the invasion, the United States and many of its allies continued to sell arms to his regime while turning a blind eye to its serious human rights abuses.

As war became more likely, I consulted widely — with labour and peace groups, with military analysts and experts on sanctions. I talked to social democratic leaders in Europe in search of more information and a different perspective, among them former German chancellor Willy Brandt, the president of the Socialist International, and Swedish prime minister Ingvar Carlsson. And I was in touch with Democratic leaders of the United States Congress. The overwhelming weight of opinion from the sources I trusted was that, given time, sanctions would work.

It's easy to forget now, but many members of the U.S. Congress and quite a few members of the military establishment opposed going to war in January. In testimony before the Senate Armed Services Committee in late November, Admiral William J. Crowe, Jr., said, "If, in fact, the sanctions will work in twelve to eighteen months instead of six months, a trade-off of avoiding war, with its attendant sacrifices and uncertainties, would in my estimation be more than worth it." Right up to the eve of the air war, many of the most respected politicians in Washington argued, as the Europeans did, for giving sanctions more time.

In fact, no more complete trade embargo had ever been undertaken than the one aimed at Iraq. There was general agreement among the experts that more than 90 percent of Iraq's imports and 97 percent of its exports had been cut off. Oil exports, almost its total source of foreign exchange, had been stopped cold. Essential services would soon begin to grind to a halt.

To quote Kimberly Elliott, Gary Hufbauer, and Jeffrey Schott, authors of a book on sanctions, "Even the tightest sanctions take time to work." In an article published in the *Washington Post* in December 1990, they went on to say, "Evidence from previous cases suggests that it would be unfair to claim the embargo of Iraq has failed until at least a year has passed . . . If after a year or two the sanctions are judged to be inadequate, the military option will still be there and Saddam's forces will be weakened by lack of supplies. The key question is whether the price of patience would be higher than the economic and human costs of going to war soon." They pointed out that less stringent sanctions had worked to move Rhodesia towards majority rule and to persuade South Africa to grant independence to Namibia. It was only a matter of time, they argued, but time was the one thing George Bush seemed unwilling to provide.

Like many other Canadians, I didn't spend a very easy Christmas in 1990, with war looming. In early January, last-minute hopes for movement on the diplomatic front were dashed. It was clear the United States was not interested in a negotiated settlement. Unless Hussein backed down, war appeared inevitable. On January 12, after passionate and often eloquent debate, the U.S. Senate and House of Representatives narrowly adopted a joint resolution authorizing the president to use military force against Iraq. From that moment, the voices counselling caution and patience were stilled. The warmongers took control of the floor.

In the preceding weeks, we had held special meeting after special meeting as the caucus agonized over whether or not to support the war — if it came to that. I believe that there are circumstances in which armed force is the only option, but force must be used only as a last resort. In order to vote for offensive military action against Iraq I would have to be convinced that all measures short of war had been given a fair chance and had failed, that war was the only possible alternative. And I wasn't convinced. Not everyone in the caucus agreed with me at first, but painfully we reached a consensus to hold firm and oppose any offensive action until sanctions and diplomacy had been given more time to work. If war was declared, we would not jump on the military bandwagon.

Even after this position took hold in the caucus, I wanted to be certain we were doing the right thing. On January 14, 1991, one day before the U.N. deadline, Les Campbell and I flew to Washington for talks with Middle East experts and congressional leaders. Committees of the House and the Senate had conducted far more exhaustive hearings than we had in Canada. Before our decision became irrevocable, I wanted to be sure we had all the facts in our hands.

I met with some of the influential Democrats who had opposed this rush into war, including Senator Edward Kennedy. They had been bruised by the political battle they'd just lost, but nonetheless took the time to meet with the leader of a Canadian third party. Kennedy was cordial and supportive. We discussed the Senate's narrow passage of the January 12 pro-war resolution by a margin of only 52 to 47. But he was frank about how difficult it would be to continue to oppose the president once war began. After our meeting, he insisted I pose with him for a photograph beside a bust of JFK, then he went out with me to talk to reporters, and to reiterate his opposition to war.

My afternoon meeting with Democratic Senator George Mitchell, the Senate Majority Leader, had to be postponed until evening because he'd been called to the White House, which meant an unplanned stay overnight in Washington for Les and me. It had already been a long and tiring day, but we didn't want to leave without talking to the most powerful Democrat in the Senate.

All in all, the visit had gone well — the only irritant being the unwelcome attention we had received from the Canadian Embassy. As expected, the embassy had helped set up my Washington appointments and I'd had a pleasant meeting with Ambassador Derek Burney that morning. What I didn't like was that at least one and sometimes two people from the embassy staff accompanied us to every meeting, despite our strenuous objections. Obviously they were there to make sure we didn't say or do anything that would undermine Canada's official all-out support for George Bush. We ignored them as best we could and certainly didn't censor ourselves, but by 6 p.m., as we were preparing to visit Senator Mitchell, I'd had enough.

I turned to the embassy official who had clung to us all afternoon and told him that I'd like him to call it a day. He refused, saying, "We always did this for John Turner." This was the worst argument he could have used. "Well, you don't need to do it for me," I snapped back. He replied that if I had any complaints I could "take them up with the ambassador," but that he was accompanying us to our next appointment. Our discussion became so heated that the chauffeur decided it would be more comfortable to wait outside the limousine until we had finished.

In the end I decided there was no point in turning this into an international incident. The embassy official was simply doing what he'd been told to do. But I deeply resented the implication that I had to be kept under surveillance by the Canadian government. I have been treated with courtesy by many Canadian embassies during my visits to foreign capitals, but after this I questioned whether I would ever call on an embassy's help again — at least as long as I'm an opposition leader.

As we drove by the White House on our way to the Capitol Building, I was struck by how quiet and normal everything looked. Yet behind that tranquil white facade, Bush and his advisers were planning a war. Inside the Capitol, the carpeted corridors were hushed and, despite the number of people still at work in the Senate Majority Leader's spacious offices, the mood was distinctly subdued.

Senator Mitchell greeted us in a small, elegantly furnished meeting room accompanied by his foreign policy adviser. For someone who probably hadn't slept much in several days and who had just come from a meeting with the president where he had undoubtedly been briefed on the imminent air attack, he was surprisingly relaxed. Before turning to the topic on both our minds, he spoke knowledgeably of Canadian politics (as a senator from Maine he was better informed on matters Canadian than most). He congratulated us on the September election that had brought Bob Rae and the NDP to power in Ontario.

When we began to talk about the Gulf, however, I sensed his weariness and sadness. Like Kennedy, he recognized that once the war began, he would have little choice but to express his support for American troops and for the president. To do otherwise would be seen as unpatriotic. (Indeed, on January 17, the day after Desert Storm was launched, the Senate would unanimously adopt a resolution commending and supporting "the efforts and leadership of the president in the Persian Gulf hostilities." But as Mitchell made clear during that debate, he still believed that "the decision to authorize war at this time was premature.")

That evening in his office, Mitchell was frank about how he felt. And he confirmed my worst suspicions: the president's decision was political. Sanctions had not been given a chance. When I asked him, "Were sanctions working?" his reply was unequivocal: "Yes, they were the way to go." When we parted, I had the sense that this man envied me in a way. I now had more freedom than he did to speak the truth as I saw it.

When Les and I boarded the plane early Tuesday morning, we felt ragged and discouraged. Because we hadn't planned to stay over in Washington, neither of us had brought a change of clothes, but we didn't dwell on these trivial irritants. The previous day Joe Clark, then minister of external affairs, had introduced a motion reaffirming Canada's support for the use of force in the Gulf. Later that morning, debate on the motion would resume in the House. Any remaining doubt about my response had vanished in George Mitchell's office. I could not support this war.

As the plane flew north, I drafted the remarks I would be making in a few hours. I knew exactly what I wanted to say. A war in the Middle East would, regardless of the outcome, carry with it grave costs and unpredictable consequences. There was the potentially devastating effect on the environment, from fires in the oil fields and the use of chemical weapons. There was a near certainty that the defeat of Iraq would do nothing to increase stability in the region. Above all there was the human cost, not only to allied forces but to the people of Iraq who would inevitably die in great numbers.

When I rose in the House shortly after noon, my fatigue fell away. "Mr. Speaker," I began, "the question is purely and simply this: Is Canada going to support a declaration of war?" I went on to argue that sanctions and diplomacy had not been properly tested and then to speak of the incalculable human factor. "The human cost, of course the most important consideration, is impossible for any of us to grasp. . . . We are not debating today whether Saddam Hussein is taking an evil action. He is. But to punish evil and immoral action with tens of thousands of other mortalities does not make sense. . . ."

As I said that day, this should not have been treated as a partisan issue, but as an issue of conscience, and I called for a free vote in the House — every MP voting according to his or her conscience — an idea opposed by both the Tories and the Liberals. (In my own caucus, the vote had been free, although in the end everyone stood together.) I said that no one knew the absolute right or wrong of the question before us, but one thing was sure: anyone who claimed certainty, who claimed to have all the answers and to occupy the moral high ground was self-deluded. At a time such as this, elected politicians have to take a stand — however lonely it may be.

After all the speeches had been made and the final vote recorded, the members of our party did indeed stand alone in opposing the government resolution. Although Jean Chrétien and the Liberals had also argued that sanctions needed to be given more time, when the crunch came, they sided with the government — and with George Bush.

Just after 7 p.m., Ottawa time, on January 16, American and allied planes and missiles began the air war on Iraq, dubbed Operation Desert Storm. That night I watched the television footage of missiles exploding on their targets, the surreal scenes of Baghdad under night bombardment. The media presented the air war as a triumph of American military technology. One CNN commentator described the city as "lit up like a Christmas tree." It had the look and feel of a video game. But as I watched the carefully selected images, all I could think of were the people who'd been edited out. People down there were dying.

In the days that followed, the NDP protested when Canadian CF-18 fighter planes, which had originally been sent to the Gulf only for defensive purposes, were authorized to participate in bombing raids over Iraq. As the devastation of Iraq mounted, we urged the government to support new attempts at negotiating an end to the war. These stands were not particularly popular at the time. According to opinion polls, a substantial majority of Canadians supported the government's handling of the war. Many people have told me since, however, that they thought my speech in the House on the evening of January 15 was one of the best I've ever made and that this was one of the NDP's finest hours. I was struck by the number of Canadian veterans of previous wars who congratulated me on our stand. Some observers were reminded of November 4, 1970, when Tommy Douglas and his caucus voted against the imposition of the War Measures Act. Tommy said, "We cannot protect democratic freedoms by restricting, limiting, and destroying democratic freedoms." In January 1991, when my party stood alone against the Gulf War, we were saying a similar thing: you can rarely promote peace by making war.

Someone once said that truth is the first casualty of war. The accuracy of this adage has seldom been more evident than in the war in the Gulf. The military might of Saddam Hussein was exaggerated out of all proportion. Is it conceivable that American intelligence didn't know the real military situation? And if they did, why did they not report it accurately? Is it possible that the pro-war factions in the military were manipulating world opinion to support unnecessary armed aggression?

Almost two years after the war ended, no one knows how many casualties were suffered — the Pentagon has estimated that 150,000 Iraqi soldiers were killed, some of them buried alive by the allies' bulldozers. The civilian death toll — always underestimated or dismissed — is even more cloudy, but certainly in the tens of thousands, given that 92 percent of the bombs dropped were "dumb bombs" with an accuracy rate of only 25 percent, not the high-tech superstars that got all the media play. A medical team from Harvard that visited Iraq after the war predicted that 170,000 children under the age of five could die because of the post-war conditions — scanty food, poor sanitation, lack of medical care — but we may never know the final figures. In addition, the Middle East suffered the world's worst environmental disaster since Chernobyl. The U.S. National Science Foundation estimated that at their peak, the oil well fires were spewing between one and two million tons of carbon dioxide per day into the earth's atmosphere — the equivalent of 46 million diesel trucks continuously travelling at thirty miles an hour for twenty-four hours.

The "new world order," at least in the Middle East, is an utter sham: Hussein's regime is still in power, still committing atrocities against its own people. I doubt many people in the Middle East see George Bush as their saviour from Saddam Hussein. For them, the "facts" of the Gulf War are very different from the "facts" in the West. But then facts depend on who is interpreting them. If you are one of the 350,000 Palestinians deported from Kuwait, you may not see the Gulf War as a war of liberation. If you are a Kurd in the Iraqi north or a Shiite Muslim in the south, you probably don't think the war is over yet.

• • •

I learned that facts are not always what they seem when I lived for the first time in a totally different culture. This was when I spent three years with my husband and two small children in the young African nation of Ghana, which had been granted independence from Great Britain in 1957. The truth as seen from North America is not necessarily the same truth as seen from the developing world.

There are two ways of approaching a different culture. One is to judge the place by your own values and standards, to compare its people to yourself and its customs to those of your home country. The other is to suspend judgement — as much as possible — and to learn as much as you can, to see with different eyes. My instinctive approach to something new seems to be this second way. When I'm confronted by something I don't understand, I ask questions and try to listen to the answers.

It's a mistake, however, to think that you can ever become the other, an idea I call the beads and buckskin fallacy. I've seen it operate with white people who get involved — with the best of motives — in aboriginal organizations in Canada. No matter how hard they try to become Indians, they can't; the beads and buckskin can only be costumes for them. When they forget this, they end up patronizing the very people they want to help.

Although I had done some reading about Ghanaian politics and culture and religion, I really had no idea what to expect when our plane touched down in Accra that summer day in 1964. On this occasion, we didn't see much of the capital. The school headmaster, Mr. Robert Orleans Pobee, met us at the airport and whisked us off to Adisadel College in Ghana's second city, Cape Coast, several hours' drive away. This was where my husband, Don, was to teach math and science for the next three years.

The headmaster, who wore a suit and tie despite the heat, turned out to be a fascinating and impressive man. I suppose in many ways he epitomized the contradictions of his country, which had been independent for fewer than ten years. He was a classics scholar who had graduated from an English university, a member of the elite class of native Ghanaians created during the British colonial administration. As well as running the school, he taught Latin to the boys. He was the headmaster of a boarding school that in most respects was a carbon copy of an English boys' school and yet he was a staunch Ghanaian nationalist. He was a traditionalist, but he was not afraid to try something new.

During the drive, Mr. Pobee discovered that I had a university degree in English. "We are short an English teacher," he told me. "Would you be willing to take on the job?" It turned out the school was having trouble keeping staff. The political climate in Ghana had turned tense. The uneasy alliance between the president, Kwame Nkrumah, and the Ghanaian elite was crumbling as Nkrumah took power into his own hands and began to imprison opponents. The head of the English department had recently left the country because of the worsening political situation. Although my only teaching experience was as an occasional supply teacher around Wroxeter while I was finishing up my undergraduate degree, I jumped at the opportunity.

In my memory, Adisadel College is a beautiful place, although the architecture was plain and the amenities were few. It comprised a group of mostly white-stuccoed buildings with red trim and unpainted tin roofs, perched high on a hill overlooking the port town of Cape Coast and the Atlantic Ocean. Louvred shutters kept out the wet but let in the breeze during the rainy season. The buildings were mostly two or three storeys and of very simple construction — the original buildings had been built by boys from the school back in the 1930s when it was founded by the Church of England. The surrounding vegetation was lush, and the school grounds included many flowering trees — frangipani, bougainvillaea, flame trees, and others whose names I did not know.

Adisadel College exhibited something of a split personality — part British, part Ghanaian. Although it was being operated as a state school, it retained its Anglican trappings and much of its pre-independence character. Roughly half the teachers were white Englishmen. Each morning, after rising around 6 a.m., the boys trooped into chapel to sing Anglican hymns and listen to a few words of scripture from the school chaplain, Father Gillette, and on Friday evenings the whole school gathered for Vespers, singing hymns as the sun went down. (This was an absolutely magical moment, with the boys' voices wafting into the gentle African evening, out towards the distant sea.) The male teachers — along with me there were two other conscripted wives — were addressed as "sir" and the lessons came out of English textbooks. Cricket, English football (soccer), and cross-country running were the main sports. Yet this was a boys' college that was training the future teachers, lawyers, administrators, and politicians of a new African nation. It took them all the way from the equivalent of our grade nine to the British upper sixth form, the equivalent of first-year university in Canada.

Some of the British expatriates, or "expats," still clung to colonial attitudes, but the majority were wonderful people who loved the country and wanted it to succeed. Truly a breed apart was the Russian couple from Gorky, who both taught science. Although they had studied English, they spoke it with difficulty. So each night they had to sit down and write out the next day's lessons, something I would sometimes help them with. They were kind and generous people, but they had a woefully narrow concept of what Africa was. Theirs was in some ways still the Africa of Joseph Conrad, the colonial Africa of the nineteenth century.

The head of the English department in our first year was a young Canadian named Dave Godfrey, who had been promoted when the previous head left the country unexpectedly. Dave went on to write a novel set in Ghana called *The New Ancestors*, which won the 1970 Governor General's Award for fiction. He and his wife, Ellen — she taught at the local Catholic boys' school — helped ease my transition into this new world. They'd already been in Ghana for a couple of years and knew the ropes.

Ellen warned me that it would be difficult for a woman to be accepted by the boys. They weren't used to having female teachers, and they could be brutal if you failed to win their respect. In colonial Ghana, teaching had been one of the few good jobs open to native Ghanaians, which meant that primarily men had become teachers. A woman was seen to be stepping out of place. Ellen gave me two pieces of advice: "Always wear your skirts below your knees and never smile." I followed the first piece, but once I'd become comfortable with my students, I abandoned the second.

Though every culture is unique, certain universals seem to apply to youngsters in school no matter where you are. I noticed the same mischievous looks, the same schoolboy pranks, and the same testing of authority I had observed in Canada. On the first day of class, the boys dutifully sat in their seats in alphabetical order. When I called the roll, I simply went down the rows in order. The next time I did roll call, everyone had changed seats. Just like in Canada.

I did find it difficult at first as the boys probed for my weaknesses. One of the big problems was getting them to stop talking and pay attention while I was teaching, but I discovered the remedy. I told them, "Okay, if you want to talk so much then you can stay after school and talk for an hour. Then I'll be happy to listen to what you have to say." The problem soon disappeared.

Perhaps because I offered them my respect as well as expecting respect from them, my discipline problems diminished. (This was fortunate for me; the previous year, the school's first woman teacher had been treated so badly she had been virtually driven from the classroom.) I was firm, but I refused to resort to the ultimate punishment, sending a boy to the headmaster to be caned. The key, I think, was that I did not present myself as a know-it-all foreigner come to teach them my culture, but as a visitor interested in theirs. I asked about their lives, their backgrounds, their ways of seeing things. Before long we could laugh together at some of the absurdities of teaching European literature to Ghanaians. Over time, in fact, the older boys began to treat me somewhat protectively and would knock the younger boys back into line when they strayed too far.

Teaching English literature to Ghanaian teenagers in 1964 was a disorienting experience that starkly illustrated the legacy of colonialism. There I was trying to explain to black Africans the work of writers who had lived in a totally alien culture. I particularly remember the absurdity I felt teaching T. S. Eliot's *The Wasteland*. Not that this poem's stark view of modern human alienation had nothing to say to the boys. But the language and cultural references were very hard for them to understand. What did it mean to a Ghanaian teenager to talk of "measuring out your life by coffee spoons"?

There were no African writers at all on the English curriculum, not even Ghana's great novelist, Chinua Achebe. One reason was the post-colonial inferiority complex: no African writer could be as great as a British writer. But it was also a practical matter. In order to graduate, these boys had to sit for the standardized examinations used in British schools, O levels and A levels. To gain admittance to the university in Accra — or to one in England — they had to think and write like English schoolboys.

However, by the time of our sojourn, the real Ghana had begun to show up in the school's extra-curricular life. Interestingly enough, the main catalyst was Dave Godfrey. He started the school's first band, which played jazz and also Ghanaian high-life music. This band became so popular that it soon was imitated at other schools and was even invited to play for Nkrumah himself.

The real Ghana also showed up in the plays Dave directed. The year before I arrived, he and his students performed an African version of *Julius Caesar*, written in vernacular blank verse by a student who had been inspired by novelist Achebe when he spoke at the school. It was a risqué production with a very subversive political subtext, but Headmaster Pobee didn't object.

Dave drew me into the school's theatrical life. My first year, which was his last, I had a small part in his production of *Twelfth Night* (Shakespeare was able to leap over the cultural barriers, perhaps because he explores such elemental themes and tells such universal stories). After Dave left, I achieved the pinnacle of my amateur acting career when I played Lady Macbeth. Although we stuck to the English text, the costumes and sets were African. As I recall, I wore seven different Ghanaian costumes over the course of the play. The audience seemed to be as interested in whether I would successfully complete my costume changes, which involved much wrapping and unwrapping of skirts and headscarves, as in the outcome of the action.

Among the few things I didn't like about Africa were the poisonous snakes and scorpions. One night not long after we arrived, we found a spitting cobra in the kitchen of our bungalow. This is a large snake that spits in your eyes and blinds you — temporarily, if you're lucky and can get medical help in time. Don killed it before it hurt anyone, but we were all shaken.

My family was happy in Ghana. David was eight and Tracy six the year we arrived, and they adapted quickly to their new surroundings, attending local schools and making friends easily. Tracy, who had white-blonde hair, was our entrée everywhere. If Tracy was with us, we were immediately drawn into local events. In Cape Coast children were welcome everywhere, as if they all belonged to one extended family. They wandered freely from house to house and accompanied their parents to what in Canada would have been adult social events. It was my first experience of a truly child-caring society.

Although it had been my idea to leave Canada and come to Africa, Don, who'd been teaching only a few years, also found it very stimulating. In the summers and during school breaks, we took trips in our Volkswagen to neighbouring countries such as Ivory Coast, Upper Volta (Burkina Faso since 1960), Niger, and Nigeria. We flew to East Africa and explored its famous national parks and reserves. We saw as much of Africa as we could, and I soaked up the cultures, learning about the different tribes and religions. This only reinforced my perception that there is no one right way: each place has its own wisdom as well as its own set of biases and blind spots.

Although Ghana was a culture apparently dominated by men, I have vivid images of the strength of the women. The people in power — the politicians and chiefs and civil servants — were all male, yet there was a sense that the women really ran the place. Women drove trucks and worked on construction sites and ruled in the outdoor markets, the heartbeat of Ghanaian society. The power of Ghanaian women wasn't apparent if you just read newspapers and looked at statistics. You could get a sense of it, though, from Margaret Laurence's wonderful short stories — *The Tomorrow-Tamer* — written when she spent several years in Ghana in the 1950s.

My time in Ghana contributed to my political awareness — if any place would make you political, Ghana would. It was a society going through upheaval. A place like Adisadel College with its strict rules and British ways was an island of relative calm, but not totally insulated from the tremors shaking the world outside.

There was little overt criticism of the Nkrumah regime, although by the time we arrived he had become increasingly unpopular and dictatorial, obsessed with the dream of pan-Africanism and of Ghana as the centre of this movement. In many ways he was a great man, but by his last years his reach had exceeded his grasp. Ghanaians had a saying, "His soup is on the fire," by which they meant that Nkrumah was in control, and so the wise course was to keep criticism to yourself. This does not mean that indirect criticism, such as the Adisadel student production of *Julius Caesar*, didn't surface. Once, when Dave Godfrey asked one of his students to give an example of the literary device known as personification, which means treating an abstract concept as if it were a person, his answer was: "In Ghana, justice is a detainee." The detainees were people Nkrumah had thrown in jail for political reasons.

Nkrumah's soup got knocked off the fire in 1966, while he was on an official visit to Peking. He was overthrown in a bloodless coup and replaced by a military council chaired by a general. For a while, there were soldiers everywhere and road-blocks, but life at Adisadel didn't change. The new government came from the old black colonial elite that felt it was losing its status under his regime. Most of our students came from this same class. Their fathers were soldiers, civil servants, lawyers, and policemen, the people who supported the coup and benefited from it.

As Nkrumah neared the end, he started to censor the press. *Time* magazine would sometimes arrive with whole articles sliced out because the president didn't like the way he was portrayed. I don't condone this suppression of free speech, but the articles weren't innocent, either. They reflected not the realities of Ghana, but rather western assumptions and interpretations.

We used to receive our Canadian newspapers many months late and often many weeks' issues arrived together. Between times, our main source of news was the BBC, which told us little about Canada. Reading several weeks of newspapers in a few days revealed how distorted the news can be. It was fascinating to read the pundits' predictions and analyses long after an event had proved them wrong. This experience helped teach me to be sceptical of the media and of conventional wisdom in general. It also gave me a regular topic of discussion with my students: how events are interpreted and how the interpretation creates new "facts."

When I arrived in West Africa, I was in my late twenties. I had just earned a university degree and begun to question many of the assumptions of my own society. But it was in Ghana that I learned to question more deeply. A lot of what I'd been taught in university didn't make much sense in Ghana. After three years in a Ghanaian classroom, I saw that every educational system has its built-in cultural bias. One of the great challenges for a teacher is to reveal this truth to her students, to help them see that their way is neither right nor wrong, but simply different — unique.

Ghana also gave me a taste for the unknown, for learning about other realities. Every such journey has its snakes and scorpions — the fears you must overcome. But if you can overcome them, the rewards are enormous.

• • •

My experience in Africa in the mid-1960s helped me see the world through different eyes. My subsequent travels, especially my work in the Caribbean and my trip through South and Central America in 1986-87, exposed me even more starkly to the enormous problems of the developing world — poverty, environmental devastation, and abuse of human rights. But these experiences also taught me to value local cultures and to respect the centuries of wisdom they have built up. I came to realize that if you really listen to what other people have to say, to how they define a problem, the solution is often apparent.

Since becoming leader of the NDP, I've talked to many

national leaders and foreign policy experts about the complexities of international relations in the post-Cold War world, a world facing seemingly insurmountable environmental and economic problems. The ideas I want to put forward in the closing section of this chapter will strike some as impractical, but I believe we had better find a way to make this particular dream a reality unless we want our children to live a nightmare. I am not so naive as to think that we can wish away weapons and wars. But I do believe the nations of the world now have one of those rare opportunities to turn assumptions on their heads and make a fundamental shift in the way human beings share the planet. What I envisage won't be easy to achieve, and it won't happen without many stops and starts along the way, but it is possible. And we've got to try to achieve it. There is no choice.

I believe that Canada has an important role to play in this work of international realignment. But we need to chart a very different course in foreign policy, the outlines of which I'll present here. For the last few years, our course seems to have been almost entirely determined by our desire to please the United States. The last Liberal government permitted Cruise missile tests and allowed American nuclear warships in Canadian ports. The Tory government endorsed the American invasions of Grenada and of Panama. It took its cues from the United States in responding to the changes in the Soviet Union. During the Gulf War, it never deviated from supporting U.S. policy, converting our purely defensive role in the Gulf in support of United Nations sanctions against Iraq into an offensive combat role in an American-led military alliance.

But what role *should* Canada play? George Bush and Brian Mulroney like to talk about a "new world order," yet the phrase has suspect connotations. The word "new" suggests that things are going to change, but the word "order" suggests a hierarchical ranking, a power structure with some countries on top and some on the bottom. History and experience both tell us that any "new" order is likely to be run by the industrialized nations in their own interests and at the expense of the developing nations — just as the old order was. And this would guarantee that the greater part of humanity will continue to live in poverty and insecurity. Ultimately I think it would guarantee the decline and fall of the industrialized countries themselves. Rigid hierarchical orders have a way of collapsing, and the world has become far too interdependent for such narrow, self-interested thinking.

I believe that Canada should be promoting an alternative vision, not of a new world order but of a new world *community*. This is more than a mere change of language — although language can be important. A community is a coming together of equals, a place of mutual respect and co-operation. These principles must replace the old principles of endless competition to get and keep the most power, to exploit the weak for the greatest temporary advantage, if a world community is to take shape. The challenge is to conduct global relations in a new way, one that includes countries and groups within countries that traditionally have had little or no power.

The underpinning of this new world community is the concept of common security. This is not a new idea, but now that two superpowers are no longer locked in a nuclear stand-off, it is an idea whose time has come. The argument summed up in the phrase "common security" starts with the observation that more and more weapons have not made the world a safer place. Our security cannot be built on the insecurity of others. Each individual nation is secure only when all other nations in the global community feel secure. If there is famine in the Horn of Africa or civil war in Yugoslavia, then Canadian security is endangered. If the Black Forest is dying from acid rain or the Amazonian rainforest is being cut down, then Canada is not safe. If citizens are being tortured in Guatemala or held without trial in China, then Canadians, too, are not safe.

The idea of common security gained international currency in 1982, when the Cold War was raging, in a report prepared by a commission chaired by Olof Palme, the Social Democratic prime minister of Sweden. The authors of that report, entitled *Common Security: A Blueprint for Survival*, could see beyond the nuclear threat that still preoccupied them. As former U.S. secretary of state Cyrus Vance wrote in the introduction, "There is one overriding truth in the nuclear age — no nation can achieve true security by itself. . . . Both we and the Soviet Union are, and will remain, vulnerable to nuclear attack. . . . To guarantee our own security in this nuclear age, we must therefore face these realities and work together with other nations to achieve common security. For security in the nuclear age *means* common security."

Now that the threat of nuclear war is greatly diminished (although not absent), the principle of common security is even more valid. Without nuclear missiles staring us in the face, we can look beyond the terror they instilled to the underlying problems that cause insecurity in individual countries, and work to achieve real security by solving those problems. Take the environment. The report of the World Commission on the Environment and Development, known as the Brundtland Report after its chair, Norwegian prime minister Gro Harlem Brundtland, points out: "The deepening and widening environmental crisis presents a threat to national security — and even survival — that may be greater than well-armed, ill-disposed neighbours and unfriendly alliances."

The greatest threat to world security today is economic inequality. And the gravest manifestation of economic inequality is poverty, primarily in the developing world. Not long ago, John Kenneth Galbraith gave a speech recalling the Atlantic Charter of 1941, in which Franklin Delano Roosevelt and Winston Churchill expressed their aims for the shape of the post-war world. The charter was shaped by what Roosevelt called the "four freedoms," freedom of speech and of expression, freedom to worship God in your own way, freedom from fear, and freedom from want. As Galbraith argued, the first three freedoms are meaningless without the fourth. Furthermore, where poverty is most intense, whether within our own "rich" societies or in "poor" nations, human rights are weakest and insecurity greatest.

A foreign policy based on common security means that we would no longer think of defence policy as separate from foreign aid policy, or disarmament policy as separate from trade policy.

All these areas are inextricably linked to global peace and security. Common security recognizes that our best defence is to promote mechanisms for the elimination of inequality and injustice. In the post-Cold War era, rethinking the kind of defence we need can permit us to free up dollars to help developing countries.

Canada currently spends $12.8 billion annually on defence. This is four times more than we spend on foreign aid and eleven times more than we spend on the environment. (The entire amount the government says it will spend on the six-year Green Plan is $3 billion.) Clearly something is wrong with our priorities. I believe we should reduce and realign the defence budget, diverting any "peace dividend" into areas that address global disparities. Of course, with the cuts must come programs to help defence industries convert to profitable non-military production and provisions for retraining soldiers returning to civilian life.

One major saving will come with the withdrawal of our troops from Europe, a commitment that now costs about $1 billion annually. For many years, the NDP has opposed Canada's membership in NATO, but until the end of the Cold War our policy was viewed as a political liability. NATO is now itself a liability, an organization that has outlived its purpose, a creature of entrenched military interests that should be disbanded. It might be replaced with a much smaller organization responsible for co-ordinating security between Europe (including Eastern Europe) and North America — and possibly Japan. But surely what is needed now is not another rich nations club, but a global peace and development alliance that would bring the nations of North and South together.

The North American Aerospace Defense Agreement, or NORAD, is another vestige of Cold War thinking. Withdrawing from NORAD won't save a lot of money, but NORAD should be replaced with a new circumpolar security arrangement, involving all the countries that encircle the North Pole. They should work towards the complete demilitarization of the region. (In my view, the nearly $1 billion already spent by the government as Canada's share of a new early warning system to replace the

DEW line has been wasted.) Not only does the recent agreement between Russia and the United States to pursue a modified version of the Strategic Defense Initiative (Star Wars) leave out other polar nations, it is the wrong way to promote security in the region.

I believe that Canada's domestic military role should focus on our ability to maintain sovereignty over our own territory and patrol our territorial waters, not on any offensive capabilities. Our military should also maintain its important role in search and rescue. And we should continue to send troops abroad as peacekeepers, a traditional Canadian specialty that we could practise as part of an even greater commitment to the co-operative resolution of international conflicts.

As traditional military defence becomes less important, the Canadian military could serve other purposes. One possibility is to use the armed forces to monitor the environment and to design and help construct public works in isolated parts of the country. Such activities could make the military a cost-effective training school in various technical and professional fields, thus making a positive contribution to restructuring the Canadian economy.

And surely the time has come to declare Canada a nuclear-weapons-free zone. This would be more than a symbolic move. It would mean banning nuclear weapons and nuclear-powered vessels from Canadian soil and Canadian waters and forbidding the transit of nuclear weapons through Canadian territory. It would also ban anything to do with the research for, production of, or testing of nuclear-weapons systems in Canada. And it would prohibit Canadians from operating support systems for nuclear weapons. Then we could work towards a nuclear-free zone that would include all our northern neighbours. Canada could also lead a new global initiative for a comprehensive nuclear test ban treaty and a chemical weapons ban. Such a policy would be a powerful signal that we believe common security must be based on something other than military might.

Another important disarmament challenge is the demilitarization of space. Since 1958, more than 2,500 military-oriented satellites have been placed into orbit. Meanwhile U.S. Star Wars

research continues. Canada could send a strong signal by pro-
hibiting Canadian companies from further involvement in space-
related military projects. We could also work for a ban on the
testing and deployment of all weapons in space.

But if common security is really based on the security of
others, we will have to do much more than reduce arms and
armaments. We will have to work to correct the economic imbal-
ance between North and South, between the developed and the
underdeveloped world. To this end, much of Canada's peace
dividend could be directed to increasing the level of our foreign
aid. However, simply increasing the quantity isn't enough. Too
much of our aid is tied to our own economic benefit, to what
Canadian businesses want to sell rather than what the developing country needs. I believe we must find better methods of
targetting aid to reach the people who need it. One way is to
channel more aid through Canadian and foreign non-governmental organizations that are close to the grassroots. And govern-
ment-to-government aid should not be given to repressive
regimes that abuse human rights — except for humanitarian aid
such as food and medicine.

Furthermore, we have to stop thinking of aid as a one-way
street and start thinking of ways to use aid to stimulate our trade
with the countries of the developing world. These countries want
to become our trading partners, not just recipients of handouts.
It's a relationship that would benefit both parties, not only
promoting badly needed diversification of Canadian trade, but
giving a lasting boost to developing economies.

Common security can never be achieved by individual nations acting alone, however nobly. The most difficult challenge
for the new world community will be to invent or reinvent the
international organizations and achieve the binding international agreements that will begin to address crushing global
problems — above all, poverty, the environment, and human
rights.

As we work towards common security, however, there will
still be wars and the threat of wars. Economic sanctions, diplomacy, and peacekeeping can prevent or end many conflicts;

others will simply wither away as we begin to suffocate the arms trade; but it's unrealistic to expect an end to war. Military action occasionally may be needed to end local conflicts or control an aggressor, but it should never come from one or a few nations acting as global policemen. Rather it should be undertaken collectively under the auspices of a reformed and strengthened United Nations.

With the collapse of the Soviet Union, the United Nations Security Council has become a virtual rubber stamp for U.S. policy, as the Gulf War showed. A major overhaul of the organization is needed, something many countries are working towards with the U.N.'s fiftieth anniversary in 1995 as the target. Canada should be a forceful advocate for reforms that will lead to a more democratic United Nations that is more representative of its member countries, including increased representation of indigenous peoples. Among the aims of any restructuring should be reducing the power of the Security Council while broadening its membership, perhaps reserving some seats for non-governmental organizations and probably restricting the use of the veto. And women must play a much larger role, both in national delegations and in the U.N. bureaucracy, which remains dominated by a male elite. Only when the United Nations becomes a truly representative world parliament will its full potential be realized.

A more democratic, more activist United Nations will play an even greater role in preventing regional conflicts and in elevating the rule of international law. This may sometimes mean activities that transcend national sovereignty: protecting the Kurds in northern Iraq, making sure relief supplies reach the victims of the Yugoslavian conflict, and overseeing Cambodia's peaceful transition to democracy are some recent examples of this broader mandate. As well, the U.N.'s responsibility for addressing the world's social, economic, and environmental problems must be preserved and strengthened. This is particularly important at a time when some would like to see these responsibilities devolve to organizations, such as the International Monetary Fund and the World Bank, that are controlled by the industrialized nations.

These international financial organizations must meanwhile be held accountable. The World Bank should not be helping to build megaprojects, such as huge hydro-electric dams that ravage third world environments, displace indigenous people, but do little to address underlying problems of poverty and inequity. The IMF must cease the so-called "structural adjustment programs" that punish the weakest and poorest nations. IMF-mandated restructuring has mostly meant greater poverty and injustice.

If we can move towards a world community where co-operation replaces competition as the organizing principle, the rule of international law will become increasingly important. As countries work together for the common good, they will have to relinquish some national sovereignty. This may sound unlikely in a period of renewed nationalism in many parts of the world, but it must happen if global problems are to find global solutions. It is already happening within the European Economic Community.

The road I'm proposing is not a smooth one. Many countries and their elites — including the business elites of multinational corporations — would naturally resist the move towards a community of equals and away from a world order where the powerful few dominate the weak majority. The developed world makes huge profits from the wars that continue to rage, mostly in the developing world. But the alternative is little more than lip-service to international co-operation: no concrete action while the crises deepen. With the end of the Soviet-American stand-off, at a time when assumptions about international relations are being turned upside down, the world has a rare opportunity to try another way. I believe we must seize the moment before it is lost.

•   •   •

One of the few possessions that I really cherish is a carving I brought back from Ghana in 1967. It depicts a common Ghanaian sight — a woman carrying a baby on her back. The carving was made by a local carver from a mahogany tree that stood in Black Star Square in Accra — freedom square. It's a lovely pale yellow-brown and stands six feet tall. I've taken it with me wherever I've moved.

Some people see the sculpture as a symbol of oppression — of woman's burden and the weight of colonialism. But it is the woman's strength that impresses me, her solidness. Her strength is the strength we must build on, the strength to carry her responsibilities with courage and dignity, a strength that quietly proclaims her right to a life of safety, productivity, and justice.

REMAKING THE COUNTRY

A S I WRITE THESE WORDS, in the late summer of 1992, a constitutional accord has just been reached between the federal government, the provinces, the territories, and aboriginal peoples. It remains to be seen how this agreement will be received by the people of Canada and whether it will be ratified. But there does now seem to be real hope that we will soon lay our constitutional agonizings to rest and get on with the important business of running the country and solving its many problems. In this chapter I'd like to reflect on the long process we've been through and draw some lessons for the future.

Lost in the recent discussions has been any clear sense of why we have a constitution in the first place. There are countries, such as Great Britain, that seem to operate quite well without a written constitution. However, I believe that there are two important reasons for having a written set of fundamental principles of government in a federal state. The first is that a constitution lays out publicly, for all the citizens of a nation to see, the framework within which a country operates. It balances competing interests and defines our relationships to one another. The second purpose is to proclaim our values and goals as a nation, to define the kind of country we want Canada to be. In 1982, during the debate that led to the enshrining of women's equality in the Constitution, we were engaged in fundamental self-definition as a nation. During recent months, as I've watched the latest constitutional process unfold, I've often shaken my head at how often we seem to have lost sight of such fundamentals.

A second question worth asking is why amend the Constitution we've already got. The document signed in 1867 and amended once, in 1982, has served our country well. It is a flexible contract that has allowed the relationship between the federal government and the provinces to evolve in positive ways — permitting Ottawa to delegate powers to provincial governments where it seemed sensible to do so. Most countries with written constitutions rarely open them up for major amendment. There were, however, good reasons for the recent series of negotiations.

First of all, when the Constitution was brought home to Canada in 1982, it was amended without Quebec's signature, a fact that only increased that province's sense of exclusion and alienation. Back then, I was not yet an elected politician, but I followed the process with considerable interest. In principle it seemed like a good idea to end the last vestige of Canada's colonial status. But I found it incomprehensible that the deed was done without the agreement of Quebec. What was the dreadful urgency? If the agreement reached in Charlottetown on August 28, 1992, is indeed ratified in every part of Canada, we will have finally finished what was left undone ten years ago.

It was also long past time to end the exclusion of First Nations, whose inherent right to self-government is part of the new constitutional package. As I pointed out earlier, the entrenchment of this right will finally redress a historic grievance and recognize that the First Nations, the first inhabitants of this country, are not conquered peoples and that their political rights have an ancient legitimacy that precedes Confederation. If and when the package becomes law, this will be one of its most significant achievements.

Finally, Canada has changed greatly since 1867. The relationship between the provinces and territories and the federal government has developed over time into a social compact by which the federal government sets national goals and works with the provinces to achieve them. At a time when many of the social standards we have evolved over the decades seem threatened, it makes sense to enshrine them in our Constitution. Furthermore, our current Constitution does not begin to reflect the immense diversity of this country. We are no longer simply a coming together of two founding peoples — or three when we include the First Nations — but of many peoples.

So, yes, despite the seeming endlessness of the process and the pettiness and parochialism often in evidence, I do believe the exercise has been worth it.

At the heart of our recent constitutional discussions has been an argument over the distribution of powers. This argument has often degenerated into a narrow debate that pitted territorial, provincial, and regional interests against those of the federal government. It sometimes seemed to me that the bargaining had turned into a kind of winner-take-all game with the press keeping score: How many powers did the provinces win today? What did the feds give away? Which region is on top? In the heat of the contest the most fundamental questions often got lost: What would work best for Canada as a whole? Which level of government can best solve which problems to everyone's benefit? How do we organize decision making so that all citizens get the best services to meet their regional and individual needs? How much must the federal government be able to do to ensure the kind of country we want?

I believe that the federal government must retain the power to set national goals and to initiate national programs that address inequities at every level. In short, the federal government must always be able to undertake major initiatives on behalf of the country as a whole, and not be reduced to a kind of high court for settling disputes between territories and provinces and regions. Although the recent agreement does give some new powers to the provinces, it does not seem to seriously undermine the federal government's ability to act in the national interest. Of course, only after the legal wording is settled and has been interpreted over time will the whole story be revealed.

I'm not opposed to devolving powers as a matter of principle. Living in the Yukon has given me a clear sense of what happens when too much power is in the hands of a distant government. As someone once said, trying to govern the Yukon from Ottawa was like driving a wagon with the reins three thousand miles long. I believe that a high proportion of decisions are best made at the local and regional levels.

The NDP is traditionally thought of as the party that pushes for greater centralization of power, but this was never true in any simple sense, and certainly isn't true now. We believe that what's important is to come up with a distribution of powers that gives the provinces and the territories the ability to set priorities and solve problems without making the federal government meaningless. The key to this apparent contradiction between a strong enough federal role and high degree of local control is shared responsibility. Under the existing constitutional arrangement, much power is already in the hands of the provinces, not just because of formal provisions but also because of the more recent devolution of administrative control in some jurisdictions. Alberta and Quebec, for example, have long exerted some control over family allowances, and Quebec administers its own pension plan. We tend to forget that Canada is already one of the most decentralized countries in the world and that federalism is a co-operative system. In light of modern realities, it undoubtedly makes sense to hand over some powers to the territories and provinces, but the federal government should continue to exercise its leadership in areas of national interest. It must be able, for example, to define new economic policy directions through the negotiation of trading agreements and the creation of a national industrial strategy. I would even argue that in some areas, for instance education and training, the federal government should have more power, not less. Canada is the only developed country I know of in which the national government does not have the power to develop and implement a national education plan, something we desperately need as our economy is forced to restructure in the face of changing global circumstances. This is not to imply that any such strategy should be undertaken except in conjunction with the provinces and territories.

These observations about the distribution of government powers lead directly back to the other fundamental reason for having a constitution: our national values and goals. The federal government must have enough power to safeguard our collective values and to work towards collective goals. As a nation we seem to have agreed that the federal government will guarantee some minimum standard of social and economic security through such measures as the Canada Pension Plan, a system of universal health care, a system of unemployment insurance, and through transfer payments that address regional economic disparities. Underlying these measures is the still-distant goal of equity — in Canada we work to make sure that no person or region is left out of the general progress of the nation or suffers unduly when times are hard. When I talk to Canadians, no matter what part of the country they live in, these national social programs are seen as basic to the kind of country we have become. They make Canada much more than the sum of its parts.

As a social democrat, I believe that one crucial reason for having a central government is so that there is one part of the system concerned with balancing the competing interests and unequal strengths of the others to achieve a more equitable outcome for all, whether on the level of regional economies or individual social and economic choices. I want to support and promote this country's diversity while working to end social and economic disparities. As poet and constitutional scholar F.R. Scott once said, "No citizen's right can be greater than that of the least protected group."

The new elected Senate will certainly be an improvement on the old appointed body that my party has long favoured abolishing. However, it has the potential to become much more than an expression of regional equality. A truly equal Senate would be structured so that 50 percent of the seats are held by women and would have mechanisms to ensure that minorities are well represented — which might be achieved through some form of proportional representation. As the final details of how the Senate is to be elected are worked out, I will continue to push to make it equal in every sense of the word.

In future constitutional debates — and there will be others in the years ahead — I hope we won't lose sight of the most important question of all: What kind of country do we want Canada to be? More than ten years ago, in his book *Fragile Freedoms, Human Rights and Dissent in Canada*, Thomas Berger wrote: "Why do we believe in Canada? What are the things that are most important in our shared history? Why is Canada worth preserving?" He answered by suggesting that Canada had evolved a unique legal and political order that was the product of the historical encounter between English-speaking, French-speaking and aboriginal peoples in North America. When we look back on 1992, I hope we will judge that that unique order has been advanced, not diminished.

• • •

Back in the fall of 1990, after the death of the Meech Lake Accord, but before the latest constitutional round had got under way, I asked myself and others how the federal NDP could introduce fresh thinking into the forthcoming national debate, ideas that could help shape the agenda. I was looking for a way to move away from the "politics of resentment" that had characterized the Meech Lake process and towards a politics of generosity and openness — towards a discussion of the shared values that unite us rather than an obsession with what divides us. At the same time, I hoped we might make the debate more meaningful for the vast majority of citizens who were frustrated with perpetual talk of amending formulas and the distribution of powers, legal talking points that didn't directly touch daily lives.

One of those I talked to was Allan Blakeney, the former premier of Saskatchewan, who now teaches constitutional law at the University of Saskatchewan. I suggested to Allan that we had to come up with a social democratic component in the constitutional debate, something that would embody the collective rights and aspirations of Canadians. His initial response was, "Well, I don't want to see another Charter in the Constitution." (During the negotiations leading up to the 1982 patriation of the Constitution, Blakeney had opposed entrenching individual rights in the Charter of Rights and Freedoms because this would transfer power from parliament to the courts.) But now that the Charter was a fact of life, I argued, wouldn't it make sense to also have a statement of collective rights — shared rights such as the right to health care.

As we talked, he became intrigued by my suggestion. The Charter protects individual rights, including the rights of corporations, so why not balance this with a charter of collective rights to protect groups of people from the abuse of privately held power or government neglect in the way that the current Charter protects individuals from the abuse of government power? Allan and I both felt the Constitution as amended in 1982, with its strong protection of individual rights in the Charter, needed a strong statement of collective rights.

The more we talked, the more excited we became about a charter of collective or shared rights — a social charter. It seemed an idea whose time had come, a way of spelling out those common ideas and values that should be an essential part of a constitution. We thought it might take as its starting point the guarantee of basic social benefits, such as universal access to medical care, that are fundamental to Canadian society. Before we parted that day, Allan offered to draft a sample social charter for discussion. He was good to his word.

Blakeney based his draft charter on the United Nations Universal Declaration of Human Rights, to which Canada is a signatory. Like the U.N. declaration, it included the following elements: the right to social security; the right to equal pay for equal work and the right to form or join trade unions; the right to an adequate standard of living; the right to an adequate education; the right to freely participate in the cultural life of the community.

The idea soon gathered steam, and the notion of spelling out collective rights in the Constitution became part of the NDP's constitutional discussion paper released in March of 1991. That paper cited as a model the European Social Charter adopted by the members of the EEC in 1989. This charter guarantees social rights, such as equitable wages, social security for workers, freedom of association and collective bargaining, universal access to public job placement services, and the integration of people with disabilities.

This discussion paper eventually evolved into a specific proposal to amend section 36 (1) of the Constitution Act, the section that deals with equalization and regional development, to include a statement that Canadian governments have the responsibility to ensure the following: full employment and fair working conditions; income security for all Canadians; health care that is publicly administered, comprehensive, portable, and accessible; adequate food, clothing, and shelter; security and dignity of the person; a quality education; a clean environment and a sustainable economy. Rather than have this social charter adjudicated by the courts, we proposed that a commission of eminent Canadians be appointed to oversee its application and to exert moral and political pressure on governments to live up to its provisions. Although this body could be independent of parliament, I favour one composed of members of a reformed Senate, in the event such a Senate comes into being. I based my choice on the assumption that a reformed Senate will not only more fairly represent the regions but be more truly representative of the Canadian population.

The social charter concept was given a significant boost later in 1991 when Ontario premier Bob Rae released a discussion paper on the subject. As premier of the largest province, Rae would be a major player in the constitutional negotiations to come; his championing of the social charter gave it extra weight. This important idea, now called the social covenant, found its way to the bargaining table and was included in the August 28 package, which includes a guarantee of the right to health care, to social services, and to education, as well as workers' rights and the protection of the environment. Regardless of the final outcome of the negotiations, I think it's fair to say that New Democrats did significantly reshape the constitutional agenda in this respect — thus bringing a discussion of shared values and goals into the debate.

We also played a role in opening up the negotiating process. During the Meech Lake debates, I was one of many people who decried the secretive and exclusive process and called for a more open and accountable form of constitution making. From the day Meech died, I argued for the convening of a constituent assembly that would come up with a package of recommendations for constitutional reform. I envisaged this as a broad gathering that would include elected politicians from the federal, provincial, and municipal levels and representatives nominated by various national organizations. The assembly would be designed to include groups and communities not usually represented in constitutional discussions. In short, it would be reflective of the regional, ethnic, and cultural diversity of Canada.

Not surprisingly, this idea was dismissed as "impractical" by those with a vested interest in doing things the old way — federal government politicians, as well as most Liberals and the constitutional experts. They claimed it was too complex and would never work, that it would be impossible to come up with a satisfactory formula for electing or appointing the members. In fact, of course, they were afraid to take the risk of giving even advisory powers to a group they wouldn't be able to control.

I thought the federal Liberals and Tories were tremendously arrogant in the way they reacted to the constituent assembly proposal. After all, they were the ones who had bungled the last two attempts at national self-definition, and produced what? — a constitution patriated without Quebec and the Meech Lake fiasco. It was one of the clearest examples I've encountered since becoming leader of why the system has got to change. These men were still operating back in the political culture of 1972, not the political reality of 1992. Despite the evidence that their approach had failed miserably, their attitudes hadn't changed. Despite their protests, there is nothing in the current Constitution's amending formula that necessitates secret negotiations between premiers and the prime minister. It just happens to be the way it has always been done.

However, the press and the public and some provincial politicians reacted warmly to the idea. Columnists and editorialists and many citizens' groups endorsed the concept of a constituent assembly. There was a widespread sentiment that more people had to participate in the constitutional process. The government bowed to this reality when it announced the Citizens' Forum on Canada's future, the Spicer Commission. Although the commission was ill-conceived and its final report virtually ignored, many Canadians put thought and energy into their submissions. They demonstrated a genuine yearning for a more open, democratic process.

This yearning was partially satisfied early in 1992, when the government convened a series of six constitutional conferences in major cities across Canada, each on a different constitutional theme. Hastily organized and imperfect as these meetings were, they belatedly recognized the need for a broadly based public forum to debate constitutional change. The conferences would not have occurred at all without some bargaining between our party and constitutional affairs minister Joe Clark. Late in the fall of 1991, it became clear that the government's latest attempt at consultation by parliamentary committee, the Special Joint Committee on a Renewed Canada, chaired by MP Dorothy Dobbie and Senator Claude Castonguay, had degenerated into a disorganized shambles. After a particularly disastrous hearing in Manitoba in late November, we withdrew our members from the committee and were soon followed by the Liberals. Faced with the collapse of the government's process, Clark asked us what it would take for us to rejoin the committee. Simple, we told him: we want what we've been arguing for all along — a constituent assembly. He wasn't willing to go that far; we compromised on the idea of the constitutional conferences.

Once Clark agreed to the conferences, we fought to make them as representative as possible. (They started out with a fairly broad mix of politicians and individual citizens and representatives of various interest groups and minority groups.) At the first conference, in Halifax, women made up only about 30 percent of the delegates. But as the conferences progressed, we put constant pressure on the Tories to achieve gender parity — to make sure that the voices of women were heard. We insisted that the conferences be televised, that their proceedings be as open as possible.

Although these conferences fell far short of the idea of a constituent assembly, they proved two important things. They showed that when Canadians from different parts of the country and different cultural and linguistic backgrounds got together, they were able to move beyond entrenched positions to reach common understandings. They also showed that it's sometimes easier for non-politicians to rise above regional interests and to see the whole picture. At one conference, people were willing to talk seriously about asymmetrical federalism — the idea that one province, Quebec, should perhaps have some powers that other provinces don't. (This idea didn't last long once the premiers took over the process.) At another, a clear consensus was reached on the desirability of a social charter, placing this item firmly on the constitutional agenda. In sum, I believe the constitutional conferences proved that a constituent assembly could have worked — and worked much better than the traditional process.

Nonetheless, in the late spring of 1992, as the next deadline approached, the premiers met once more behind closed doors, resorting to the old way of reforming the Constitution. However, the process had been somewhat more open. Instead of being handed a done deal, which we could argue about but not change, there had been nine months of public hearings and six constitutional conferences leading up to the final series of high-level negotiations. And for the first time, women sat at the constitutional table. Rosemary Kuptana, Nellie Cournoyea, and Mary Simon of the Inuit Tapirisat were among the aboriginal representatives. When the agreement on self-government was reached, they emerged to announce that they had become the first "mothers of Confederation," a wonderful moment in Canadian history.

But imagine how different the process could have been. Acting strictly on the consensus reached at a broad-based constituent assembly, an all-party committee of the House of Commons could have drafted a constitutional resolution to be debated in the House and subjected to a free vote. The final resolution could have been submitted to the provinces and territories for ratification in their legislatures. Such an open process would have a much better chance of yielding a result that is good for all of Canada.

In the most recent constitutional round, we have heard much talk of redistributing power and very little about what kind of country we want to live in. As I've argued from the beginning, this means we've been doing our constitution making upside down, trying to find a barely acceptable "bottom line" instead of articulating a shared positive vision. The Meech Lake Accord amounted to a list of concessions English Canada felt it could make to Quebec to keep it in Canada. And underlying the current constitutional round has been the idea that English Canada has to come up with a minimum package that Quebec can accept — perhaps inevitably so, given the psychic wounds Meech inflicted in Quebec. But lost in the discussion has been the possibility of a more positive formulation: the building blocks for a country we're sure Quebec will want to remain part of, the country we all want to be part of.

In the spring of 1991, as this latest round of constitution making was getting under way, I travelled around the country giving speeches about my party's recently released discussion paper on the Constitution. In my remarks, I often referred to an Alberta woman I once met who used a lovely metaphor to describe Canada. To her the country was a multi-coloured quilt made up of different patches stitched together by a strong and almost invisible thread. As in all quilts, she said, there is a distinctiveness, a beauty in each individual patch. But the true beauty and purpose of the quilt lies in its wholeness, in the fact that each piece contributes to something greater and more beautiful. In Canada in recent years we seem to have lost track of the whole. The thread has slipped out of our fingers and we have been left fumbling for the means to remake our country. What we've lost is the binding thread of commonalities and the healing thread of respect for each other's uniqueness. By the time you read these words, perhaps we will know if these threads have again been found.

C H A P T E R   E I G H T

A F U T U R E   T H A T   W O R K S

AFTER WATCHING QUESTION PERIOD from the House of Commons Visitors' Gallery, a seventeen-year-old constituent of mine told me he now understands how this daily parliamentary ritual got its name. He said, "It must be called Question Period because there sure are no answers." Indeed, there is a strong sense among the people I talk to around the country that we politicians have lost our way and that no person or party has the solutions to our current problems. Although I have never claimed to have all the answers — and distrust any politician who does — I do believe that social democrats have a wide-ranging and pragmatic alternative to the policies that have got us into our current economic mess.

Some will consider it brash or foolhardy for a federal NDP leader to tackle economics in a book of this sort. Traditionally, our party scores poorly in public opinion polls when it comes to managing the economy. During election campaigns, our candidates tend to emphasize our strengths in social policy and the environment and downplay our economic thinking. We have sometimes been reluctant to face up to serious economic problems such as the federal debt or the need for economic restructuring in the face of fundamental shifts in the global economy.

In fact, however, social democrats have a strong record as economic managers, one we should be boasting about. CCF and NDP governments have successfully managed provincial and territorial economies going back to Tommy Douglas's first administration in Saskatchewan in the 1940s. And some of the most successful national economies today — for example, those in Sweden and Germany — have been led for long stretches of the post-war period by social democratic governments. But we have failed to get out the message that there is a coherent social democratic alternative to the painful economic policies currently in vogue in Canada and many other western nations.

Not long ago I sat in the waiting room of the intensive care unit of a hospital in Regina, Saskatchewan, where my mother had just had an operation for lung cancer. There was anxiety in the faces of all the people in the room, each of us wondering if a loved one would make it through to the next day. I looked into the lively eyes of a prairie farmer, his big hands rough and gnarled from years of physical work, and listened as he spoke of his love for his wife who lay nearby on the edge between life and death. They had been planning a cruise to celebrate their fiftieth anniversary. Now he wondered if there would be an anniversary to celebrate.

But even in the middle of this anguish and worry, I could not help thinking about the kind of conversations we would have been having in an American hospital waiting room. Would we have been talking about our loved ones or wondering how we were going to pay the bills? These reflections led me to think back to my family's huge celebration the year I turned ten. That was when my mother and father finally paid off the medical bills accumulated just after my birth because of my mother's mastectomy and her lengthy stay in hospital. My father had a relatively good job, but we owned neither house nor car because the monthly medical payment took such a chunk of his earnings.

My mother's lung surgery was successful and the farmer's wife recovered — the cruise they'd planned would take place after all. How different these stories might have been without our system of universal health care. As far as I'm concerned, high-quality health care is not a privilege, it is a right of citizenship in a country like ours. This is to defend not every aspect of the present system, but rather the principle of universal health care itself. That system, not just in its details but at its core, is under threat in Canada, as is the safety net of social programs that makes our nation one of the most progressive on earth. This troubling development is a symptom of something deeper and even more serious, the gradual abandonment by Canadian governments of their responsibility to act in the public interest.

In this chapter, I'm going to depart from the autobiographical mode of this book to talk about my ideas for revitalizing the Canadian economy. What follows is a roadmap, not a detailed plan or election platform. I've begun with a personal anecdote about Canadian health care because I believe governments must begin to treat social programs and economic policies as part of an integrated strategy for managing the economy. Economic productivity and social justice are inextricably linked. Prosperity that comes at the expense of the social safety net is not true prosperity — and it will not last. As I see it, the challenge is to devise an economic future that not only works for the few but produces benefits for everyone. Can we achieve prosperity and fairness at the same time? I'm convinced the answer is yes.

• • •

There seems to be general agreement across the political spectrum that Canada must restructure its economy to become more successful in the face of globalization. Stripped of its mystique, the word "globalization" describes a fairly straightforward phenomenon. In the words of economist and political scientist James Laxer, "all it means is that, because of the technological revolution and the intermingling of national markets, we now live in

the era of the global marketplace. This transformation has re-
sulted in a severe limiting of national sovereignty and the demise
of the old idea that a nation should try to be economically
self-sufficient. Now the goal is to specialize in something that
will provide access to wider markets." We can no longer rely on
selling our traditional goods and services to our traditional
customers: these markets are either becoming much more competitive or are disappearing. And we can no longer rely on trade
barriers that insulate certain industries from the world at large.

Interestingly, there also seems to be agreement among economists, both on the left and right, about the kind of economy we
must build if we're going to meet the challenge of globalization
and preserve our standard of living. The disagreement is over
how to get there. It's clear we can't continue to depend on cheap
natural resources as the basis for our prosperity. These resources
are no longer inexpensive relative to those of other countries.
And our traditional manufacturing base is being eroded by a
world-wide phenomenon that has seen many industries migrate
to the newly industrializing nations of the developing world
where labour costs are much lower. In our case, this trend has
been exaggerated by the Canada-U.S. Free Trade Agreement.
The consensus seems to be that Canada, and other developed
nations, must move towards what economists call a high-value-
added, high-skill economy, one that exports finished products,
not jobs. (Democratic presidential candidate Bill Clinton, in his
acceptance speech at the recent Democratic Convention in New
York, used similar language to describe the kind of economic
transformation he hopes to bring about in the United States.)

"High-value-added" is one of those jargon phrases economists love, but it boils down to common sense. Value is added
to a product at each stage of processing. In other words, the more
"processed" a commodity is, the greater its value. The more
value that has been added, the higher the price it can command
in the marketplace. To move towards a high-value-added economy means to move away from types of economic activity that
involve little processing — to stop simply extracting a resource
and shipping it somewhere else for processing, for example —

to types of economic activity that produce sophisticated finished products. A chair has far more value added than raw lumber; a computer more value added than a computer chip. This transition is already taking place. More Canadians now work in the electronics industry than in the pulp and paper industry, and the communications and telecommunications sector is larger than our petroleum and mining sectors combined.

The "high-skill" part follows logically from "high-value-added." The more processed a product, the higher the degree of technological advancement needed to produce it. The more advanced the technology, the higher the skills required of workers. Thus a high-value-added, high-skill economy benefits both business and labour. Business is producing products that command a high price in the global economy. Workers with higher skills command higher wages. Society benefits because higher wages and more profitable companies help maintain the broad tax base that pays for our social programs. (There's an added advantage of a well-paid workforce: it creates an incentive for business to come up with even more efficient and less expensive processes that keep us at the forefront of technological innovation. I don't buy the argument that increased efficiency ultimately means fewer jobs; in a vibrant, high-skill economy many more jobs will be created than will be lost.)

Given this general goal, the question becomes where the Canadian economy should specialize. Clearly we can't compete successfully in every sector; the key is to concentrate in those sectors where we can gain a competitive advantage. What are the areas towards which Canada can best direct its economic energies? Professors Joseph d'Cruz and Alan Rugman of the University of Toronto in a recent study on international competitiveness for Kodak Canada identified ten key "strategic clusters," groups of firms within a small geographic region "all of which participate in the same industry or a closely related industry." For example, they single out a western Canada forest products cluster and a southwest Ontario automotive cluster. Their idea is to build on these areas where Canada is already strong by encouraging co-operation among suppliers, customers, and competitors within each cluster. This is exactly how Japanese business has operated for years and in part accounts for its success in the international marketplace.

Canadian businesses must seek focused markets, specialized niches in which their products can compete in both quality and price with any in the world. Many of these will grow out of existing strengths in the sectors that built our country, such as transportation, communications, energy, engineering, and construction services. Some Canadian companies have already become global players — for instance, Northern Telecom in communications and Bombardier in transportation. Others will need to identify a market niche and move quickly to occupy it. Bombardier now does 54 percent of its business in Europe, where it is the leading manufacturer of two-stroke engines and is providing double-deck shuttle-train cars for the soon-to-be-completed "Chunnel" linking France and Britain. It has recently developed the Canadair Regional Jet, capacity fifty passengers, the only entry in this market niche. Smaller Canadian companies are also seizing global opportunities — for instance, Ottawa's fast-growing Corel Corporation, which specializes in computer software for designers and illustrators. And Adco Enterprises of Alberta has built on experience in the Canadian oil industry to win contracts in the Middle East, Algeria, and Mexico. Its main product is a "relocatable shelter unit," a mobile office trailer suitable for oil drilling and other nomadic enterprises.

One of the most promising areas for Canadian firms is in new environmental technologies. There is a growing market for technologies that either help clean up existing environmental damage or reduce the environmental impact of products and processes. For example, hazardous waste clean-up costs in the United States are expected to go as high as $200 billion. By the year 2000, the U.S. government will have to spend $60 billion to live up to the terms of the Clean Water Act. It is estimated that by the end of this decade, the Clean Air Act will require U.S. industry to spend $25 billion annually. Western Europe, with some of the strictest environmental standards anywhere, represents another huge potential market. And there are major

opportunities in the Asia-Pacific region where South Korea and
Taiwan have already announced major environmental spending
programs. This sector of the Canadian economy now has sales
estimated at $6 billion, and the potential for growth is enormous.
The countries that lead the way in environmental technologies
are Germany and Japan; both have an enviable record of anticipating world economic trends.

Canada is also well placed to take advantage of emerging
markets for socially useful technologies. Because of the demo-
graphic trend towards an older population throughout the developed world, there will be increasing demand for health-care
products and services. Canadian expertise developed as we move
to a more decentralized, user-based system could help reduce
costs in the U.S., which now spends $600 billion annually on a
system in which more than 32 million American citizens aren't
even included.

These are a few examples of areas where Canada could
specialize. Experts are only beginning to identify the most promising. But we have a limited time before we are left behind by
countries that move more quickly to seize the opportunities of
globalization.

•   •   •

Although there is broad agreement about the challenge globalization represents and the ultimate goal of restructuring the
economy, there is serious disagreement about the process for
reaching the goal. The neo-conservative approach, epitomized
by the policies put into place by the Tory government over the
last few years, might be characterized as economic restructuring
by default — widespread plant closings and horrendous job
losses without the offsetting creation of new businesses or new
jobs, and without the government's promised adjustment programs to help workers through the transition. We are told this is
short-term pain while our economy goes through the necessary
changes that will ensure long-range prosperity. The companies

that survive this dog-eat-dog process will in theory be "leaner and meaner" and will thrive.

These government measures have included a disastrous free trade deal with the United States, unnecessarily high interest rates — leading to an artificially high dollar and high rates of unemployment — and the GST. On the evidence so far, these policies have actually hurt our ability to compete. Their architects have blindly followed the neo-conservative ideology that has wreaked social havoc in Britain and the United States. This ideology is a narrow, selfish one that favours the wealthy and makes multinational corporations even more powerful while undermining Canada's ability to determine its own social and economic priorities.

Even before the U.S.-Canada Free Trade Agreement (FTA), Canada had lost much of its economic self-determination. Our economy has long had one of the highest rates of foreign ownership in the world, levels that would be considered intolerable in other developed countries. In 1987 — the last year for which government figures are available — 32 percent of all Canadian non-financial industries was in foreign hands. In comparison, the figure for the United States was 5 percent, Japan 3 percent, and the European Community 9 percent. Of the top five hundred corporations in Canada, 49 percent were under foreign control. This degree of foreign ownership has meant a huge loss of government revenue in the form of profits that leave Canada untaxed. In the decade ending in 1990, $50 billion was sent out of the country in the form of dividends to foreign owners.

The FTA could well lead to an even higher degree of foreign ownership, unless the federal government steps in. The agreement has already cost hundreds of thousands of jobs, especially in manufacturing, as many branch plants closed up shop when parent companies realized they could serve the Canadian market from south of the border. At the same time, the trade deal removed barriers that protected our natural resources, such as oil and gas — a primary goal of American negotiators — ending our ability to have priority use of these resources. Probably worst of all, it has served to further tie our economy with that of the

United States at a time when many believe our neighbour to the south has embarked on a long economic decline while other parts of the world, notably Europe and Japan, are becoming the new economic powerhouses.

As the economy staggered, the government raised no protest against the Bank of Canada's high-interest-rate policy, followed slavishly until 1992 in order to "fight inflation." Not only has this policy contributed to high unemployment by discouraging domestic investment and dampening consumer demand, it has kept the value of the dollar high relative to other currencies, thus making our goods less competitive, not more.

The neo-conservatives argue that government is "too big" and living beyond its means. They claim the main reason the deficit is now more than $30 billion annually is that we are spending too much on government programs, especially social programs. In fact, as Statistics Canada revealed in a report released in 1991, most of the increase in the debt between 1975 and 1990 was caused by tax breaks for big business and very wealthy individuals, unnecessarily high interest rates, interest payments on the debt, and the transfer of tax points to the provinces. During that same period, spending on social programs as a percentage of the Gross National Product had not increased at all. As Duncan Cameron pointed out in the September 1990 issue of the *Canadian Forum* — before the worst of the recession hit — "the Tories have been taking in more money in taxes than they have been spending on government programs for the last three fiscal years. Increases in the deficit are due strictly to interest payments on the national debt, i.e., higher than necessary interest rates paid on accumulated past deficits." In other words, had the government pursued a lower interest-rate policy, which would also have helped ease the impact of the recession, the deficit would now be much lower and we would have more room to initiate the new programs that are needed.

The size of the debt is largely the Tories' own fault, and it is a serious problem. When you are trying to manage a huge debt, your options in other areas are extremely limited because interest payments become such a dominant item in the federal budget. However, although the debt now stands at more than $400 billion, alternative policies could steadily lower our annual deficit without requiring cuts in social programs at a time when people need them most. For one thing, a fairer tax structure, along the lines discussed in an earlier chapter, would increase government revenue without hurting those who can least afford to pay. And lower interest rates would further reduce our debt payments. Although rates have dropped lower than they have been in many years, they are still high compared to those in the United States. More important, the real interest rate — the difference between the rate of inflation and the prime rate — remains high. As well, lower interest rates would make our dollar cheaper in relation to other currencies and our goods more competitive, thus speeding Canada's recovery from the recession through increased sales abroad.

The GST was supposed to help competitiveness by stimulating domestic savings and investment, thereby reducing our reliance on foreign capital. Instead it has made Canadian retailers less competitive by adding to their costs, and it has sent many Canadian shoppers south of the border to take advantage of lower GST-free U.S. prices. In sum, the tough medicine we've been asked to swallow to make our economy more competitive has actually made it less so.

• • •

Neo-conservatives believe that restructuring, like all economic decision making, is best left up to the market, that the government shouldn't get involved. The problem with this approach is that it ignores the people hurt in the transition. The current recession, in part a creation of the Tory government's mismanagement, has been devastating. Numbers can't describe human suffering, but the latest statistics are deeply disturbing. As of this writing, there were close to 1.6 million unemployed people in Canada, a figure that didn't include the 665,000 people working part-time who wanted full-time jobs or the discouraged workers who have simply given up looking — a number we estimate may be as high as 300,000. Well over 2.5 million Canadians were on welfare. During 1991, two million people used a food bank at least once, 700,000 of them children. About four million people were living below the poverty line, over a million of them children. And there were tens of thousands of homeless.

Like the human cost, the economic wastefulness is obscene. Communities and whole regions are being destabilized. People who could be contributing to our economic life are having to live off cash-strapped governments. There has got to be a better way for us to make the transition to a more successful economy.

The key to this better way is economic democracy, which means redistributing wealth more fairly and dispersing the power of economic decision making more widely. Fair taxation and adequate social programs that prevent anyone from falling into poverty are basic to economic democracy. So is our party's belief in giving workers more control over their jobs and bringing more democracy into the workplace.

There are a number of ways to encourage both public and private enterprises to become more democratic. Enhancing worker power and worker ownership is one — and I don't mean just in cases where a bankrupt company is saved by its employees, as in the recent case of Algoma Steel in Sault Ste. Marie, Ontario. Greater worker ownership could be encouraged by providing tax incentives for workers to buy into viable firms and for owners to sell to workers. Another possibility is to set aside employee seats on the boards of directors of Crown corporations and government agencies and to assure employee representation on the senior decision-making bodies of federal departments. Joint labour-management committees to plan and implement changes in workplace organization at the plant level and the sectoral level are already being experimented with in some industries. These committees should also play an important part in designing education and retraining programs that will increase worker skills and help them adjust to change. Such moves ultimately benefit everyone. When workers own a stake in their companies and/or exercise significant decision-making power, then everyone gains.

A more democratic workplace means replacing hierarchical structures where authority comes from the top down with structures where workers have greater power. One example is the concept of "group work," which is practised in German manufacturing industries. There a group of workers is assigned shared responsibility for a group of tasks (an arrangement not to be confused with the "team concept" sometimes tried in North America, which is an effort to pit one group of employees against another to increase productivity). Participation in the work group is voluntary. At weekly meetings, the group makes decisions about everything from personnel requirements to work methods and product quality. Many decisions previously made by management are made by the workers themselves, causing layers of bureaucracy to become unnecessary.

Strong unions, in themselves highly democratic organizations, are the key to successful workplace reorganization and to co-operation at every level. There's a pervasive myth in Canada that labour unions have outlived their usefulness and now do more harm than good, that they demand unduly high wages, create waste, and foster inefficiency. The facts suggest otherwise: some of the most successful economies of the world are also among the most highly unionized. In Germany, 90 percent of the workforce belongs to trade unions; in Canada, the figure is around 35 percent; in the United States, the number is closer to 17 percent. A recent study by Harvard professors Richard Freeman and James Medoff concluded that, in most sectors, unionized firms were more productive than firms operating without unions. This is because unionized firms enjoyed lower turnover rates, generally co-operative relations between plant workers and management, and better managerial performance because unions keep managers on their toes. On a broader scale, when unions are strong enough to enter into partnership with business, the adversarial aspect of industrial relations tends to ease, as it has in Sweden and other highly unionized jurisdictions.

It's instructive that it is in highly unionized sectors of the

North American economy that co-operation between labour and management is highest. In Canada, the Steelworkers joined with steel companies to form the Canadian Steel Trade and Employment Congress in 1985, a sectoral initiative that has played a crucial role in designing and implementing labour-adjustment programs in an industry going through major changes. Similar organizations have been set up in the electronics and wood products industries. And the Communications and Electrical Workers of Canada is one of the pioneers in working with management to achieve more democratic forms of workplace organization.

Increased co-operation between labour and management does not mean the adversarial nature of industrial relations will ever completely disappear, nor should it. Unions must continue to operate autonomously even as workers take a more active role in determining their own economic future through co-operation with business. To quote a recent publication from the Communications and Electrical Workers of Canada, "We are not the same team. But we have to recognize, in many ways, we share the same house."

Above all, economic democracy means making the goal of full employment the cornerstone of economic policy. It concerns me greatly that in Canada, we seem to have reached a point where high levels of unemployment are accepted as normal, an inevitable side-effect of tight monetary policies to control inflation. Such high levels aren't accepted as inevitable in Scandinavian countries. Although no country ever achieves zero unemployment, Sweden has historically had low unemployment, in the area of 1 or 2 percent. One key to this success has been labour-market adjustment — programs to train and retrain workers as the economy changes. Sweden spends three times as much on training as on unemployment insurance. In Canada, the ratio is more than reversed: we spend less than a third of the cost of unemployment insurance on retraining and employment subsidies.

Our system of helping workers adjust to changes in the economy is characterized by underinvestment but also by a lack of coherent direction. Although the recent closure of the New-foundland cod fishery wasn't the result of globalization, it demonstrates how badly we handle labour-market adjustment. The government had known the fishery was in trouble for ten years, yet when the end finally came, no plan was in place to help these workers find a different way of making a living. To avoid this sort of tragedy in future, we must not only increase our investment in education and retraining, but tie this expen-diture into our overall economic restructuring strategy. We need money and a clear plan for educating the workforce of tomorrow. Otherwise the dollars will be wasted.

Finally, economic democracy entails protecting the very net-work of social programs that the Tories and their allies in business argue is too costly to maintain as the economy adjusts to globalization. I would argue the opposite — not just because these programs are integral to Canadian life, an important ex-pression of our shared values, but because they are a vital part of what makes Canada a good place to do business. Big compa-nies in the United States are forced because of the absence of a federal health system to shoulder a large share of health care costs themselves in the form of insurance premiums for their employees. A recent study by Chrysler Corporation found that an automaker's cost of health care benefits works out to $700 for each vehicle it produces in the United States. In Germany, the figure is $337, in Japan, $246; and in Canada, $223. Given such statistics, corporations should be leading the fight to preserve our medicare system.

This is not the place to deal in detail with the kinds of reforms needed to revitalize our national system of health care, but the basic direction seems clear. For too long, most of our resources have been concentrated in large institutions. While we will continue to need well-staffed and well-equipped hospitals, we should be providing more care in smaller co-operatively run community clinics along the lines of those pioneered in Sas-katchewan in the early 1970s, long established in Quebec, and now being experimented with in several other provinces. I be-lieve we need to shift our underlying health-care philosophy from emphasizing the treatment of illness to its prevention — a wellness model similar to that now being developed in Saskatchewan. The result will be a more efficient health-care service that keeps costs down.

In sum, I can't accept any plan for restructuring the economy that doesn't maintain our strong social programs and improve on our existing system of helping workers adjust to change.

• • •

The federal government has an important role to play in helping design the transition to a high-value-added, high-skill economy. Above all, that role will involve developing an industrial strategy in a co-operative partnership with business and labour — a strategic alliance for economic change. Such partnerships have already proved their worth in Sweden, Germany, and Japan. Although there is no strong history of this sort of social contract in Canada, we must find a way to forge one.

The key to successfully restructuring the economy will be getting labour and business together as equals to help plan the transition in each industry or sector and ultimately at the national level. Each economic sector should develop a tripartite body, composed equally of representatives from business, government, and labour, to plan for the structural changes that will be needed. At the national level, a similar coalition would develop an overall restructuring strategy. This coalition would have to adhere to certain basic values such as advancing social equity and achieving sustainable economic development. It would also identify the areas where Canada needs to focus its research and development dollars. The coalition should be formalized in an Economic Restructuring Commission whose mission would be to reach a consensus and plan our transition to a more competitive economy.

In addition to helping forge a social contract between business and labour, the government must adopt other policies to encourage high-value-added economic activity. It's one thing to

agree that there is a market niche for Canadian-made environmental technology, but such technology will emerge more
quickly if government enforces rigorous environmental standards, which will act as incentives for businesses to develop
more efficient and cleaner products and processes. Beyond that,
the government should help Canadian businesses develop export
markets for environmental technologies by establishing an Environmental Technology Agency. This body would carry out
market research and disseminate information to Canadian companies. It could also actively match sellers of products and
services with prospective buyers in the public and private sectors. And it could finance, through grants and loans, research
and development, marketing, and partnership-building activities. It could even help firms obtain financing for specific projects.

Another, and even more far-reaching policy idea is the creation of a Canadian Bank for Renewal and Development, fi-
nanced by private and public pension funds as well as
government contributions, that would help facilitate the restructuring process. A national investment bank is needed, not only
because of the high concentration of foreign ownership of the
Canadian economy, but because private-sector institutions tend
to make investment decisions on the basis of short-term profit
objectives, rather than what is best for Canada in the long run.
Such a bank would invest, either alone or in partnership with
provincial investment funds, wherever the potential is greatest
for long-term value-added economic activity — especially in
flagship firms in the various strategic clusters. It would also play
an important role in fostering regional economic development by
making capital available to local organizations involved in community economic development, a subject I will return to later in
this chapter. Part of its mandate would be to create and preserve
high-skill jobs while encouraging environmentally sound economic activity and fostering increased democratic control over
strategic sectors of the Canadian economy.

The federal government should also invest in infrastructure — for example, waste treatment plants in the many cities

and towns still lacking them. Here's an example of a program that would meet more than one goal — and an example of the kind of integrated economic thinking I believe in. Treatment plants would address a chronic environmental problem — urban waste disposal — thus making a community a more attractive place to invest, while promoting local development and creating new jobs. On a broader scale, improvements in our transportation and communications networks will help make economic restructuring possible. As in so many areas, Japan leads the way in infrastructure investment, having committed itself to an accelerated public works program that will see $47 billion (U.S.) spent in the second half of 1992. (Recent reports suggest this amount will likely be almost doubled.)

Then there is the matter of trade. Clearly, with the globalization of the world economy, protectionism is not the way of the future. But because of the NDP's opposition to the Canada-U.S. Free Trade Agreement, some people mistakenly believe we are against trade liberalization. In fact, we have long supported liberalized trade through multilateral agreements such as the General Agreement on Tariffs and Trade (GATT), which was founded in 1947 on the principle that only through multinational arrangements, not bilateral deals, could lasting and equitable trade liberalization take place. Although the GATT is far from perfect, it has overseen the gradual lessening of trade barriers worldwide.

The New Democratic Party proposes to broaden Canada's trade horizons, not narrow them — as happened with the FTA. Rather than ratifying the recent North American Free Trade Agreement (NAFTA), we should move to negotiate a Western Hemisphere Trade Agreement as recently suggested by B.C. premier Mike Harcourt. The broader our trade, the more stable it is; then our fortunes no longer rise or fall with the fortunes of one or two trading partners. But any agreements we do sign must include a social and environmental charter that ensures all parties live up to certain minimum standards in areas such as working conditions, health care, and environmental regulations. This is what the members of the European Community have done in signing the European Social Charter. (Like the FTA, NAFTA fails to set such minimum standards.)

The FTA and NAFTA have done more to restructure our country in a negative way than any other policy of the current government. The FTA contains an abrogation clause: either country can terminate the agreement on six months' notice. We must exercise this clause and replace the FTA with key sectoral agreements and a broadening of our trade base beyond the U.S. and Mexico. Otherwise, it will be virtually impossible to reclaim Canada.

Finally, although government must play an active role in reshaping our economy, it must itself be restructured and renewed. It needs to work faster and more cheaply and to provide better service to its customers — Canadian citizens and businesses. Reforms to democratize the public service — giving more authority to front-line workers and eliminating unnecessary layers of management hierarchy — will help make this possible. I envisage a government that is a catalyst of change, that steers more than it rows, not bigger government but more effective government. One of its primary jobs should be to provide the policy framework and the support so that other players — business, labour, local communities — can get things done themselves.

• • •

Amid the talk about what Canada must do to improve its global competitiveness, little attention is paid to the health of regional and local economies. Yet these form the bedrock of any successful national economy. Only three of ten businesses in Canada make products for export. The vast majority of economic activity involves Canadians doing business with other Canadians.

Canada has a poor record of regional economic development. Despite a long history of massive transfer payments from the wealthier parts of the country, the poor regions tend to remain economically underdeveloped. Part of the reason is that local communities are not sufficiently involved in planning their own economic development and diversification.

I would like to see federal policy place more emphasis on community-based economic development, development that is planned and implemented locally. Only then will we see economic development that grows out of local conditions and reflects local needs. At the heart of this shift would be special support and encouragement for local development organizations — community development corporations, community-owned co-operatives, municipal councils, or local financial institutions, such as credit unions, caisses populaires, or community loan funds. About 2,000 such organizations in Canada today are already involved in community economic development.

In my view, co-operatives combine the best features of public and private enterprise. They operate as independent businesses, but every member has a vote in electing the board of directors, which appoints the management — so democratic control is assured. Forty percent of all Canadians are members of a co-operative, a credit union, or a caisse populaire, and these businesses manage assets of well over $5 billion. In some parts of Canada — notably Saskatchewan and Quebec — the co-operative sector is a primary force in regional economic development and job creation. It seems to me that strengthening this sector is the key to a successful community economic development strategy. As part of this strategy, we could not only encourage existing co-operatives but establish a network of development co-operatives whose mandate is to plan and promote community economic development. (As a positive side-effect, strengthening the co-operative sector could contribute to increased economic democracy.)

The kind of economic development I'm talking about is intended to stimulate, not stifle, individual and small-group initiative. While the main instruments of development — community development corporations, credit unions, and community loan funds — would be community owned, they would encourage private businesses as well as joint ventures that blend public and private ownership. Private entrepreneurship combined with community entrepreneurship is what will revitalize stagnant localities, as demonstrated by some of the initiatives pioneered by aboriginal communities.

In discussions about the Canadian economy, agriculture is often left out, yet it is vital to Canada's overall economic health. Agricultural products account for $11 billion of annual exports and the agricultural sector generates $11.5 billion in economic activity. Furthermore, when agriculture suffers, rural communities suffer and a whole way of life is threatened. But farming is in serious trouble in this country. Between 1986 and 1991 the number of family farms in Canada dropped from 300,000 to 280,000, and one in five farm families are now in danger of losing their farms because of debt. We will reverse this trend only if we adopt policies to stabilize farm incomes (including help for people who work a farm and hold down a separate job), that will stave off farm foreclosures, and that will aid Canadian farmers in making the transition to sustainable agricultural practices that will preserve and enhance two of our most precious natural resources — our soil and our water. The family farm is important to Canada and must not be allowed to disappear.

Improved local infrastructures and easier access to capital would be of enormous help in fostering both community economic development and restoring the agricultural economy.

●　●　●

On the subject of economic revitalization one consideration cuts across and perhaps unites all my other concerns: the environment. To paraphrase a wise aboriginal saying, we do not inherit the land from our ancestors, we borrow it from our children. If we continue the kind of wasteful and environmentally damaging behaviour that has dominated economic activity since the Industrial Revolution, our children and their children will suffer enormously. The only alternative is a system of sustainable economic development — development that does no net harm to the environment. Starting now, without any more excuses from politicians, the environment must become an integral part of every economic decision, leaving behind the traditional, hierarchical approach in which we first assess the economic benefit, then measure the environmental impact — often after the damage has been done. We must move beyond the idea that there is a simple trade-off between jobs and the environment. In fact, in the long run I believe that environmentally sound economic activity will create more jobs than it displaces. For example, the countries that take the lead in green technologies and produce the most environmentally sound products will carve out important export market niches for themselves. The countries that fall behind will become less competitive internationally as their products fail to pass increasingly strict environmental standards elsewhere.

Governments can help ensure that every economic decision factors in the environment by passing environmental laws and enforcing them vigorously. The best laws will be those written jointly by business, labour, and environmentalists. Ontario is taking a step in the right direction with its recently drafted environmental bill of rights, which among other provisions gives individual citizens the power to challenge environmental wrongdoing. And government must ensure that rigorous environmental assessments are performed in all areas of public policy.

Beyond such measures, I agree with the growing number of economists who argue it's time we rethought the traditional measurement of economic health, the Gross National Product. This system of accounting fails to "count" the losses caused by pollution of the environment or the depletion of non-renewable resources — the depreciation of a country's environmental capital. Strange as it may seem, an environmental catastrophe such as the *Exxon Valdez* oil spill off the Alaskan coast in 1989 caused a sharp increase in Alaska's GNP because of all the economic activity involved in the clean-up. The GNP calculations left out damage to wildlife and to the fishery, as well as the many permanent jobs lost. As has been pointed out by Robert Repetto of the World Resources Institute, a Washington, D.C., based environmental think tank, under this system of accounting, "natural resources are treated as gifts of nature rather than as productive assets whose value must be depreciated if they are used up. . . . A nation could exhaust its natural resources, cut down it forests, erode its soils, pollute its aquifers, hunt its wildlife to extinction, with illusory gains in income and permanent losses in wealth."

We need to replace such skewed economic accounting with a green GNP. The current Gross National Product totals the value of all the goods and services created in a country during a given year. A green GNP would also measure gains and losses to a country's natural capital — resources such as forests, lakes, clean air — and to its humanly created capital — farmland, municipal infrastructure, and so on. With this new kind of accounting, different kinds of decisions would make economic sense, decisions that would put us more in tune with the planet we inhabit and leave it in better shape for future generations.

• • •

The route to a global economy and domestic prosperity cannot be determined by some latter-day version of the doctrine of the survival of the fittest. A sound strategy for economic restructuring must also redistribute wealth more fairly and disperse economic decision making more widely. If we achieve restructuring at the price of widespread poverty and even greater inequality, the sacrifices won't have been worth it. Only if we simultaneously build a more democratic economy based on the goal of full employment, one in which the material benefits are widely enjoyed, will we truly have met the global challenge.

CHAPTER NINE

A WOMAN'S PLACE

WHEN YOU'RE ONE OF ONLY a few women in the men's club, it's easy to forget that your voice is being heard beyond the corridors of power, that women in politics are beginning to make a difference. Not long after I won the December 1989 leadership convention, Yukon premier Tony Penikett told me an amusing and gratifying story. Naturally the leadership race had been followed avidly in the territory, and Tony's twin daughters — then seven years old — had been glued to the set during the final balloting. A few days later, the girls were playing in his office while he worked. At one point he had to leave for a few minutes. When he came back, he found one daughter sitting behind his desk looking very serious while the other daughter — also engrossed in this childhood play — handed her what was clearly an important piece of paper.

"What are you kids doing?" Tony asked.

"We're playing Audrey," they replied in unison.

When I'm having a bad day, I sometimes recall this anecdote to help put things in perspective.

I've talked a little about the different ways in which men and women operate in a political setting. But just what distinguishes typical female leadership from typical male leadership? I'll hazard some generalizations, based on personal observation. There are women who try to lead in a male way — Margaret Thatcher is the best-known example — and men who exhibit female leadership traits. However, in my experience the generalizations do contain a good deal of truth.

First of all, women tend to listen, men tend to talk. There's a delightful article that appeared recently in the *Utne Reader*, entitled "The Male Answer Syndrome." Its author, Jane Campbell, defines this typically male behavioural trait as "the chronic answering of questions regardless of actual knowledge." She continues, "The compulsion to answer varies from person to person, but few men are happy saying, 'I don't know.' They prefer, 'That's not what's important here.'" Sound familiar?

Campbell gives examples of the syndrome in action. My favourite involves her friend Pauline who at the age of eight noticed that eating ice cream made her teeth hurt. When she asked her father if Eskimos suffered from the same problem, he replied, "No, they have rubber teeth." Campbell continues: "Pauline repeated this information in a geography lesson and found herself the laughingstock of her class. That was how she learned that a man, even if he is your own father, would rather make up an answer than admit to his ignorance."

While Campbell is being satiric, behind the humour lies considerable truth. For reasons that no doubt stem from both nature and nurture, when men and women are in the same room the men tend to dominate the conversation. Campbell writes, "Men can speak with such conviction that women may be fooled into thinking they actually know what they're talking about." Of course, there are women who can and do hold their own in any forum, but in general women are reluctant to push a point unless they're confident they know what they're talking about. And in my experience, women are more likely than men to modify a position after hearing a good argument.

Women's tendency to let men do the talking surely results in part from the fact that historically their opinions didn't count for much — in many cases still don't. I continue to be haunted by the women I met at the door during my first campaign in the Yukon who said, "I know you want to go to Ottawa, but will *they* listen to you?" By which they meant that nobody listened to them. Their self-depreciation wasn't surprising given the deeply rooted social attitude that women are not fully competent, more like children than adults. Not so long ago, married women were still considered to be men's property. They didn't win the right to vote until the First World War, and only in 1929 did Canadian women gain legal status as "persons." Even now the notion persists in some quarters that women are "emotional" and men "rational," meaning women can't be trusted with "real" responsibility.

Nor is this attitude a quaint relic of the past. Just before the Gulf War, I attended a meeting of social democratic leaders in Austria. That country's social democratic government had decided to allow planes destined for the Gulf to fly through Austrian airspace even though Austria is a neutral country. This decision was protested vehemently by the youth wing of the party and by many social democratic women. One evening at dinner, I asked our hosts about these protests. Their response was dismissive: "Oh, those are just the women and the kids rabble-rousing again."

Women's style of listening before talking extends into the realm of decision making. Women in leadership positions are sometimes accused of being indecisive. In part, the appearance of indecisiveness stems from our desire to know all the facts before making up our minds and in part from our reluctance to impose a decision on others. Most women would rather build a consensus than impose their point of view. We are usually prepared to take the time for divergent views to converge, something that requires patience. In general, we are less comfortable with confrontation than men.

When women are faced with a difficult issue, their instinctive response is "How do we solve this problem?" With men, more often the attitude is "How do we win this one?" or "How can I be on the winning side?" In my experience, most women feel that "winning" is less important than gaining collectively. For us, the group is more important than the individual ego.

When I approach a contentious political situation, I'm always looking for what the various sides have in common. Where can they find a basis for co-operation rather than confrontation? Even in an issue as emotional as abortion, I believe it should be possible to find common ground between the opposing camps. Since both sides presumably would like to see fewer unwanted pregnancies, we should be able to find agreement on issues such as sex education and promoting birth control. Unfortunately the temperature of the debate is so high that a reasoned discussion seldom occurs.

Given the different styles of women and men in positions of leadership, it's hardly surprising that they have very different ways of thinking about power. The traditional male definition of power is in terms of coercion, power *over*: now that I have power, I can get my way; I can get people to do things my way. Women tend to think of power in terms of responsibility. Were I to become prime minister, my first thought would be that I had been handed an enormous responsibility. When I won the NDP leadership, I was above all conscious of the responsibility I'd accepted — to my party, to my campaign team, to the many women outside the party who would be rooting for me to do well. This didn't make me particularly noble — it was a typical female response.

Most women politicians I know see power in positive, activist terms. Power is a chance to accomplish something, to advance a cause, to help the people we represent. As Marilyn French pointed out in *Beyond Power*, this is not power *over*, it is power *to*. This generalization is supported by the findings of a recently published book, *Women in Power*, written by American psychologists Dorothy Cantor and Toni Bernay and based on interviews with twenty-five successful American women politicians. The authors found amazing agreement among their subjects about the female definition of political power: "Although we interviewed the women separately, nine responded identically: Power is 'the ability to get things done.' Several other responses, although not identical, said basically the same thing. In addition to getting things done, most of the women we talked with said they used their power to make other people's lives better." To me, power in the male sense of the word, power over, is at best a fleeting possession, at worst a licence to put oneself ahead of the cause for which one is supposed to be working.

One interesting section of *Women in Power* deals with the personality traits that define successful political women. The most important characteristic Cantor and Bernay discovered is something they call "a competent self." Here's how they describe such a woman: "She does not feel defined by situations, people, or events. She doesn't feel she has to change the way she acts to please the people around her. . . . [Her] strong sense of self enables her to promote the principles she believes in even though she knows that some people will disapprove, some quite vehemently." Not surprisingly, they found that this self-esteem was usually rooted in a stable family where the messages from both parents were extremely positive: you can do anything you want to do; you can do anything boys can do.

Few women of my generation were fortunate to grow into adulthood with such a solid sense of self as the exceptional subjects of *Women in Power*. Yet many of us have managed to achieve positions of power or status. To do this, most successful women I know have had to overcome internal psychological obstacles as well as external barriers. They have relied greatly on other women for support and have sought strong female role models to balance the persistent images of women as weak, childish, irrational, not serious.

And despite the many gains women have made, in general female self-esteem remains disturbingly low. It's now commonplace to observe that as girls grow older, they tend to do more poorly in school relative to boys and that they do worst in subjects such as math and science. A recent Canadian study of high school students, commissioned by the Canadian Advisory Council on the Status of Women, found that twice as many girls as boys had negative feelings about themselves. In the words of one of the study's co-authors, "Our findings seem to suggest that young men feel entitled to a presence in the world. The young women seem to understand their presence is on sufferance."

In *Revolution from Within*, Gloria Steinem cites numerous recent American studies probing the "gender gap" between boys and girls as they progress through school. Surprisingly, even the women who succeed — who graduate as top students from high school and then do well at the post-secondary level — emerge with a sharply diminished sense of their own worth relative to men.

In Steinem's words, "The difference seemed to be that, with each additional year of higher education, the women saw less of themselves, and less chance of being themselves. In the academic canon and in the classroom, their half of the human race was underrepresented in authority, often invisible, sometimes treated with contempt, perhaps treated as if success were 'unfeminine,' and denied even the dignity of a well recognized suffering. And since the great majority were in coeducational schools — and studies report that male classrooms are more 'competitive' while female classrooms are more 'cooperative' — women of all races were having to function in an alien and often hostile culture."

This only confirms that we still have a long way to go before men and women in our society are truly equal and see themselves as equal. And although many more women now work in traditionally male areas — in business, as university professors, in trade unions — there are still far too few women in positions of authority, role models for us all to look to. Electing women political leaders and achieving 50 percent female representation in every legislature won't automatically change the world, but it will go a long way towards helping women see themselves in a more positive light — as strong, as capable of exercising power well.

Beyond that, women in politics can begin to change the image

of what it means to have power, by exercising the characteristics
I've described and insisting on respect for doing so. Someone
once asked me if I thought more women in politics would help
the cause of women in general. I replied that I thought so, but
that without any question it would improve the practice of
politics. Perhaps women can begin to change the accepted concept of leadership. And maybe we can modify the cynicism about
politicians that threatens to undermine the democratic process.

• • •

Every party leader has to adjust his or her life dramatically to
do the job. Many people ask me if it's more difficult because I'm
single. My answer is that I just don't know. One thing I do know
is that nothing could be worse than being in public life while in
a bad relationship. Politics puts an enormous stress on families.
I don't know how many marriages break up after one partner is
elected to parliament, but quite a few. If both partners have their
own lives and careers, which often means splitting up the family
geographically, the strain can just become too much.

I have great empathy for all political spouses, having been
one myself. During most of my first seven years in the Yukon, I
lived with Roger Kimmerly, a judge who became an opposition
member of the territorial legislature, then minister of justice in
the first NDP territorial government. Although ours was an equal
partnership and a very happy one, as the spouse I was seen as
the secondary person. If we went to a dinner or a reception that
had some political purpose, people would look right through me
and talk to the "real" person, the politician. This often made me
angry. But since I had my own business and my own separate
life, I didn't let it bother me for long. However, it did give me
some insight into how political wives must often feel, or male
spouses of female politicians, for that matter.

The spouse is certainly expected to keep her place when it
comes to elections. I remember how upset I was at the beginning
of Roger's first run for the legislature when I was told in no

uncertain terms that it wouldn't be appropriate for me to run his campaign. I suppose this comes from the book of conventional political wisdom that says candidates, and their spouses, are basically ignorant and should simply do what they're told because their judgement can't be trusted. I don't know who wrote this book, but I reject its message.

At any rate, by the time I received this judgement, I'd already worked very hard and recruited quite a few volunteers so I simply decided to ignore it. After I had run the campaign and Roger had won, no one raised the subject again. Success creates new truths.

Since I don't have a spouse, I rely for support on my strong network of friends. Sometimes, at the end of a long and difficult day, someone in Whitehorse will get a call and listen patiently while I unwind. And the women in the caucus are good at checking up on me to see how I'm doing. Sometimes Joy Langan or one of the others will call up my assistant, Francesca Binda, and say, "How's Audrey doing? Does she need a break? Does she have time for dinner and a movie?" Although I don't always have the time, the gesture is very important to me.

One of the funnier dilemmas facing a single woman in politics is the escort question. Like many women, I used to feel somewhat uncomfortable going to social events by myself. I was cured of this traditionalist handicap one day when the search for a suitable escort reached the realm of the ridiculous.

At home in Whitehorse I would occasionally invite a male friend to accompany me to a dance or a play or a reception. The year after I was first elected, I was in the Yukon at the time of the annual Prospectors' Ball, so I decided to attend — but not alone. However, when I checked with various male friends, none were available. Finally a friend offered her husband, a contractor. She wasn't going and Peter (who is also a good friend) loves to dance, so this seemed like the perfect solution. He agreed to meet me there.

I arrived on time. No Peter. I waited and waited. Still no Peter. Finally, Peter's wife rushed up. "Peter really wanted to come," she explained, "but he couldn't. He had to pour cement tonight." (In a Yukon summer, there's enough light for contractors to work all night if they want to.) Stood up for a load of cement! We laughed, I went in to the ball, sat with some friends, and enjoyed myself thoroughly. I haven't worried about finding an escort since.

When I ran for the leadership, I realized that for the first few years it would be an all-consuming job. Like any intense relationship, the job has its ups and downs. The toughest part is the number of people I feel responsible to: the party, the caucus, the people in my constituency. There simply aren't enough hours in the day. I work hard, but I don't think of myself as a workaholic. I sometimes go home at night with a briefcase full of reports and policy papers and instead I watch something silly on TV. I don't berate myself when I do that; I know it's occasionally necessary to just vegetate.

Maybe the most difficult aspect of being leader is the way in which I've become public property. I learned this early on when someone asked me how I was feeling. I'd probably taken the "red-eye" overnight flight from the Yukon to get back to Ottawa in time for Monday Question Period. I hadn't slept much and I felt pretty ragged. It didn't occur to me not to answer frankly, so I said, "I feel just awful." The next morning, of course, I felt fine.

Within days the word was everywhere that "Audrey's falling apart." "Audrey can't cope." "Audrey's at the end of her tether." All of a sudden I was getting phone calls from worried friends and supporters. They weren't being nasty; people were really concerned. But it made me realize how careful I had to be about what I said. A flippant remark or a joke, out of context, could do real damage. (Since becoming leader, I've come to understand why Mackenzie King talked to his dead mother: she was the only person he could trust to keep it to herself.)

In Judy Steed's biography of Ed Broadbent, she reports that when he first became leader he had to change, too. His natural instinct was to be a prankster. "Ed made faces for the cameras, walked backwards off planes," and loved practical jokes. His advisers convinced him to tone down this kind of behaviour in public — and he did, which must have been quite difficult. But he obviously understood that what would be perfectly acceptable for a private citizen wasn't appropriate for a leader, whose public actions and utterances are always scrutinized.

The danger in all this is that you will lose track of who you really are, that your public persona will no longer reflect your private self. That didn't happen in Ed's case. I remain determined it won't happen in mine, even if I now belong to other people as much as to myself. This is undoubtedly one of the reasons I get satisfaction out of ordinary, unleaderlike activities, such as doing my own laundry or spending Sunday morning cleaning my Ottawa apartment.

The sense that I've become public property undoubtedly also contributes to how fiercely I guard my own privacy and the privacy of my friends and family. There is little in this book about my mother, who's now seventy-eight, or my son and daughter, or my two grandchildren because, as I said in the preface, I believe that my decision to enter public life should not complicate their lives. I'm certainly not alone in this view. Iona Campagnolo, former Liberal cabinet minister and former president of the federal Liberal party, put it very well a few years ago when she spoke at a symposium on women in politics: "I have been very reluctant to make anything known about my children," she said. "I keep them well out of the light. Now that one has children of her own, I'm equally careful about my grandchildren. Political life is so very cruel. It seems to me, though I may be a little sensitive about it, that the children of women politicians are more seriously discriminated against than the children of male politicians. . . . There's an inordinate curiosity about women politicians. Every way that you can buttress your own personal life, quietly, in the background, is better for your children."

I sometimes find my job tough, but it has many rewards. These can be as simple as someone coming up to me in an airport with the words, "You've been saying exactly what's on my mind." I hear that often. It may be a speech that's gone well. It may be a particularly good debate in the House or a caucus meeting where we've argued long and hard and finally reached some common ground. It may be having some impact on an issue —

helping set the agenda rather than just reacting to someone else's.

I am, however, my own harshest critic. I set high standards for myself. I often don't think I've done as well as I could have or should have. And believe me, there are lots of opportunities in politics to disappoint yourself and others — and many people to point it out when you have. But I don't allow myself to feel too guilty about falling short, something I used to do when I was younger. I've learned to put both success and failure in perspective. I set high goals, but I don't torture myself when I don't attain them right away.

In this job, a lot of exhilaration and stress come from constantly doing things that are new or unfamiliar. Without question, the most stressful experience of all will be the coming election campaign. Any campaign is exhausting and draining but the leader's campaign is like being inside a pressure cooker for sixty days. Although it will be tough, I'm excited about the challenge. I love to be stretched and tested. It will also be a chance to demonstrate once again that I can take on a tough job and prove that a woman can do it.

• • •

When I search for patterns in my life, I see that each time I've taken a risk and succeeded, my success has become reinforcing. It has helped give me the confidence to confront the next challenge. If I had simply taken a few university correspondence courses and then let my education lapse, my life would surely have turned out differently. If I had not made my years in Ghana a rich learning experience, I doubt I would have later quit a good job in Toronto and moved to the Yukon. But I've also noticed that for me and other women of my generation, success often springs from what looks and feels very much like failure.

When my relationship with Roger Kimmerly ended in 1986, I was devastated. It wasn't my choice to end it, and of course, it's always harder to be the one who is left. Although I'd had some good relationships with men since my marriage had ended, my seven years with Roger were the happiest. But would I have become an MP, let alone leader of the New Democratic Party, had that relationship endured? I don't think so. Like so many women, I've tended to tie my life closely to the man I'm with. When I was with my husband, I was not the prime breadwinner; when I was with Roger, I was not the primary politician — I worked behind the scenes. After my husband and I were divorced, my career developed. After Roger and I split up, I ran for parliament and won.

I remember a woman I met in the mid-1970s, shortly after I left my job at the Children's Aid Society and took on a contract with Ontario's Department of Community and Social Services. For years she'd enjoyed what to her was an ideal family life: she had married the college football star who'd gone on to be successful in business; she'd had seven kids; she was in love with her husband. As she described it, they seemed the perfect happy family. Then one day when her youngest child was finally in school, she decided she wanted to do something for herself — go back to college for a degree in social work. Up until this point, she had felt like her husband's equal in every way, a perfectly respected partner. She had chosen to stay home and raise the kids, and she had no sense of inferiority about this.

Her husband's reaction shocked her. At first he flatly refused to go along with this change in their arrangement. When she persisted, he finally agreed that she could go to school as long as nothing changed at home — as long as she cooked and cleaned and looked after the kids. Nothing was ever the same between them after that. Eventually they separated and she did get her social work degree, but what I remember most about our conversation is how absolutely devastated she was at her husband's response. For all those years — as long as she played her role — she had thought she was an equal partner. But it wasn't true.

After Roger left, I felt I needed to get away from the Yukon for a while. It's such a small place, and everyone knew me and Roger as a couple. So I began to plan something that would stretch me in new ways. In the previous few years, I had done some volunteer work for Canadian Crossroads International, interviewing applicants for placement in Crossroads projects abroad. Crossroads is a non-profit organization dedicated to building bridges between cultures, specifically between Canadians and people in developing countries. The volunteers are expected to raise a portion of their travel and living expenses; local contacts in the host country arrange accommodation and a suitable job.

That summer I applied and was accepted for a three-and-a-half-month placement in Barbados to start in the fall. Since I was going to be in the Caribbean and had long wanted to visit South and Central America, I decided to do some travelling after my placement ended. So before I left Whitehorse, I bought a guidebook and read up on the places I planned to visit. Once I arrived in Barbados, I enrolled in Spanish classes at the university.

Although Barbados would not have been my first choice — I had hoped for a placement in Asia, which I hadn't yet experienced — my time there turned out to be very rewarding. I lived with a local family in the capital, Bridgetown, and for the first month worked with about fifteen developmentally handicapped children in a school housed in a private home. The school was run by a lovely Barbadian woman who'd lived in Canada and had a learning disabled daughter herself. Although the work was challenging — these were very difficult kids — after about a month I became restless. I wanted to experience more of the country.

Each day as I walked to the school from where my bus stopped I would pass a place with a sign that read "Women in Development." One day I walked in and introduced myself to the director, Lynn Allison, an American who had lived in Barbados for about twenty years and was married to a Canadian. We took to each other immediately. I said, "I'm here in Barbados for a couple more months. Is there anything I could do for you?" She offered me a volunteer job on the spot, so I left the school and went to work with her.

Lynn had founded the organization with the aim of helping women develop small businesses — anything from a sewing service to operating a hog farm to selling bread and pastries in the street to small childcare operations. Women in Development provided seed money to help the business get started. I took on the task of conducting case studies of women the organization had helped, studies that would be used to support applications for funding. Like all small non-governmental development organizations, this one was constantly in need of money. I was pleased to discover that Canada was one of the countries funding their efforts.

The project proved fascinating. I travelled all over the island and met many wonderful women struggling to make a small business work. The pride these women had gained by achieving some measure of economic self-sufficiency stays with me still. I was observing concrete cases of empowerment in action.

Women in Development is an example of the kind of grass-roots aid organization where foreign aid dollars truly make a difference in people's lives. The staff was small, so most of the money went not to administration but to the women who needed it. And rather than imposing a fixed idea of what kind of aid was needed, the program responded directly to the demands that were coming from the recipients themselves.

Because of my strong interest in third world development, I visited a number of foreign aid projects in Barbados. Both then and later, as I travelled through South and Central America, I was struck by how often the seemingly insignificant and small-scale types of aid were the most successful. The school I'd first worked at had bought some much needed equipment with money from the Canadian High Commission, which had a modest budget for discretionary spending. Helping a poor village dig a well or providing subsistence farmers with new machetes often makes more sense than funding an expensive megaproject. The key principle must be that the people the aid is intended to help have a strong say in the kind of aid they receive.

When my time in Barbados came to an end, I packed my belongings in a backpack and set off on a three-month journey.

My itinerary through Latin America took me from Venezuela to Brazil, then Bolivia, Peru, and Ecuador, and finally to Panama, Costa Rica, and Guatemala. I travelled almost entirely by bus or train and stayed in inexpensive hotels. I visited the main cities and took in the mandatory attractions, but I preferred the countryside and the smaller centres. As a single woman travelling alone, I took sensible precautions, avoiding the cheapest hotels in the worst parts of town and seldom going out in the evening by myself.

On the whole it was a wonderful experience. I met people and saw sights I'll carry with me always. One of my vivid recollections is of New Year's Eve in Rio de Janeiro. During the afternoon, as I was walking through the downtown area, I found myself in the middle of what seemed like a huge ticker tape parade, as people threw a snowstorm of shredded paper from their office windows: out with the old, in with the new. That evening I observed the year-end ritual practised by the followers of Macumba, the Brazilian religion that venerates both Christian saints and African gods and goddesses. After dark, devotees crowd the beaches, where tiny boats of paper and wood, each bearing a lit candle, are sent seaward in honour of the goddess Lemanja. Soon the whole of Rio's harbour was dotted with flickering lights. Then came some of the most spectacular fireworks I've ever seen.

During my trip I covered many miles and visited many places I had read about since childhood. I made it to the Galapagos, the islands that gave Darwin the evidence he needed for his theory of evolution, and climbed through the evocative Inca ruins of Machu Picchu. I went white-water rafting in Costa Rica and visited the Mayan temples of the Yucatan Peninsula. And I fulfilled a long-held dream by taking a boat trip on the Amazon — not that it was easy to organize. Before leaving Canada, I had written to a Brazilian guide who specialized in Amazon tours. He replied that he would be delighted to show me the river and suggested I call him when I reached Manaus, a city located at the confluence of the Amazon and its largest tributary, the Negro. With no more information or assurance than his letter, I took a flight from Rio to Manaus early in January of 1987.

When I landed in Manaus at four in the morning, I began to have second thoughts. The city made me think of an old Rita Hayworth movie, with steamy bars and seedy hotels strung along the edge of the river. The place has a fascinating history, having been hacked out of the jungle by the rubber barons who built an opulent nineteenth-century opera house, the Teatro Amazonas, in the middle of the jungle. But early that morning I wasn't interested in history, only in getting myself safely to a decent hotel.

If my Spanish was rudimentary, my Portuguese was non-existent, so I put my fate into the hands of a taxi driver. I simply pointed to the name of a hotel in my guidebook, and sure enough he took me there. Unfortunately it was full. Using the international language of gesture, I somehow communicated that I wanted another hotel at a similar price. Finally we found a place for me to spend the night.

The next day I met the guide with whom I had corresponded, who explained that, regrettably, his tours were completely booked. However, he introduced me to another guide named Franchesi, a short, dark-haired Brazilian man in his late thirties or early forties who seemed nice enough, but unfortunately spoke no English. Negotiating the itinerary and the final price involved a lot of hand waving and pointing at maps, but we finally came to terms for a five-day trip up the Negro. I balked, momentarily, when I discovered I would be Franchesi's only passenger. But I hadn't come this far only to turn back now.

We travelled in a small open boat — really a motorized canoe — with a canopy to ward off the sun and rain. Sometimes we would fish for piranha, which turned out to be quite tasty; occasionally we would pull ashore and explore the rainforest. Each night we stayed in a family's house on the river, both hosts and guests sleeping in hammocks in the same small room. As we left Manaus behind, the trappings of civilization became fewer and the people poorer. But above all I remember the kindness and generosity of our hosts.

One day as we were walking through the forest — just Franchesi with his machete and me — I said to myself, "Wait a minute, haven't I seen this in a movie?" If he'd wanted to take advantage of the situation in any way, he certainly had opportunities. I suppose I was taking quite a risk in trusting him, but he turned out to be a good man. We weren't able to have much in the way of conversations, but we developed an amicable enough relationship. He taught me what he could about the rainforest animals and plants, for instance how to get drinking water from certain trees. And he returned me to Manaus safe and sound. So my Amazon adventure had a happy ending.

No one can travel through this part of the world without being struck again and again by two things: the chasm between rich and poor — the incredible, devastating nature of the poverty — and the ubiquity of the military. Everywhere in Latin America there are poor people and there are soldiers.

On the train from Bolivia to Peru I met a woman biologist, a Peruvian who worked in the environmental movement. She told me that some of the most environmentally sensitive areas in Peru — the places where she and her colleagues did their work — were also areas where the Shining Path guerrillas were active. In other words, to be an environmentalist in Peru meant you might get killed. And in places like Guatemala, to be an advocate of rights for indigenous people can be to risk your life — certainly to risk imprisonment and torture. Everywhere I went, I met people who were willing to put their lives on the line for their beliefs.

My only really bad experience during those months of travel happened in Panama, a country in which I felt uncomfortable from the moment I arrived. There was so much resentment of the American military presence there that you could almost smell it in the air, especially in the capital, Panama City. One day I went to Colon, at the entrance to the canal on the Caribbean side. While I was walking through the train station, somebody ripped the purse off my shoulder and disappeared into the crowd. I was shaken, but unhurt. The only real valuables I had lost were some money and a pair of glasses; I had left my passport and most of my money at my hotel in Panama City. I was neither surprised nor shocked by this incident. I knew that as a North American travelling through Latin America, I was a target: someone was bound to steal something at some point. It was just a matter of time, since 90 percent of the people were so poor.

Looking back on the whole trip, what I found much harder to accept were the limitations on me because I was a woman. It made me angry that I didn't feel safe going out alone at night and that I felt I always had to be on guard. But how safe do women feel in Ottawa or Vancouver or Toronto or Montreal or New York City? Most of us avoid certain situations and live with a permanent undercurrent of anxiety. This is a sad reality for all women.

What I brought away with me more than anything else from my trip to Latin America was a sense of privilege. Not simply to be living in the relative safety and prosperity of Canada but to have had so many choices in my life.

• • •

In my speeches I sometimes recount an incident that occurred on a radio phone-in show in Edmonton soon after I became leader. The host, a man, didn't quite know what to make of me. In the brief interview before he started accepting calls, he asked me if I was a feminist. I don't think I've ever been asked this question in an interview when it wasn't issued as a kind of challenge — as in, "Lady, if you say yes, you'd better be ready to justify yourself." In response I don't make a big thing out of it, I just answer simply and directly. I said, "Yes, as a matter of fact, I am." "Okay," he went on, "but you're not like a hard-core feminist." Images of legions of bra burners marching on Parliament Hill were by now raging through listeners' heads. "Yes," I replied, "I'm a feminist." Still he wasn't satisfied. "Well, I guess what I'm saying is you're not an out-and-out feminist, are you?" I didn't know whether to laugh or cry. So I said it again, "Yes, I am an out-and-out feminist." End of that line of questioning.

Since he couldn't make me defensive, he moved on to another topic.

One reason I insist on using the word "feminist," apart from the fact that I am one, is that I believe we must restore the positive meaning of the word. We have to take back the language that's been stolen from us by those who would like to undermine the legitimacy of women's struggle for equality. It's not that I'm on some great crusade, but I am on a little crusade, namely to reinstate feminism as a respected label. So whenever I have the chance, I'm happy to remind people that I am a feminist and proud to be one.

To me feminism comes down to two related goals: equality and choice. Unfortunately the idea that the sexes should be treated equally and have equal choices in life still seems to be a radical notion for many. We are a long way from achieving equality for women, even in Canada, one of the most privileged societies on earth. The prime minister is fond of quoting a recent U.N. study that rates Canada's overall quality of life as the highest in the world. However, when you factor in the status of women, we drop to eighth place. Women are still paid on average 33 percent less than men doing the same job. In two-income families — where both the man and woman work — the woman still performs a disproportionate share of domestic chores — cooking, cleaning, shopping, child raising. When it comes to positions of leadership and responsibility, women still stand only on the threshold of power — the door is open a crack, but that's all. Fewer than 2 percent of the people serving on corporate boards of directors are women. In the federal civil service, despite gains in recent years, women now occupy less than 20 percent of senior positions. Not only are the prime minister's cabinet and caucus overwhelmingly male, so are the senior bureaucrats who advise him. And I hardly need to reiterate the position of women in electoral politics.

Every woman who believes in equality and choice is a feminist, whether she uses the word or not. Yet I know many women whom I would classify as feminists but who are uncomfortable wearing the label and I respect that. Maybe they feel like my friend Margaret Joe, this country's first aboriginal justice minister, who once said to me, "I've had enough labels in my life." Most of us, whether we accept the label or not, have learned about inequality from our life experience, not from books. When I was younger I did read Betty Friedan and Germaine Greer, but the origins of my feminism lie in my early years as a homemaker, working hard but having no work identity, no work status. In those days, when I was asked what I did, I inevitably said, "Oh, I do nothing. I just stay home."

My experience as a woman working in the home has made me particularly vehement in defence of the value of women's traditional work. My generation was told that raising kids didn't count, that looking after elderly relatives didn't count, that cooking and cleaning and budgeting and shopping didn't count. At the same time, I knew that what I was doing as a homemaker was important. In my unacknowledged anger and confusion lay the seed of my feminism.

Later, after I had returned from Ghana and earned my degree in social work and begun my job with the Children's Aid Society, my sense of injustice grew into something more active. Above all I was radicalized by the poor women I worked with who had never been listened to with respect, almost never been talked to as adults, virtually never been taken seriously in their entire lives. And there were also very privileged women I worked with who still thought of themselves as inferior.

I remember in particular some workshops I ran while I was director of the Metro Toronto Mental Health Association. They were for women who had stayed home to raise their children and were now thinking about returning to the workforce. These women were mostly upper middle class. Their husbands made good incomes. All of them had worked before they'd got married. Yet almost without exception they felt they had absolutely nothing to offer, not even as volunteers, whereas I knew my agency would have jumped at the chance to get them involved. These were intelligent, well-educated women who'd raised families and run households, but they saw themselves as having no use outside the home.

There is much talk these days of a backlash against women's liberation, of a kind of neo-conservative conspiracy to put women back in their traditional place. The setbacks suffered by the women's movement in the United States — the defeat of the equal rights amendment, the decreasing access to abortion — lends weight to this analysis, as does the recent revelation in this country of a "family values" caucus among federal Conservative MPs that is credited with having blocked the government's election promise to create a national childcare program. And there are many studies that suggest working mothers feel increasingly guilty about attempting to play both roles.

The fact is, however, that most working women simply don't have an option. According to Statistics Canada, 70 percent of families with children under sixteen have mothers who work. And as research done by the Vanier Institute of the Family has shown, it now takes two incomes to support most households. According to the Vanier Institute, if women dropped out of the workforce, low-income families would increase in number by about 62 percent.

Right now, women are getting a mixed message: we should be strong and independent with careers of our own and we should also be perfect mothers and nurturers. We should be tough and goal-oriented and we should also be sexy and submissive. In any bookstore you will find the self-help section packed with books telling women how to dress for success, lose weight, feel better, do more. And the authors of these books parade endlessly through the television talk shows. A woman is left with the feeling that she can never be good-looking enough, clever enough, young enough — just plain not good enough ever.

Women feel enormous pressure to respond to these messages about how we should improve ourselves. When I speak to women's groups I often say, "My first advice to you is to throw away all your self-improvement books. And if you don't have any, don't buy one. You're okay as you are." Inevitably my audiences clap like mad.

Equity for women may be under attack, but it's going to be harder to turn back the clock than at other times in our history.

There are more women in positions of power than ever before. There are more men sharing the jobs of raising children and running a household — and liking it. There are powerful networks of women working for real change. But we still have a very long way to go. Is there, for instance, less violence against women? I don't think so. How quickly are women closing the gap of economic inequality? Not very fast. The gains are real, but progress is painfully slow.

Women in politics have an important contribution to make to this continuing revolution. And by this I don't simply mean women who run for elected office. Women in advocacy politics — working with groups that advocate fundamental social change — can also have an enormous impact. Most of my early political experience was in advocacy politics. In fact, I think it's important to remember that simply electing more women won't automatically lead to the kind of change I want. Only if we elect more women who are committed to the goals of equality and who will work with others outside electoral politics will the egalitarian goal come closer to achievement.

Alexa McDonough, leader of the Nova Scotia NDP, expressed this very well when she spoke at a conference in Toronto in 1986. The conference was organized by the Committee for '94, a group of women from all three political parties who decided, after the dismal showing of women candidates in the 1984 election, that they would work to elect women to 50 percent of the seats in the Commons by 1994. Alexa said, "We are working towards, and intend to achieve, equal representation of women in the political arena. This is not only an essential means of achieving equality for ourselves, but it is also a means of achieving equality for our sisters and for the many others who suffer injustices and indignities and have less than their fair share in our society."

In this chapter, I've talked a great deal about women, but the goals of feminism are not just another version of the win-lose game: more for us, less for "them." Not at all. They are an essential part of the path towards meeting the broader goals of social justice alluded to elsewhere. In fact, I believe that feminism and social democracy are inextricably intertwined. Both strive for equality and fairness throughout society, to reduce unearned and undeserved disparities between people. In that sense, a man can be a feminist — and men have every bit as much to gain from the feminist vision as women do.

When I ran for the leadership, people often said to me, "Well, of course, you'll only talk about women's issues," by which they meant areas that are usually seen as female concerns, such as poverty and childcare and pay equity. My reply was, "You're absolutely right. I'm going to talk about trade — that's a woman's issue — I'm going to talk about unemployment and fiscal policy and tax policy — these are all women's issues. And I'm also going to talk about economic issues such as childcare and health care and pay equity." Someday I hope no issue will be regarded as being a woman's issue.

• • •

Women have traditionally faced a number of barriers when seeking public office. The most obvious is the cultural bias against women politicians, especially beyond the municipal level — where, until recently, political office was usually a poorly paid part-time job. A 1988 background paper from the Canadian Advisory Council on the Status of Women came to the same conclusion: "Politics at the federal level is still viewed as a male activity and therefore as inappropriate for women." Society also sends a strong message that family life and public life are incompatible, causing many to think twice before seeking office. (And as long as women retain the primary responsibility for running families, many will be prevented from entering the political arena.) There is also the question of money. On average, women make less than men; they also tend to have more trouble raising money, being less tied into financial networks than men are. (Only because I knew a group of women willing to raise the money I needed was I able to contemplate running for my party's nomination in the Yukon.) Since contributions to nomination campaigns aren't yet tax-deductible, this makes the monetary barrier even higher.

Combined with these factors is the natural resistance of political parties to change. Like other institutions, they tend to keep doing things the way they've been done in the past. The inevitable result is that it remains very difficult for anyone who isn't white and male to gain a party nomination in a winnable riding — a constituency the party holds or has won in the past. Even in the NDP, which is dedicated to egalitarian goals, the statistics tell the story: in the more than sixty years since the party was founded, we have elected only eleven women, three aboriginal people, and one member of a visible minority to the House of Commons.

The progress of women in electoral politics — especially at the federal level — has been glacial. In the United States, where much lip-service is paid to "equality of opportunity," women have fared even worse than in Canada. According to one recent calculation, at the current rate of increase it will take 410 years before the U.S. Congress achieves gender parity. At the current rate in Canada it will be at least fifty years before we approach an equal number of women and men — and that projection assumes no effective backlash. To quote Judge Rosalie Abella, in her Royal Commission report on Equality in Employment, "It is not that individuals in the designated groups [women and minorities] are inherently unable to achieve equality on their own, it is that the obstacles in their way are so formidable and self-perpetuating that they cannot be overcome without intervention." Changes to structures of power don't just happen, even with "good will." They have to be made to happen.

The route to reform of the political structure is unquestionably through changing the way candidates are nominated. According to the 1992 Royal Commission on Electoral Reform and Party Financing, "in countries where women are now a strong force in elected politics . . . mandatory requirements within political parties to correct the historical underrepresentation of women have been the principal cause." The best example of this today is Norway, where 59 of the 165 MPs are women, slightly more than 35 percent. The shift began in 1983 when the Norwegian Labour Party adopted a rule that no fewer than 40 percent and no more than 60 percent of its nominees must be women.

Other parties soon followed. Norwegian prime minister Gro Harlem Brundtland heads a cabinet that is 50 percent female, and two of the main opposition leaders are also women. In other words, affirmative action is necessary if the Canadian House of Commons is soon to reflect the population.

Following the 1988 election, when our party failed to increase the number of women and minority candidates elected, many of us argued that the time had come to introduce a strong affirmative action policy for such candidates. After I became leader in 1989, I encouraged this movement at every opportunity, arguing that it was time for a real revolution in the way candidates were nominated. If we succeeded, it would mean that the NDP would have the first affirmative action policy ever put in place by a federal party in Canada.

Naturally there were New Democrats who objected to the idea. Their arguments were familiar ones. It would mean we were going to nominate inferior or incompetent people (I always find this one particularly insulting, since it's predicated on the notion that we won't be able to find a woman or an aboriginal or a disabled person who's capable of handling political office). The media coverage focused primarily on this same issue: competence. Time and again the journalists who interviewed me about our policy would ask, "But won't you be nominating unqualified people?" This shows an enormous blind spot in our national press, which has in essence bought the establishment line: the outsiders are on the outside because they aren't good enough. It just isn't true.

A more valid worry within the party was that the policy would be anti-democratic, taking away the decision-making power from the riding associations. (The policy we've ended up with does not impose decisions from above; it simply requires a much broader candidate search process.) And finally, the argument of last resort: it's a great idea but "the time isn't right."

This is the argument that's been used as long as anyone can remember to keep the powerless in their place. It was used in the nineteenth century against those who fought to abolish child labour: we admit child labour is a bad thing but to eliminate it now would be too costly in economic terms; we should wait until the economy is stronger. And it was used by those who wanted to preserve slavery: without slaves, there would be no one to do the work and the economic system would collapse. The same argument is used today against legislation requiring equal pay for work of equal value: good in principle but it will cost too much money in these difficult economic times. For how long have aboriginal people been told the time wasn't right for recognition of their inherent right to self-government? The fact is, the timing is never right. At some point you have to simply say, "This situation is wrong and we're going to change it." And that's what the NDP finally did with affirmative action.

Many people in our party worked long and hard to come up with a policy that would have real teeth but that would not usurp the right of the riding associations to choose their candidates democratically. I'm proud of the result. Our target is to nominate women in at least 50 percent of federal ridings. In winnable ridings, including ridings where an incumbent NDP member is retiring, the policy calls for 60 percent women and 15 percent other affirmative action candidates. But just as important as these targets is the process for reaching them. We've subdivided the federal ridings into small clusters. Each of these groups must work together to make sure that a broad-based candidate search takes place. Only when a cluster has demonstrated that it has actively recruited qualified women, visible minorities, aboriginal people, and people with disabilities to run will the federal office lift the freeze on nominations in the cluster. In effect this policy lays out a mandatory process, but does not mandate the outcome. As this book goes to press it's too early to say what the final result will be, but the early evidence suggests that the new policy is working beyond our expectations.

Although our new affirmative action policy is a giant step in the right direction, more must be done to remove the barriers facing women and others. Several excellent ideas came from the recent Royal Commission on Electoral Reform. It recommended strict spending limits on nomination contests — something that is already part of NDP policy. It also called for extending the political tax credit for donations to political parties to include donations to nomination campaigns. This would mean many more people would be able to afford to run for a nomination. More novel is a suggestion that the more women a party elects, the greater should be its reimbursement for election expenses. I support this idea.

It's time to push open the doors. The current situation is wrong and must be changed. With our affirmative action plan, that's what my party and I are trying to do.

• • •

Many people ask me if I really want to become prime minister. On the surface, the question seems to mean: "Do you want that horrible job?" But often I think it carries a more critical underlying question: "Would you know what to do? Are you capable of handling it?"

One might well ask why anyone would want to take on the responsibility of trying to lead this country at the present time. Our social, economic and environmental problems appear so daunting. On the international front, the situation seems to be spiralling out of control — war, famine, overpopulation, vast disparities between rich and poor countries.

Certainly I have no desire to become prime minister for its own sake, for the perceived perks and privileges. I have no interest in living in a mansion or driving around in a limousine. I sometimes joke that if I won the next election I would turn 24 Sussex Drive into a home for battered women. As it is now, it's the most expensive social housing in Canada. (One election promise I can safely make is that I won't redecorate the prime minister's residence — that should automatically save Canadian taxpayers about a million dollars.)

I want to become prime minister because I believe it's time we tried a new approach to governing this country. There's a saying that whoever defines the problems defines the solutions. Well, the people who have been defining the problems in Canada for as long as I can remember must not have been defining them correctly because they certainly haven't come up with adequate solutions. To my mind, the fundamental problem we face is inequality and how to diminish it. Tommy Douglas once said that we should not judge a nation by the height of its skyscrapers or the depth of its gold reserves, but by the way in which its citizens treat each other. Our challenge is to build a country that is not only economically strong but socially just.

People are cynical about politics, in large part because they feel that all governments, and especially the federal government, have lost touch with their realities and concerns. Government seems alien and distant, but it needn't be that way. A New Democratic government would mean much more than new faces sitting around the cabinet table — although I can guarantee many of those faces would be new in more ways than one. It would entail transforming the way government operates, the way it relates to Canadian citizens. One of my first priorities as prime minister would be to begin making the structure of government more democratic and its proceedings less secret. Changing the way government works — making it more open and inclusive — will not just lead to better solutions; it is actually part of the solution. But beyond making government more open and accessible, a prime minister needs a clear sense of direction. In this book I've outlined some of the paths I would take — the idea of common security in foreign policy, of economic democracy as the basis for a revitalization of the economy. In the coming election campaign, my party's candidates will elaborate on these and many other ideas we have been developing over the past several years — good ideas that spring from our fundamental commitment to the principles of social democracy: equality and fairness.

Social democrats believe in a mixed economy, where public and private enterprise work together to create wealth but where government has a responsibility to make sure that wealth is distributed fairly. We believe government must intervene to see that social inequities are reduced — whether they are based on income, race, gender, sexual orientation, or any other factor. We believe in a central government with enough power to set and maintain national standards in areas such as health care, pensions, and unemployment insurance. We believe in an international order founded on co-operation rather than competition.

But any politician who tells you she has all the answers is lying. Personally I distrust messiahs and I have no desire to pass myself off as one. I don't see myself as a saviour but as a nurturer of change.

The next election will be about the kind of country we want Canada to become. We have just passed our 125th birthday. At our 150th, will we look back at 1992 as a step forward or a step back? One evening this past summer as I was walking home from work, an elderly man approached me. He had been born in Eritrea, he told me, but was now a citizen of Canada. His words were simple: "Please don't let this country go. You cannot know how precious what we have here is." I do know. But I also know that however much we have, our country remains deeply flawed and in need of transformation.

Despite our many problems, I remain an optimist. I see a revolution trying to happen in this country — a positive non-violent revolution that will bring the people who have been left on the outside into the system, creating in the process a new kind of society. For much of my life I was one of those on the outside, pushing on the doors, attempting to force them open. Now I want to help pull them open from the inside. I want to bring the outsiders in.

So the answer to the question is, yes, I want the job of prime minister. As to whether I'm up to the task, I can only answer that I believe I am. During my life I've taken on challenges that looked difficult or impossible at the time. Yet over and over again I've succeeded in meeting them. I've proved that I can operate in many different contexts and communicate with many different types of people. But when electing a prime minister, the ultimate question each voter must ask is: "Does this person have the qualities of heart as well as mind that I want in a leader?"

It's a question only you can answer.

This book is typeset in Bodoni Book,
a typeface introduced in 1909 by Morris Fuller Benton
and based on the classic design of Giambattista Bodoni.

Typeset by Tony Gordon Limited
Text design by Styles Design Inc.
Printed and bound in Canada by union labour
at John Deyell Limited